A THEORY OF THE GOOD

ALSO BY
CHRISTOPHER KELLY

⊙

The Song of Songs, of Solomon (2015)

The Tangle (2018)

A
THEORY
OF THE GOOD

A New Account of the Value of Life, Love,
Freedom, Knowledge, Beauty,
and the Environment

◉

Christopher Kelly, Ph.D.

Now Experience Books
Los Angeles, California

TOG@nowexperience.com

ISBN 978-0-9861230-1-6

Book Design by *CSK*

For my grandfather
Robert Kelly
(who taught me how to think)

TABLE OF CONTENTS

acknowledgements

All the members of my dissertation committee: Professors Bob Pasnau, Luc Bovens, Michael Tooley, Bud Coleman, Michael Huemer, and Graham Oddie.

Stan Godlovitch in whose Environment Ethics seminar I first conceived this idea. His passion required response.

Rachel Singpurwalla whose scholarship, hard work, and true curiosity stretched my thinking in many ways.

Gregory Mikkelson for digging my obscure dissertation out of the stacks and encouraging me to keep working on it.

The Boulder Bookend, though it no longer exists, was a fabulous place to write, think, drink tea, and eat pie.

Will Hickman for always being willing to read.

Michael Huemer for the clarity, simplicity, and depth of his thought.

Jessica Graham for her constant magic.

And, my advisor and friend, Graham Oddie for the inspiration of his work and far-reaching mind, and for the constant support and encouragement over the many years.

INTRODUCTION

"One can say that he who acts perfectly is like an excellent geometer who knows how to find the best constructions for a problem; or like a good architect who utilizes his site and the funds destined for the building in the most advantageous manner, leaving nothing which offends or which falls short of the beauty of which it is susceptible; like a good paterfamilias who puts his capital to use in such a way that nothing is left waste or barren; like a skillful engineer who makes his effect by choosing the least difficult way; like a talented author who encloses a maximum of realities in the least possible volume. Now the most perfect of all beings and those which occupy the least possible volume, that is to say which hinder each other least, are spirits, and their perfections are the virtues..."

"God has chosen the [rule] which is the most perfect, that is to say the one which is at the same time the simplest in hypotheses and the richest in phenomena, as a geometrical line might be, of which the construction was easy and the properties and effects very admirable and of great extent." Leibniz[1]

A s a child I used to play a game I called "Let's Count the Things in the World." I never got far; it is a wide and varied world, after all. But I did make some progress. The game began as nothing other than a listing of particulars: this purple blanket, me, *Green Eggs and Ham*, the moon. But gradually, the listing became more general: blankets, people, books, planets and so on. And more abstract: purple things, round things, talking things, distant things. One night, I remember, I ended the listing in the following manner: there are difficult things, there are dangerous things, there are good

---

1[Leibniz, 1953; 9]

things. Which are the difficult things? Tests and vegetables. Which are the dangerous things? Crossing streets and operations. Which are the good things? I'd like to answer that question in this essay.

There are many ways of being good in this world, of course, but I want to argue that all these ways are valuable in virtue of having one property, a property I call *richness*.[2] Things are rich when they contain a large variety of elements properly unified. He who acts perfectly, says Leibniz, 'encloses the maximum of realities in the least possible volume.' This is the best universe, he says, because it is 'the simplest in hypotheses and the richest in phenomena.' It is this density of reality, this simple line connecting the widest variety of phenomena, that is richness. All things that are good in this world – beauty, knowledge, persons – are good due to being rich. To fix all facts about richness is to have fixed the value structure of the world.

There is an alternative approach; I might claim there are *no* good things at all, not truly, that goodness is a fiction like the interplanetary ether or the vital spirit. This view has become commonplace in many academic fields and even some philosophy departments. 'Good' is nothing other than a word for objectifying our subjective preferences, some say. It is not even that, others say; it is merely in an inappropriate way of talking due to our need for societal norms. Though I think there are good arguments against such views of value and good arguments for being a value realist, such arguments are to the side of the immediate aim of this essay. Here, I assume without argument that goodness is as real as table-ness and blanket-ness, as roundness and thickness. One way of framing the question of this essay: given the meaning of 'good' and the variety of ways that it is applied in the world, what must the good be to be at all? Whether it does exist, then, is a question for another day.

On the other hand, if the thesis of this essay can be made plausible, it presents, on its own, some not insignificant evidence for value realism. The best explanation for the fact that richness is the only

2[Editor's Note. Only years after writing this was the work of Peter Miller brought to my attention. He also defended a theory of "value as richness." Although I decided on the term 'richness' independently, and our definitions are somewhat different, I believe we are both trying to capture the same property and for similar reasons. So credit where credit is due.]

thing people really value seems likely to be that richness *is* valuable. Without some other explanation for the uniformity of what we value – an evolutionary explanation for example – the uniformity itself suggests that valuers agree because valuers have access to a real property of the value world. As such, the present project is part of a larger project attempting to show the objectivity of value.

If value is real, there are few more important projects than finding out what it is. Value talk permeates our lives. We talk of good theories and good actions and good paintings. To establish a value theory will alter or affirm the way we do economics, environmental ethics, theology, epistemology and moral theory. It will give us insight into debates on euthanasia, capital punishment, abortion, democracy and many others. 'What should one do?' is a question that all our actions implicitly answer. Wouldn't it be nice to know if we were answering it well? One way to answer this fundamental ethical question is to answer the other question first: 'What is good?' It is arguable that we do little else than try to answer this question and bring its answer to some sort of fruition in our lives.

What might make one think richness is a plausible answer? The value of richness is most obvious with respect to aesthetic value. There is a long tradition that puts richness (usually identified as 'organic unity') at the center of aesthetic value, beginning most likely with Plato and Aristotle, explored in detail by Plotinus,[3] and brought into the foundations of modern aesthetics through Leibniz, Baumgarten, Hutcheson, and Coleridge.[4] Beautiful art is art that brings some portion of the multitude of human experiences together in a harmonious way, or that brings the variety of color, or sound, or meaning or shape together so that it is *one* thing.

The value of richness outside of aesthetics is not without mention. A fairly common interpretation of Plato's *Republic* has it that Plato thought the good was order or unity or, possibly, uniformity.[5] I have argued elsewhere that this cannot be the full story, and that Plato's conception of the good must be very much like richness, not just

---

3[Plotinus, 1957 18: I. vi]
4[Brown, 1967]
5[Hitchcock, 1985], [Fine, 1989], [Cooper, 1984]

unity but the unity of a variety.[6] A couple of millennia later, Leibniz bases an argument that this is the best of all possible worlds on the fact that it is the richest (in my sense of the word). And recently, in both *Philosophical Explanations* and *The Examined Life* Robert Nozick has put forward the conjecture that the property of richness (what he calls organic unity) underlies most of the value structure of the world.[7]

What are rich objects, then? The aesthetic literature almost invariably points to living organisms as prototypical examples of rich objects. What is it about living objects that makes them rich? Rich things are, at the very least, some form of unified variety: one thing with a whole bunch going on inside it. Often, living objects and other rich states are described as wholes whose parts are tightly interdependent: the heart does not function as a heart unless the lungs are functioning as the lungs; the first line of the poem does not function without the last; the rabbits cannot survive without the dandelions which cannot survive without the bees which cannot survive without the rabbits. Another suggestive property of living organisms is that they appear *designed*. Most – if not all – rich objects seem similarly designed; it doesn't seem as if they could have been an accident; they require explanation. Many things seem, at first glance, to be unified varieties in this sense, appearing designed, made of tightly interdependent parts: art, yes, but also human minds, eco-systems, human relationships, societies, intellectual systems and so on.

The aim of this essay, then, is to make plausible that everything of value is a unified variety of a particular sort. To show this beyond

---

6It is true that Plato thinks that the best psychology is one that is ordered according to reason, and that the best city is one that is unified, with all its parts working together toward one goal, but he can't think that the unity is the only important feature. It is also important that the psychology be complex to some degree; it is not sufficient for the personality to be reduced to a single urge; it must be that all of the personality's potentials are brought together. In the best city, we want all of the talents being used to their highest compossible degree. All of this suggests that it is not only unity that matters, but what is unified as well. Gail Fine has argued that the good is the (teleological) ordering of the Forms. But as in Plato's view, the Forms are the only things that *really* exist then this is the rational ordering of everything that exists (*and* everything that is possible). Mere order is not the highest good; the highest good is the ordering of the maximal variety. [Kelly, 2001]

7Though, notably, he seems to think it unlikely to be the *only* thing of value. [Nozick, 1981: 418-435], [Nozick, 1989: 162-169]

a shadow of doubt is unlikely here. Value is integral to all aspects of our lives. We talk about good theorizing and good manners. We talk of beauty and morality. We talk of rightness and appropriateness. To fully explain it all in a handful of pages, to *prove* that all of it is rich, is, I admit, beyond me now. The goal of this essay, then, is slightly less ambitious. I hope to show the enormous promise of the program of study, to show the advantages such a theory has over other existing theories of value, and to show that we should fully explore the concept of richness and its connections to the things we value. Along the way, I reach intermediary conclusions that, if correct, are of worth in their own right: a defense of monism, analyses of love, pleasure, and suffering, and a solution to the problem of moral motivation, among other things.

In Chapter 1, after working out a usable definition of richness, I present some of the elements of my methodology. I argue that a good value theorist needs to explain what people desire and what people value. She needs to explain our desiring because our desires are our perceptions of value; and she needs to explain our valuing because our values are our best theories of value built from the evidence of our desires. The evidence of our desires and values is a significant burden for the theory of value presented here: how to explain the multitude of different desires and values that people have all in terms of one property, all in terms of richness? As part of a response to this worry, I argue that monistic theories of value are greatly preferable to pluralistic theories of value. I do this by first refuting the thesis that values are incommensurable, and then by showing that there are significant methodological reasons for preferring monism to any version of commensurable pluralism.

In Chapter 2, I begin the attempt to meet the evidentiary burden. I survey a number of things generally held to be valuable and attempt to show both that these things are rich and that we value them for their richness. I look at knowledge, consciousness, beauty, persons, social structures, life, desire-satisfaction and some values from environmental ethics. Though this chapter is of necessity a bit shallow, I hope it demonstrates the plausibility and promise of explaining the value of these things through richness while also presenting a methodology for broadening the project to other things of apparent value.

In Chapter 3, I look at a meta-ethical argument for the claim that richness is the good. There are necessary connections between certain of our psychological attitudes and the good. I argue that one of these connections – namely that the best love is love of the good – gives us strong reason to think that richness is the good. To show this, I first present an analysis of love. Given this analysis, I argue that the only proper objects of love will be rich things. As the proper objects of love are also good things, richness must be necessary for the good. The best explanation for this fact, I suggest, is that richness *is* the good. I also show how richness accounts for the intrinsic value of love itself.

Finally, in Chapter 4, I consider the two strongest counterexamples to my theory of value. First, pleasure. At first glance, pleasure appears a simple – that is, non-rich – experience. But pleasure is one of the great (and obvious) goods, isn't it? How can the theory presented here explain the apparent value of pleasure? Second, pain and suffering. My theory entails that there is no absolute bad in the world. But pain and suffering, at the very least, seem strong counterexamples to such a claim. In response to these two objections, I give analyses of pleasure, pain, suffering, enjoyment, and unpleasantness. Using these analyses, I explain away the intuition that pleasures are always valuable and pains always disvaluable. I suggest, on the other hand, that only pleasure in the good (in richness) is always good and this is because it is a rich state of affairs; and that suffering, though not an absolute bad, is a consistently *instrumental* bad due to its invariably reducing the richness of our experiences.

1
DEFINITIONS AND METHODS

1.1 Toward a Definition of Richness

> "We in the back are all agreed that your theory is crazy. But what divides us is whether your theory is crazy enough!"
> Niels Bohr to Wolfgang Pauli

Broadly speaking, theories can fail in two ways: they can be too crazy or not crazy enough. A theory is *too crazy* when it belies uncontroversial evidence. The theory that the Adam's apple is a firm and edible fruit lodged in the throat is too crazy. A few millennia of investigation into human corpses and the like firmly confute the theory. A theory can fail to be *crazy enough* in one of two ways. A theory may be trivially true, may fail to say anything crazy; or it may be unfalsifiable, may fail to take any (crazy) risks. The theory that all bachelors are males is an example of a trivial theory. The thesis that there is an, in principle, undetectable lizard on each person's shoulder controlling his or her thoughts is an example of an unfalsifiable theory. No observation could ever disprove it. Though it sounds crazy, it takes no real risks.

I am happy to say that I am proposing a crazy theory. I claim that all the good in the world can be explained by accounting for all the unified variety in the world. I call this property of unified variety, *richness*. I claim that the value of life, beauty, consciousness, kindness, knowledge, ove and all other valuable things is due to their richness. I claim that when we combine the lists of what everyone truly values (or might in the future truly value) into a single list, we will find only rich things there. Furthermore, I claim that when we order that list's members according to their degree of value, we will also have ordered them according to their degree of richness. These are not trivial claims.

The reader's immediate concern is probably that this theory is too crazy, and much of this essay will be an attempt to defend the thesis' merely moderate wildness. Initially, though, I am more worried that the theory is not crazy enough. A similar theory of aesthetic value has been floating around for a couple of millennia: thinkers from Plato through Coleridge have toyed with the idea that beauty is unified variety (richness). To my mind, this theory's greatest weakness has been its (cowardly) mutability. Isn't most *everything* unified to some degree? Isn't most everything varied to some degree? What does one mean by unified variety anyway? Is it so vague that it applies to everything? Despite its long history in aesthetics, 'richness' has rarely received explicit definition, and the few attempts have resulted in vague and, for the purposes of being crazy enough, unsatisfactory results. In this section, I want to sharpen the term richness to the point where it might just make a value theory centered on the notion a bit dangerous to wield.

1.1.1 Boundary Conditions: Perfect Simplicity, Perfect Randomness

Let's begin by identifying those things that clearly fail to be rich. Take seriously this notion that richness is unified variety. Any good definition will have it, therefore, that some amount of unity and some amount of variety are necessary conditions of richness. If a thing is without variety, it is minimally rich. Likewise, if a thing is without unity, it is, also, minimally rich. Perfectly simple and perfectly random objects supply, therefore, boundary conditions on the concept. Richness falls somewhere in between. For an example of each these two failures, consider, on the one hand, Birkhoff's Aesthetic Measure and, on the other, Kolmogorov complexity.

George D. Birkhoff cited 'unity in variety' as motivation for the following equation in which M represents the 'aesthetic measure' (beauty), C represents complexity and O represents order:

$$M = O/C$$

The beauty of any object O is proportional to the magnitude of O's order and inversely proportional to the magnitude of O's complexity. The consequences of the equation are most easily seen by Birkhoff's ordering of polygons according to their beauty (with exact numbers!): for Birkhoff, a square has an aesthetic value of 1.5, an equilateral triangle 1.16, a Star of Jerusalem 1.00, a Greek cross .62, a swastika (Birkhoff is writing pre-Nazi) .33 and more complex shapes even less value.

Intuitively, M fails to be a good measure of either beauty or unified variety. By M, the reduction of complexity to arbitrarily close to zero makes the aesthetic measure arbitrarily large. For Birkhoff, the simpler, more symmetrical an object, the more beautiful. Birkhoff's measure is a method for measuring *unity* then; variety is only measured in as much as it gets in the way. Surely 'Mary Had A Little Lamb' is not vastly superior to *Ulysses*? Surely a simple spherical marble is not significantly more attractive than a Rembrandt? From Plato onward, one natural value theory associated the good with order and harmony, but order without anything of interest ordered is unlikely to be a unity of variety.

I am not being entirely fair to Birkhoff because the manner in which he measures order seems, sometimes, to sneak some variety in through the backdoor (though clearly not in the case of polygons). For instance, he measures a melody's order by twelve different standards, and the melody's order gets 'points' for the times that these standards are met. To have maximum order then one must be doing a full variety of ordering. And that, at least, seems correct. But it is a roundabout and inadequate way to capture the value of variety.

Consider, then, a definition that fails in the other direction. Rich things are complex things, like human beings and Rembrandts and the novel *Ulysses*. So, a natural approach to defining richness might be to look at definitions of complexity. Consider, for instance, the widely accepted definition of complexity in information theory called Kolmogorov complexity.

To measure the Kolmogorov complexity of a string of information you measure the length of the shortest program that could generate that information. For instance, consider two strings of information:

catcatcatcatcatcatcatcatcatcatcatcatcatcatcatcatcatcatcatcat-catcatcatcatcatcatcatcatcat

26539190327641278889921039392811043219076365746652110079899 82318768

The first string can be captured by the simple 'program:' *repeat 'cat' thirty times*. On the other hand, there is no obvious way of reducing the second string to something more manageable. The description length of the second string is longer than the first; therefore, the second string has greater Kolmogorov complexity. Kolmogorov complexity is useful for determining how difficult it would be to communicate a particular string of information. This accords with our intuition that Ulysses would be difficult to communicate over the phone, that rich things are not easily reducible. So, it gets that right. Unfortunately, Kolmogorov complexity entails that maximal complexity occurs in *random* strings of information, strings that are entirely unordered. But surely, *Ulysses* is richer than a random collection of letters of similar length? Random things are entirely *without* unity and, so, are *minimally* rich.

1.1.2 Unity and Variety

Francis Hutcheson defined beauty as a "compound ratio of uniformity and variety: so that where the uniformity of bodies is equal, the beauty is as the variety; and where the variety is equal the beauty is as the uniformity." Nozick took a nearly identical tack.

I borrow their approach for defining richness. A state-of-affairs is richer the more it increases in unity without any corresponding decrease in variety or the more it increases in variety without any corresponding decrease in unity.

This might be captured by the following equation:

$$R = UV$$

This captures the limiting cases. When unity is zero (randomness), richness is zero no matter how much variety there is. When variety is zero (perfect simplicity), richness is also zero no matter how much unity there is. This still suffers from considerable vagueness. What are unity and variety? How do we go about measuring their values?

In analyzing unity, it pays, I suggest, to consider closely related, if not synonymous, terms, such as, order, simplicity, uniformity, harmony, coherence. What do these concepts have in common? All of them imply a *limitation* on the number of properties in a state-of-affairs. This is straightforwardly true of simplicity and uniformity. But the same is true for unity and order.

It is in virtue of the parts of a whole sharing properties that wholes become unified. One way of putting this is that the number of *determinates* exhibited for a particular *determinable* is minimized. A determinate is a specific way of being a determinable; *scarlet* and *carmine* are both determinates of the determinable *red*; they are ways of being red. A collection of Americans is a somewhat ordered state because regardless of all the differences among individuals in the collection, they all share a property, namely, that of being citizens of the United States. The determinable of *citizenship* is fixed, limited to one determinate, and this is what the order of that collection consists in. The more determinables we fix or limit in our collection, the more ordered it becomes. A determinable need not be limited to only one determinate to unify some state. A house that is red and blue is unified by that color scheme: the determinable color is limited to only two of its many determinates. A maximally unified state is one in which all the parts of the collection share all their properties. Presumably, this state consists of something like one indivisible concrete particular (or a collection of concrete particulars indiscernible from each other). The minimally unified state consists, presumably, of a large collection of objects that share as few properties as is possible. Suppose then that the unity axis of richness is a measure of the *limitation* on the number of determinates instantiated for some determinable.

An increase in variety, on the other hand, is a *reduction of limitations* on determinables. The more varied a state is, intuitively, the *greater the number* of each possible determinate for each determinable is exhibited. The most varied state with respect to the determinable 'hair color' is one that presents all possible determinates, all possible hair colors. A collection of Americans that exhibited all colors of hair would be more varied than one that presented only two colors of hair. And a collection of persons that exhibited all possible citizenships and all possible hair colors would be a more varied state than one that exhibited only Americans of many different hair colors. If this is right, variety and unity vary inversely. Variety is lack of unity and unity is lack of variety.

This causes serious problems. Hutcheson's formula (as I've interpreted it), **UV**, is not going to be a good measure of anything. **UV** will always equal 1 (or some other constant). Variety will never increase without a corresponding decrease in unity and *vice versa*

Perhaps, then, (in defense of Hutcheson's and Nozick's take) variety and unity within richness should be maximized over different determinables. For instance, a collection of Americans all with the same hair color is unified under two determinables and varied to some extent under all others. On this account, if variety were increased in those other determinables, we would increase the rich-ness. This move could preserve a form of the original definition. For some whole $\mathbf{W}$ that exhibits two sets of determinables $\mathbf{U}$ and $\mathbf{V}$, rich-ness is that property that increases in whole $\mathbf{W}$ when the unity with respect to determinables $\mathbf{U}$ increases while the variety with respect to determinables $\mathbf{V}$ remains constant, *or* that property that increases in whole $\mathbf{W}$ when the variety with respect to some determinables $\mathbf{V}$ increases while the unity with respect to some determinables $\mathbf{U}$ remains constant. So:

$$\mathbf{R}_w = \mathbf{U}_u \mathbf{V}_v$$

Good. But which determinables to put in set $\mathbf{U}$ and which in set $\mathbf{V}$? One can't pick the sets arbitrarily. Presumably, the members of $\mathbf{U}$ need to be the more unified determinables over $\mathbf{W}$ and the members of $\mathbf{V}$ need to be the more varied. We won't be measuring richness if we measure the unity of non-unified determinables in $\mathbf{W}$ or the vari-ety of non-varied determinables in $\mathbf{W}$. Unfortunately, though, unity and variety vary inversely; every determinable is varied *and* unified to some degree. Consider the set of determinables $\mathbf{D} = \{\mathbf{d}_1, \mathbf{d}_2, \mathbf{d}_3 \dots \mathbf{d}_{n-1}, \mathbf{d}_n\}$. Suppose these are ordered by degree of unity; so, $\mathbf{d}_1$ is the most unified determinable and $\mathbf{d}_n$ is the most varied. This leaves us with only arbitrary methods for placing the rest of the determinables in $\mathbf{U}$ and $\mathbf{V}$. What justification could one give for putting $\mathbf{d}_{14}$ in $\mathbf{U}$, but not $\mathbf{d}_{15}$? This view gives us too many different but equally good accounts of how rich a particular state is.

We might try, then, confining the determinables in $\mathbf{U}$ to those that are maximally unified over $\mathbf{W}$ and confining the determinables in $\mathbf{V}$ to those that are maximally varied over $\mathbf{W}$.

This can't be right either, though. An object doesn't need to be perfectly varied or perfectly unified to have any richness (or beauty or value). A novel's variety with respect to character adds to its value even if the novel is not *fully* varied with respect to character (indeed, it would be monstrous if it were). Conversely, maximal unity over some determinable may be irrelevant to evaluating the richness or beauty of the whole within which it is in. Imagine a novel in which every third word started with a 'p' or in which all the typewritten words were black. These *may* add something to the unity of the novel, but clearly nothing significant. Supposing, though, that those were the *only* maximally unified determinables within the novel, the present analysis of richness would take *only* the 'p' repetitions and blackness of the letters into account no matter how greatly unified other aspects of the novel were. That can't be right.

1.1.3 Unities of Variety

This problem is not insurmountable. Here are two promising avenues of escape: (1) Certain *types* of determinables are those to be used to measure the richness–creating unity of an object, and other types of determinables are those to be used to measure the variety. The repetition of p-words is not the right type of determinable. (2) Richness requires some connection between unity and variety; a common referrer for the property is, after all, 'unified variety.' It is not sufficient that unity and variety co–occur within some **W**; the variety must be unified in some manner. The repetition of p-words does not unify the novel properly because it is unconnected to the variety in the novel.

One can tease a solution from Leibniz that captures the force of these two suggestions. He says with respect to the perfection of this universe, "As concerns the simplicity of God's ways, this holds properly with regards to *means*, as on the contrary the variety, richness and abundance in them hold with regard to *ends or effects*"{italics mine}.

For Leibniz the proper unity of richness resides in the simplicity of the *means* that created the richness, and the proper variety in richness resides in the variety of the *ends*. So,

$$R_w = U_{means} V_{effect.}$$

This view entails a tight connection between the variety of a rich whole and its unity. The variety in a rich whole is created by unified means. The repetition of p-words was not part of (or was only a meager part of) the means for creating the variety of the novel, and this is why it does not properly unify the novel.

The problem here is that the richness of **W** should not generally be dependent on how **W** *actually* came about. Richness is a structural feature of a whole; if the structure of the whole itself can be considered without knowing its history (a sculpture, a blade of grass, a sunset, a human being), then its richness should be independent of its history. If, due to some accident of quantum mechanics and the improbable conjunction of all the proper molecules, Joyce's *Portrait of the Artist as Young Man* appeared fully formed from a gaseous swamp, it would still be a rich and beautiful object.

Further, and even more worrisomely, it seems unlikely that the actual creation history of most rich objects *is* simple. The creations of humans and novels are generally not simple affairs. Indeed, one might think that rich objects are precisely those that are hard to make, that would require quite a bit of work to create.

Briefly, let's turn back to the literature on complexity. Lloyd and Pagel's definition of physical complexity turns on this notion that complex things require quite a bit of work to make. They define the physical complexity of **O** as **O**'s 'thermodynamic depth.' The thermodynamic depth of **O** is a measure of how much entropy was created in the creation of **O**. Why would we think this would have anything to do with the complexity of an object? Entropy is a measure of disorder. If work is done, it increases the amount of entropy in the world. So, an object with quite a bit of thermodynamic depth required quite a bit of work to make.

Though this view captures the fact that it is, generally, hard to create rich objects, it fails to answer the objection that the actual history of an object is irrelevant to whether the object is itself rich.

Charles Bennett, noting these weaknesses (and the weaknesses in Kolmogorov complexity), favors a definition of complexity he calls *logical depth*. The logical depth of a system is the execution time required to produce that system given a (near) incompressible universal computer program. Recall the **cat** series from earlier. That string could be compressed to a string that gave the order to repeat **cat** 29 times. Think of the incompressible universal computer program to be the best theory of how the system came about. The system is complex, then, according to the amount of work it would take to produce that system on that theory.

Definitions along these lines have a number of advantages. 1) It gives an explicit method (if often impractical) for ranking the complexity of systems. 2) The notion of unity is captured by the notion of an incompressible universal computer program – the system is unified by the fact that the entire system can be seen to arise from a single simpler source. 3) It captures the intuition that a complex system is an unlikely one, that it, generally, requires significant work to create such a system. 4) It explains the connection between the unity of a system and its variety.

Here are three prominent worries about such an account: 1) Can all systems that we want to rank for complexity be replicated by Turing Machines? There are a number of physical scientists who think so. But there are many who think not. It would be nice if we could capture the notion of richness in terms at least nominally neutral on what the final theory of physics will look like. 2) What about the complexity of incompressible strings with truly random elements? Consider, for example, the following method for producing a string of numbers. Find the first number using a truly random event or a series of truly random events to elect between 1, 2, and 3. Find the second number by randomly choosing between 2, 3, and 4, and the third by choosing between 3, 4, and 5 and so on to infinity. The resultant string, because random, is not compressible in the normal manner. On the above definition, then, it would be no more complex than a completely random sequence. But clearly this is not a *completely* random sequence; it exhibits more structure and, thus, more complexity (richness) than a completely random sequence. It has unifying properties that a random sequence does not. For instance, it is a fact about whatever this sequence turns out to be that the addition of any three consecutive numbers in this sequence is always greater than twice the first of the three numbers. It has order that no purely random sequence has. (3) Take two different strings **S** and **T**, one that is compressible to s and the other that is compressible to t. Consider the string **U** that is the result of appending **T** to **S**. The tightest compression of **U** will often be merely some fairly simple joining of t and s. Does this mean that **U** is unified? If we think of s as the explanation for **S** and t as the explanation for **T**, then the proper conjunction of s and t *is* an explanation of **U**. But it is clearly not a unified explanation of **U** and so seems unlikely to be a good unification of **U**.

But looking at Bennett points us to a central aspect of what it is to be rich. For any information string, the shortest program that generates that string functions much like the 'best explanation' for that string. It is not the *means* that we need to unify, but the *explanation*. So:

$$R_w = U_{explanation} V_{explanandum}$$

The richness of **W** is the variety in the object times the unity of the best explanation for the variety of the object. We must restrict the types of explanations, though. Often the best explanation for many, if not most, states-of-affairs would lie in the causal history leading to that state-of-affairs, but we established the causal history of **W** isn't necessary for determining the richness of **W**. We are looking for explanations that capture not the history of the explananda but the *patterns* in the explananda. We need *nomic* explanations, that is, explanations that look like laws.

Start with a simple example. The following famous series can be seen as unified by the fact that it suggests a *nomic* explanation.

(F) 1 1 2 3 5 8 13 21 34 55 89 144 233 377 610 987 1597....

There are many explanations for how these numbers might appear on the page. Explanations about how the printer copied them from the galleys or how I learned them in discrete mathematics in junior high school or some story about an Italian named Fibonacci or an account of the history of the Golden Ratio. None of these serve the present need; none of them are *nomic* in nature. Here, though, is a possible *explanatory law*: if y is in the (n–1) ordinal position of (**F**) and x is in the (n–2) ordinal position, then the number in the nth position of (**F**) will equal x+y. This is a law–like explanation of all elements of the series other than the first two; moreover, *it is precisely the reason that we see this series of numbers as unified.*

Now for a significantly more complicated example. James Joyce's novel *Portrait of the Artist as a Young Man* was, for its time, radically structured. The novel progresses in voice and tone throughout the body of the work, gradually passing from a child-like voice to the voice of an intelligent, rebellious young man. Many of the traditional unities of the novel are broken: tone, diction, even subject matter to a large extent. The reader accepts this variety because she largely understands the reason for it, because, I suggest, she senses a law–like explanation for this variety. The reader grows up with the protagonist and the language does as well. The law is something like: if the protoganist is of age x he will write like someone of age x. What we ask for in an artwork (and in richness) is not just variety, but a non-arbitrary variety. We need a reason for the variety, an explanation for the way the artwork is. And for what kind of explanation are we looking? It is closely connected to the artist's intentions, of course, but, again, a good novel should not depend for its enjoyment on our knowing what the actual genesis of the words was. Rather, we want to know if the novel, all by itself, is intelligible. I suggest that there is a method for explaining each of Joyce's choices, a method that does not require us knowing that he was drinking coffee while he wrote chapter four. We need only discern the 'laws' of the book; we need discern the rules governing the choices. These rules are grammatical, semantic, representational, dramatic.... among others no doubt. They are for the most part not deterministic and the *actual* rules that Joyce used are, of course, somewhat inaccessible to us. But, nonetheless, the unity we require of an artwork is just the sense that there *are* rules governing the choices; that there are structural reasons for why the novel is the way it is, for why the particular words are where they are. In the end, we want the sense that the work has some unitary explanation.

We look for law-like explanations for the variety in a rich object just as theoretical physicists are looking for law-like explanations for the variety of phenomena that makes up our world (which is also, clearly, a rich object). To be unified is to follow rules, but not just any rules, remember, but *explanatory* rules. It may be that *Portrait* obeys the following rule: **(R1)** There shall be no less than ten instantiations of the letter 'e' on any one page. This rule fails to be explanatory; it is *ad hoc*. Nothing about the fact of ten e's on each page makes us think that such a rule played any role in the genesis of the book. It is, therefore, not a properly unifying property of the book. On the other hand, if every word starts with a 'p', then we are tempted to think that was no accident, that it could only be explained by someone or something following a rule that entailed such a pattern.

This distinction between an explanatory rule and a non-explanatory rule give us one method for understanding Aristotle's claim (and those of Leibniz and Coleridge) that "the whole is prior to its parts" in rich objects. It is plausible to think that rich wholes are wholes in virtue of the rules governing them. Without those rules the parts would *not* be parts of any whole because they would not be unified by anything. "Only when the whole has been dissolved will they [the parts] attain actuality," says Aristotle. Explanations are prior in some difficult to define sense to what they explain. Non-explanatory rules are not prior to what they attempt to explain (hence, the sense that they are *ad hoc*, that they are added on afterward). And, so, an explanatory unification is prior to the variety it explains.

Let me recap what's been done so far. On the one hand, progress has been made; I've narrowed the problem of analyzing richness a great deal. Take some **W**. Determine a law–like explanation **E** for **W**. Establish which of the determinables **D** in **W** are governed by **E**. Evaluate the unity of **E**. Evaluate the variety of **D** (determine how many of the determinates for each determinable in **D** are instantiated). Multiply the variety by the unity.

On the other hand, I am about to run hip deep into three famous problems in epistemology and, more particularly, the philosophy of science.

1) One needs an account, now, of how to measure the unity of an explanation; this is tightly connected if not identical to the problem of determining the simplicity of a theory, of defining Occam's Razor. This is a notoriously thorny bramble. It is hard to find any theory–maker who does not accept the governing norm of simplicity in their work, and yet several decades of attempts to give accounts of simplicity (and unity) in theory–making have yet to reach consensus. Indeed, they don't even seem to be converging. Some think the simpler theory is the one with greatest prior probability; others think it is the theory with smallest prior probability; some think it is the theory with fewest variable parameters; others that it's the one that makes the fewest substantive assumptions; some have thought that a unified theory is the one that is the most fruitful in its consequences and this list goes on and on. Some like Eliot Sober seem to think that the intransigence of this debate means there will never be a 'unified' account of simplicity.

2) Not all determinables can matter in the measuring of variety. Consider, for example, the problems that arise due to Goodman's famous neologism, 'grue'. Something is grue if it is green and the date is before 2025 or blue and the date is after 2025. Something is 'bleen' if it is blue before 2025 and green afterward. Suppose I am considering the richness of my house, particularly the variety of its colorations. My house is green and blue and it is 2004; therefore, my house is somewhat varied with respect to color. But my house is also grue and bleen and so is somewhat varied with respect to 'gruler'. More importantly, there is an infinite number of other strange properties that I might ascribe to my house or any other object. Without an account of which determinables matter, any object will be varied over an infinite number of determinables; and, so, all **W**'s will be equally and maximally varied. To solve this problem requires some account of basic or natural properties.

3) Finally, we need to worry about what is called the 'goodness of fit' problem. For any data set one can come up with an account that is as accurate as you'd like as long as you're willing to sacrifice simplicity. Consider, for instance, Ptolemy's cosmology. To get the Earth at the center of the universe and circular orbits and to accurately track the increasingly detailed motions of all the planets, the Ptolemaic system needed an elaborate system of 'epicycles,' little backward circles in the general orbit. The more accurate the theory was made, the more inelegant it became. A similar problem applies to the present method of evaluating richness; suppose **E** is the most unified law–like explanation of some of the variety in a whole **W**, and **F** is a slightly less unified law–like explanation of *more* of the variety in a whole **W**. As long as both **E** and **F** count as law-like explanations of **W**, the present method does not tell us which to choose. And there is no reason to think that these two measures of the richness in **W** will give identical magnitudes. Which is the right account?

Before saying something substantive about the first problem, let me point out that, despite the obstinacy of these problems, this is a good place for us to be. Each of these three problems are solved in practice by scientists and philosophers all the time. Theory-makers know simplicity when they see it; they understand which properties matter and which don't; they continually balance elegance versus explanatory power. If value theorists find that their worst problems are those faced by practicing physicists, biologists, and chemists, then we should count ourselves in good epistemological company.

I am going to spend the rest of this section giving us some rules of thumb for identifying explanatory unity. This will be important so that we can evaluate whether valuable things are, indeed, rich things and whether more valuable things are, indeed, richer things.

I suggest that there are three variables important for determining how unifying an explanation is: 1) the explanation's simplicity, 2) the explanation's indeterminacy and 3) the completeness of the explanatory rules.

Simplicity first. Clearly a theory **T** is unified is if **T** consists of only one rule. But theories that have more than one rule can also unify a set of phenomena. It is clear that Newton's three laws is a somewhat unified explanation of the movement of the solar system. All other things being equal, the number of basic claims in a theory, the simplicity of the theory, is a measure of how unified a theory is. A theory is simpler the smaller the set of possible partitions of the theory. This all depends, of course, on knowing when we have one rule rather than two, and that single rules themselves cannot be more or less simple in important ways. Let us suppose, for now though, that we theorists can identify the simpler of two theories in most relevant cases and we will use the partition rule as a rule of thumb for getting in the right ballpark.

Theories can be equally simple and not be equally unifying. Consider two series of numbers: 1) an infinite series in which each element in the series is a number between 1 and 1000; and 2) an infinite series in which each element in the series is a number between 1 and 5. For example:

Series 1: 982 221 339 920 12 453 99 678 561 229 111 902 397....

Series 2: 1 5 3 4 2 1 3 4 2 2 3 5 1 1 3 2 4 3 4 5 2 1 2 1 1 3 5 5 3....

Clearly, the second set of numbers is more tightly unified by its rule. The numbers in the first set can be anything between 1 and 1000, those in the second can only be one of five numbers. A set of Americans and Germans is more unified than a set of anyone from North American and Europe (all other things equal). This suggests that the degree of *indeterminacy* in a rule is a measure of how unifying that rule is. All other things being equal, an explanatory set of rules that completely determines all the parts unifies the object more than one that does not. If the rules require that the thing be exactly the thing it is, the rules are deterministic, have minimal indeterminacy, and maximally unify (along this dimension) the thing they explain. The more the rules allow, the more *lenient* the rules are, the more indeterminacy in the rules, the less unifying they are.

I should note how stringent this condition is. Though most scientists genuinely aim for the simplest theory possible, none that I know of, aim for a maximally deterministic one. For one thing, even those theories that are considered deterministic (being such that given any earlier state one can determine any later state), require one to specify the initial conditions, that is, the laws leave the initial condiditons indeterminate. Relativity is a deterministic explanation of why the universe looks the way it does, given certain starting conditions (is the universe flat, compressed etc....). Grant that most theories will not specify their own starting conditions, still they don't achieve perfect determinism in the sense I am suggesting. Yes, many theories will determine the complete state of a system at time t given the complete state of the system at time t–1. A truly deterministic system, though, (even supposing it doesn't explain initial conditions) would have it such that *any* partial description of the system at *any* time would be sufficient given the explanatory laws for determining the complete state of the system at *all other times.* Such a system would be truly unified by its explanation. Every element would necessarily belong with every other. It is fascinating to note that Leibniz who believed that this universe was the richest imaginable seemed also to suggest that this universe was completely deterministic in the sense I am describing. For Leibniz, the universe was built up entirely out of monads and within each monad was a description of the entire universe; therefore, given the smallest bit of the universe, one would have the entire thing.

Now, imagine a whole **W** that is split into three parts, **A**, **B**, and **C**. Most of the whole consists of **A** and **B**. **C** is just a small part of the whole, a part that conjoins **A** to **B**. Suppose rule **E** explains **A** all by itself and Rule **F** explains **B** all by itself, but rules **E** and **F** together are required to explain **C**.

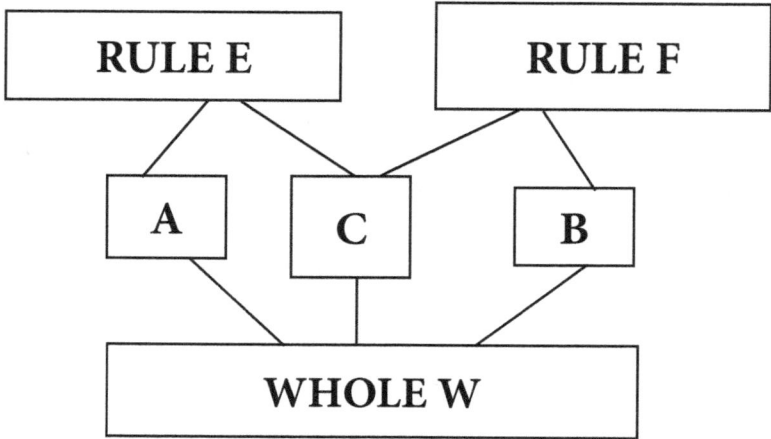

Suppose **E** and **F** are completely deterministic. This whole is still not entirely unified because the rules that govern it, **E** and **F**, are, more or less, operating independently of each other; it is only over **C** that they come together. It is not as unified, say, as a whole made of **A** and **B** in which *both* **E** and **F** are required to explain *both* **A** and **B**. This suggests one final measure I will call the *completeness* of the rules. An explanatory rule is complete if it governs, at least partially, all parts of the object. The rules are more unified, the more complete all of the rules are.

To see how this all works, consider the following Shakespearean sonnet. I assert dogmatically that the following sets of rules govern this sonnet: grammatical rules, semantic rules, metric rules, rhyming rules, and intensional rules (the intensional rules are the rules that govern whether elements of the poem are helping to achieve the overall 'purpose' of a poem: the poem is supposed to put forth an idea, or tell a story, or paint a picture, or create a feeling, or make an argument etc…). Shakespeare's sonnet would not seem an inexplicable collection of words even if one knew nothing of Shakespeare or the historical events that gave rise to the sonnet. Notice how the rules I've suggested would count as an explanation for the (complete) structure of this sonnet.

CXVI

Let me not to the marriage of true minds
Admit impediments. Love is not love
Which alters when it alteration finds,
Or bends with the remover to remove:
O, no! it is an ever-fixed mark,
That looks on tempests and is never shaken;
It is the star to every wandering bark,
Whose worth's unknown, although his height be taken.
Love's not Time's fool, though rosy lips and cheeks
Within his bending sickle's compass come;
Love alters not with his brief hours and weeks,
But bears it out even to the edge of doom.
If this be error and upon me proved,
I never writ, nor no man ever loved.

The rules that govern the poem are not spectacularly simple –
there are several rules, after all – but they are quite complete. Only
the rhyming rule seems to clearly fail the completeness test because
the rhyming rule does not explicitly have anything to say about any
of the words that are not at the end of the sentences. This rule is not a
complete rule for the sonnet because it is not part of the governance
for every part of the sonnet. On the other hand, the grammatical
rules as a whole do cover all of the sonnet (although the individual rules that make up grammar, of course, do not). The metrical
rules and semantic rules also cover each part of the poem. Most
importantly, the poem's point is brought forth through all the parts
of the poem (though this is a matter of some judgment). The poem
as a whole has a high degree of completeness, though clearly not
maximal. (In addition, it is interesting to note that the greatest art
makes the less complete rules seem unnecessary. One may feel that
the poem *had* to rhyme given the other rules – *even if the rhyming
rule were not present*: the naturalness of the meter and language and
meaning is so perfect that the poem seems as if it had to rhyme for
reasons independent of the rhyming rule. But if the rhyming rule

becomes unnecessary to explain the poem as a whole, the poem is made more complete and the rules simpler.)

Turn now to the degree of indeterminacy. Consider all possible arrangements of the sonnet with only one word missing. For instance, imagine it with 'find' missing or with the last word, 'loved,' missing or the first word, 'Let,' missing. It is plausible to think that the rules (given a modest understanding of the poem's point) above would entail – for whichever word you take out – what the remaining word must be. Given all the other words and the rules, 'find' must go at position **P**. Given all the other words and the rules, 'loved' must end the poem. The consequences of these rules are non-trivial; they have a significant logical strength; they make significant requirements on the structure of the poem.

Now, consider a different poem, **A**, in which the rules entail that given *any single word* in the structure and its place, the rest of the words are fixed. In **A**, if you have the first word or the last word or some word in the middle and you have the rules, you can deduce all the rest of the words. The rules of **A** clearly require much more of the poem than the sonnet above, and, therefore, unify the poem more significantly than the rules of the Shakespearean sonnet unify it. The words of that poem *belong* together.

Finally, imagine a complete set of rules for a poem **B** that entailed *all the words* in a poem. Given the rules, **B** has to be the way it is. Intuitively, this poem is extremely unified: there is a good and completely deterministic explanation for why all the words are where they are. These words *have* to come together. And this is why the degree of indeterminacy is a good measure of the unity of a poem.

Finally, let me use this example to make a point about how we look for a *nomic* explanation. Imagine a world much like ours in which Newton's laws are the correct and final theory of the universe. These laws are fairly simple, have maximal logical strength and are likely to be nearly complete. Given certain initial conditions *everything* is explained by Newton's laws; so, Newton's laws also explain Shakespeare's sonnet. If this were true everything would be equally unified.

The mistake here is that Newton's Laws do not explain the sonnet given *just the evidence of the sonnet*. Nothing about the structure of the sonnet suggests Newton's Law of Inertia, for instance. And none of Newton's laws explain why 'loved' must end the poem given everything that came before *in the poem*. To borrow and expand on a term from Stephen Yablo, the best nomic explanation for **F** must be the explanation most *proportional* to **F**. An explanation is proportional when it neither explains too much nor too little. An explanation like Newton's theory explains too much – it purports to explain everything – it is not an explanation specifically for the sonnet. And, clearly, explanations that fail to explain the full sonnet – for instance an explanation that only referred to the grammatical rules of English – explains too little, it is not a full explanation of the sonnet. A maximally proportional explanation of x will be a unified explanation of x and of nothing else.[1] So, when we evaluate the richness of an object, we look first for the most proportional *nomic* explanation of that object. Then we ask if that explanation is unified.

So, the unifying power of an explanation is a function of simplicity (**S**), indeterminacy (**I**) and completeness (**C**). Richness then is

$$R = U_{explanation}(S, I, C)\, V_{explanandum}.$$

There is clearly much more work to be done here, even supposing one had solutions to problems **1**, **2**, and **3**. What matters more, the variety within a determinable or the variety of the determinables? This can be put another way. My household has a variety of determinants for the determinable 'human:' my mother, father, and sister. It is also has a variety of determinants for the determinable 'mammal:' human, cat, and dog. Determinables can be determinants of other more general determinables. Is the generality of the determinable important to measuring the variety? How do (**S**), (**I**) and (**C**) form the unity function or is there a more *unified* way of capturing unity? What is the relation between the value a part has in a whole and the value that part has when considered alone? How do we form natural

---

1 [Yablo, 1997]

partitions of our *nomic* explanations? What is the most natural way to break a whole into its parts?

Rather perversely, I find it appealing that the final definition will require more work. It should be considered a positive feature of the definition and the definitional refinements to come that they require subtlety. If value is an objective feature of the world like electrons are an objective feature of the world, we would expect that the final theory of value would be something a bit separated from appearance; something that can *explain* appearance but is nonetheless not immediately apparent from experience. That is, we don't just *know* what richness is by seeing it; we don't just *know* what makes something good. We have to look around; we have to theorize; we have to struggle to unify our evidence of value. If value is as much a part of the 'fabric of reality' as CD players and we only access it through fallible human perceptions, we should expect to have some work to do to figure out what it is. It should not be surprising, then, that the good is not pleasure or happiness or reason or some set of socially constructed right actions, but something a little less obvious. I am confident that what I have presented here is an improvement on what has come before, and is enough to make the arguments that follow, but it is only a first pass. I fully expect the definition to face revision as evidence is gathered.

1.1.4 Part and Whole

Is a part of a valuable whole valuable in virtue of being part of that whole? An important aspect of the concept of richness is that it is both an intrinsic property of a whole and a relation between the parts. The intrinsic property of richness is defined as that property a whole has when its parts are in the unity-variety relation. R_{whole} $=_{def} UV(p_1, p_2, p_3 \cdots p_n)$. R is a property of wholes. UV is a relation between parts. This is nice because it explains why the parts of a valuable whole get value without the need to appeal to some notion other than richness.

So how do we find the value of a part in a whole? I suggest that the value of part of a rich whole is the variety that part adds to the whole times the unity of the whole, in other words:

$$R_{part} = U_{explanation\ of\ whole}\ V_{part\ in\ explained\ whole}$$

This entails that the value of the whole is the unity of the whole times the sum the variety of the parts *adds to the whole*:

$$R_{whole} = U_{explanation\ of\ whole}\ (V_{p1} + V_{p2} + V_{p3} \cdots V_{pn}).$$

Why should we think this is right? Intuitively, the richness of most wholes is not spread out evenly. In Hemingway, a huge chunk of the richness is located in the characters rather than the language, while in Joyce the language itself adds a great deal to the richness. Hemingway's language is simple and not very varied, but his characters are deep and unique. Joyce's language is like nothing else ever written, ranging from the straightest prose to the most outlandish verse.

So, the importance of a part to the value of the whole seems to be about the variety it brings to the whole. On the other hand, if something doesn't add to the variety it is not of much value in the work. Considered alone, a reproduction of a Rembrandt has some value; it is a unified variety. Call this **V**. But now consider a booklet made of three hundred copies of the same Rembrandt. What is the value of this whole? It is certainly *not* 300**V**. The repetition of the same painting (in the absence of some other rich reason for this repetition) clearly *reduces* the value of each individual copy. This is captured by the equation above: the variety each painting adds to the whole is minimal and so the value of each painting in that whole is minimal.[2][3]

---

2 Abstruse worry: do any of the paintings add variety to the whole? If the answer is no, then the value of the whole is reduced to near zero. The whole book isn't 300**V**, but it should be at least **V**, right? Answer: the Rembrandts by themselves do not exhaust the parts of the whole. There are also relations between those Rembrandts that need to be taken into account: any variety within the painting by itself can be matched by a relational property that governs aspects of all the paintings. For instance, suppose there is a similarity in color between the top corner of the painting and the bottom. That relation's instantiation in any particular reproduction adds no variety to the whole (accept for its being instantiated at a different *position*) because it is instantiated three hundred times. But there is an isomorphic relation that does add to the variety of the whole, namely the color in the upper left hand corner of *all* the paintings is similar to the color on the bottom of *all* the paintings. This relation *can* add variety and is a legitimate part of the whole.

3 Also, while we're here: is value additive? Value is additive if the sum of the value of the parts is equal to the whole. In one sense, we are tempted to say 'No.' If you take a certain amount of richness and then you add it to another chunk of richness, you will not, in general, have the value of the first richness plus the value of the second richness. This is exemplified by the three hundred Rembrandts. Or imagine putting together the two halves of Shakespeare's sonnet. It is clear that the value of the whole sonnet is greater than the value of the two halves by themselves. There is apparent organic unity of value everywhere, and this is captured by our definition of richness. But there is another sense in which value *must be* additive. We have defined the value of the parts in such a way that they must add up to the value of the whole. When two richnesses are brought together, new relations that are not present in either richness appear. These relations are part of the final whole and can be bearers of value.

1.2 The Experience Conjecture

1.2.1 The Conjecture

When fashioning a theory of the good, what is it that our theory needs explain? What evidence are we required to take into account? How will we know when we have a *good* theory of the good? The purpose of this section is to answer these questions. I will be arguing that, ultimately, a good value theorist needs to explain why people desire what they do and why they value what they do.

A scientific theory is judged, at least in part, by its empirical adequacy, by its ability to explain the evidence presented to our senses. I suggest that the same is, more or less, true of a value theory. How can this be? Do we have *perceptions* of value in the same way that we have visual perceptions and auditory perceptions? This sounds, at first, a bit mysterious.

Graham Oddie has argued recently that, yes, we do have perceptions of value, and that there is nothing mysterious about them because our perceptions of value are just our *desires*.[4] When we see (perceive, experience) x as good, we desire x; when we desire x, we see it as good. Oddie calls this the Experience Conjecture. That is:

(EC) To experience X as good $=_{id}$ To desire that X.

If desires just are perceptions of value, then desires are an excellent candidate to ground an investigation into value. An adequate theory of the good will explain why it is that we desire the things that we do by showing that those things are good. (An important side project, of course, will be to explain our misperceptions of the good – why we can desire things that are not good. I will look at this at the end of this section.)

---

4 [Oddie, 2003]

What reason do we have to hold (**EC**)? First and foremost, (**EC**) gives us an excellent solution to the problem of moral motivation. The good is, by its nature, an action-guiding thing; but if, as is commonly believed, we can only be motivated by our desires, then the good can have no purchase on how we actually act. The problem of moral motivation is fairly simple then: how can the good motivate us? (**EC**) gives us an answer: our desires – the only things that motivate us – are perceptions of the good. Let's make this plausible.

I have an undergraduate degree in physics and some unspectacular knowledge of how quantum mechanics is used to build a CD player. Specifically, I know **P**: "A CD player works according to the laws of quantum mechanics." This bit of knowledge is mildly interesting, but I take no great pride in it: it is not grounded in any great understanding. Indeed, anyone could know **P** if some trustworthy expert were to tell him it was true. But my knowledge of **P** can improve. I have a friend who is a physicist. I ask my friend to explain to me exactly how the CD player works. My friend agrees and begins my instruction. At some point in his teaching, assuming my ability to follow, I will *see* how it is that certain rules of quantum mechanics allow for the functioning of the CD player. I will see what makes **P** true. When I do see it, I *understand how* **P**. When this occurs, my knowledge will have a particular *seeming*, a seeming that I understand **P**.[5] I started out with a bit of knowledge, a single propositional belief. After explanation, I had understanding. I had a model for the truth of **P**. This is a common enough experience. Most learning that is not just memorization is built out of understandings of this sort. Call this seeing what makes something true *understanding how*.

Two things before proceeding: first, I do not intend this to map onto the familiar distinction between 'knowing that' and 'knowing how' often brought up with respect to Frank Jackson's Mary argument – though, I am not ruling out some connection. Second, I have no intention of claiming that understanding-how is non-propositional. I do want to suggest, though, that understandings-how

---

5 Peter Forrest suggests that this 'seeming' is necessary for understanding (though, of course, not sufficient). [Forrest, 1991]

must involve a particular seeming. It would not be sufficient for me to have memorized the list of propositions that my friend tells me about the relation between quantum mechanics and CD players nor to consciously recite statements that expressed those propositions. That would not entail that I understood how quantum mechanics makes my CD player work. To truly understand how, I must bring those propositions together in awareness in some manner. The simplest, least mysterious, explanation of this phenomena is to say that I become aware of the logical relations between the facts my friend is telling me and the proposition **P**, namely, that those facts entail (or make more likely) **P**.

So, consider a second friend of mine. This friend has excellent taste in classical music. He has recommended many composers to me who have all proven to be good. Sometimes, at first, I don't like the pieces he suggests; but invariably, after a time, sometimes with work, I do come to like the pieces. At some point in my self-education, I start to see (hear) the good in them. The harmonies click, the melodies come clear, the counterpoint is evident, and I begin to enjoy the music. Recently, he recommended another composer, **M**, to me. Again, I trust him completely, but *as of this moment*, I just can't see what is good about **M**'s music. I believe that **M** is a good composer, but I have yet to see it; I have yet to understand how **M** is good.

The psychology of this is interesting. Right now, while I merely *believe* that **M** is good, but don't *see* it as good, it is rather difficult for me to listen to **M**; it is work. Without my friend's recommendation, I would have given up long ago. I only keep listening because I know **M** is good – my friend told me so – and I know that it will be worth it when I finally *do* get it. For now, though, I really don't feel like listening to **M**. On the other hand, I know from past experience that the moment I really do begin to *hear* the good in **M**, in that moment, I will *want* to listen to **M**. It won't be a chore. Rather, it will be a pleasure to listen to **M**. So, at some point, I will be listening to **M** and I will have that experience (or many small ones) where my many listenings to **M** are brought together and unified; suddenly I will see

M as good.[6]

It is immediately apparent that the sudden seeing of something as good is psychologically similar to the sudden *understanding how* something is true, but the case of the composer M suggests that understanding how something is *good* involves more than other understandings how. Seeing something as good involves not only a qualitative attention shift, but also a motivational shift. This is key. Before I perceive M as good and after I perceive M as good, I *believe* that M is good. But only after seeing M as good do I really understand how M is good, do I really see the good in M; only then do I find M motivational. Only then am I *drawn* to M. Moreover, I am not really seeing M as good unless I *am* drawn to it. This suggests a biconditional between seeing M as good and being motivated by M, a biconditional most easily explained by (EC).[7]

This also defeats the following type of objection. Yes, one might object, certain things Y give rise to desire. But this isn't because we are perceiving value; it's because we have a pre-existing desire for

---

6 Why do I try and listen to M at all? I must be motivated to some extent; I must have some desire. So, if (EC) is correct, I must see listening to M as good to some degree. What I desire, I suspect, is to have an experience similar to the experiences I've had listening to other recommendations of my friend. In general, I've seen that following my friend's advice has led me to these experiences and so, because listening to M is likely to lead me to something I desire, I see listening to it as desirable for instrumental reasons. It is not a strong motivation because the good of listening to M is (1) only probable – there is only a probable connection between listening to M and receiving the good listening experiences. The more faith I have in my friend the easier it will be to listen to M. (2) I cannot fully *see* the connections between listening to M now and the good listening experiences I will get later on. I understand how giving money to a cashier is likely to get me the ice cream I've asked for. The person will turn around and make it because it is part of a fairly explicit agreement between customer and store that a certain price will get a certain product. On the other hand, I don't fully understand how my listening to M now is going to lead me to the good experiences later – this is because I don't understand how the music is good. I have some understanding of how this is going to work – things I haven't noticed before will become salient, certain melodies will become comprehensible, but I don't *fully* understand how this will happen – I don't know which melodies these will be, for instance; I don't know how much work I'm going to have to do etc....

7 Grant Sterling has a similar view [Sterling, 1994, Ch.5]. He argues that desires necessarily give rise to perceptions of value (he calls them quasi-beliefs). Though this ends up having similar consequences, it is less explanatory than (EC). How do we explain the necessary connection between desire and perception of value? (EC) is an elegant and fundamental explanation.

things of type **Y**. We find out that **P** is **Y** and so we desire it. We all start out with some desires and we use those to form the remainder of our desires and it has nothing to do with the actual value of things in the world (unless, we got lucky, and our innate desires mapped onto the good). But this can't be right: merely believing – merely getting knowledge that **P** is **Y** is insufficient to make us desire it, *even if I do have a pre-existing desire for things of type* **Y**. I have a pre-existing desire to listen to good music; I come to find out that **M**'s music is good music. This on its own cannot make me want to listen to **M**'s music in the face of my failure to experience **M**'s music as good. I have to, first, *perceive* listening to **M**'s music as good.

To see all this more clearly, note the following variations on examples from Oddie: "I believe that giving to charity would the best thing to do, but I can't seem to muster any desire for it" and "Right now, I really *see the value* in giving money to charity (or alternatively, right now, I am *really valuing* giving money to charity), but I can't muster any desire to do it." The first sounds odd, but if we accept the possibility of the weakness of will, we don't think it is a logical contradiction. Indeed, the oddness may be entirely due to the bald-faced admission of weakness. The second claim on the other hand seems downright contradictory. How could I really be seeing it as good, how could I really be valuing it *right now* if I wasn't drawn to do it in any way?

Why should this be? The connection between the good and our motivations has always been one of the great challenges of meta-ethics. The good by its action-directing nature *must* have some motivational power. Socrates famously argued that only ignorance of the good explained immorality.[8] If, Socrates claimed, we really knew what the good was, we would always do it. But why should the *having* of any belief (namely, one about what is good) entail the *having* of any desire? Indeed, as Oddie points out, the having of a particular belief doesn't even entail the having of any other *belief*, even if those beliefs *logically* entail each other.[9] Though Euclid believed his axi-

---

8 [Plato, 1976: 352-8]

9 [Oddie, 2003, 28] Though we may think deductions due to containment relations

oms, he did not believe all propositions deducible from them. How much less plausible it is to think that the having of a belief must entail the having of a desire.

The simplest way out of this for the Socratic would be to claim that value beliefs just are desires (motivations) of a sort. Call this the Socratic Conjecture (**SC**). There are two rather powerful reasons to think (**SC**) unlikely. First, desires and beliefs are very different things, both in the way they function and in the way that they feel. Anscombe distinguished between beliefs and desires by their *directions of fit*.[10] A belief is a mental state that must fit the world. A desire, on the other hand, is a mental state with which the world 'must' fit. Michael Smith put this in the form of a counterfactual: If you find out not **P**, you stop believing **P**, but you don't stop desiring **P**.[11] Beliefs and desires have different directions of fit, so they can't be the same thing. Furthermore, most of us – though, notably, not Michael Smith – are willing to accept that desires are *warm* mental states (they feel like something) while beliefs are not.

A second important – and, perhaps, more conclusive – reason to doubt (**SC**) is that our desires and our beliefs about value can come apart; we can have a belief about value without the corresponding desire or a desire without the corresponding belief about value. This is called weakness of will and is, on the face of it, quite common. I can believe that it would be best for me to abstain from eating the layered strawberries and cream double devil cake, but still eat the cake due to overpowering desire for the cake. Though I know what I should do, my will is weak. Harry can believe that it is right to give 20% of his income to charity, but not do it because he feels no motivation. Though he knows what he should do, his will is weak. Surely, situations like these occur all the time. But if desires *are nothing other than* value beliefs, weakness of will appears impossible.[12]

---

between propositions do necessarily occur. Doesn't believing 'Bachelors are unmarried males,' entail that I believe 'Bachelors are males?'

10 [Anscombe, 1957]

11 [Smith, 1995: 116-129]

12 This is, of course, an incredibly brief outline of a very long and complex debate. For other reading see [Smith, 1995], [Williams, 1985], [Hume, 1964], [Scanlon, 1998], [Sin-

Experiences of the good are, on the other hand, not beliefs: they are a type of perception. So (EC) doesn't face the same objections as (SC). First, the experience conjecture allows for genuine weakness of will because, as we noted above, we can believe that something is good without seeing it as good. Second, it is much more plausible to think that a desire is an experience and that to experience something as good is to desire it than it is to think that a desire is a belief or that a belief (that something is good) is a desire. Indeed, one reason to think that beliefs are not desires is that desires have a warmth – a *quale* – that beliefs need not. Experiences, by their nature, *do* have that warmth. In addition, it is uncontroversial that part of having a desire *is* seeing something good in the object of our desire; we must be feeling *something* positive for the object to be desiring it. This, as well, is explained by (EC).

(EC) allows us, then, to mediate the debate between the Humeans and the Rationalists, the two main camps in the debate over moral motivation. Humeans claim that we can only be motivated by our desires, never by beliefs alone; for the truest Humeans, even our desires can only be motivated by our desires. The Rationalists deny this claim, wanting to leave room for our apparent ability to reason about the good and have the conclusions of that reasoning motivate us even in the presence of contrary desires. (EC) gives us a way to accommodate both of these positions.

To get their strong thesis of the ground, Humeans must make a (plausible) distinction between causation and motivation. The cause of a desire need not be the motivation for that desire. Likewise, the cause of an action need not be a motivation for that action. I might act because of a microchip implanted in my brain, but it is a stretch of the language to say that microchip *motivated* me. A motivation must, at the least, be a causal *mental state* of some sort, probably a conscious mental state (I have just argued, for example, that a motivation is a perception). The Humean needs this distinction; otherwise, her thesis that desires are always necessary to motivate is entirely implausible. Clearly, I have desires and take actions that are

purwalla, 2002]

caused by things other than desires. To establish this, consider the fact that everyone must have had a *first* desire (or set of desires). Assuming, this desire had a cause, its cause must be something other than a desire. The Humean, then, allows for unmotivated desires and actions, desires and actions that are caused by things other than desires.

Recall, now, the two different ways I can believe that quantum mechanics is a good explanation for my CD player. I can believe **P** or I can believe **P** while understanding how **P**. I can call to mind the bare belief **P** or I can call to mind the model that was created when I understood how it was true. The second is clearly a much richer mental state than the first (I will discuss this further in §2.2.1). In the second, I can, metaphorically speaking, *see* the truth of **P**. I can do the same with my value beliefs. If I call to mind my belief that **M**'s works are good in the first sense, as I must do before I've come to see them as good myself, my value beliefs are, more or less, motivationally inert. If I call it to mind in the second sense, coming to awareness of the full model of **M**'s goodness, I will, under normal conditions, perceive it as good and be motivated to listen.[13]

So, yes, we can say that only desires are motivational. Neither our desires nor our actions can be *motivated* by anything other than desire. The Humean is right on this. That is only half of the debate, though. The other question is whether our reasoning about the good, and, more importantly, the good itself can ever lead us to act or desire in accordance with it. The Rationalist core contention is that even in the presence of a strong desire to do the bad, our reasoning about the good can lead us to act contrary to that desire, even absent some preexisting desire to do the good.

Can I accommodate the Rationalists, then? Yes, to a large degree. Our desires are perceptions and our perceptions can be *caused* by events in the world. More importantly, they can be caused by the true nature of things, by what is really good (assuming we have some accurate value perceptions). No, they cannot be *motivated* by anything other than our desires. My perception of the words I

---

13 [Oddie, 2003, 177-185]

am writing right now are not *motivated* by the words on the screen. Nonetheless, *evidence* of what is good and bad can be the source of our motivations to act. This is a key element in the Rationalist picture of moral psychology. In addition, as we can have perceptions of value with respect to imagined states of affairs, mental states other than desires can *cause* our desires (I can imagine sitting in the Rockies among the aspens turning, and this can motivate me to go to the Rockies this fall). This means that the conclusions of our reasoning about the good can motivates us. If we reason to conclusions that some g is good and we also understand how that something is good (maybe, because our reasoning is based on direct evidence from our value senses), our reason can be the ultimate cause of our desires. And so important aspects of Rationalism are correct as well.

(This does suggest some interesting theses about moral argumentation. If we are intending to persuade and motivate, our arguments must, in the end, paint pictures, evoke models, and give details of particular situations. This is not at all surprising, really. It is commonplace of moral motivation that one use examples, to make comparisons to situations that you know your interlocutor is familiar with, to ask your interlocutor to bring to mind what happened the *last* time they did this etc.... It is also a commonplace of moral argumentation to use detailed stories as evidence of good or bad. This suggests that imagination of a sort is key to moral progress. If we are incapable of imagining how the world is or how it will be as a result of certain actions, we will not be motivated to act correctly. An inability to picture situations, or to model all facets of a situation leaves us with an inability to *want* the right things. It is the development of this imaginative faculty that allows for us to have strong motivations toward the good, motivations to do the right thing, even if the good is in the distant future.)

All of this gives us good reason to use desires as evidence for the good. If our perceptions of value are desires, then desires are the ground for our moral epistemology in much the same way that sensory perceptions ground our empirical epistemology.[14] Absent

---

14 This is not to say that there are not moral intuitions in the normal sense of philo-

defeaters, a desire for x is a good reason for thinking that x is good.

Furthermore, what we desire is tightly connected, hopefully, to what we value; therefore, our values are also a good source of value evidence. One aspect of valuing x is to believe that x is good, but this is not the full story. You don't genuinely value x if x does not motivate you at all, even if you do truly believe x is good. Before seeing the good of **M**'s music, I don't value his music (despite believing it good). Value beliefs that are genuine values are beliefs about the good that are connected to our motivations. We know, now, which beliefs those are. Our beliefs about the good are genuine values when they are accompanied by full-bodied understandings of how the object of our belief is good, of perceptions of the value of that object. x is a value for a person **P** if **P** believes that x is good and **P** *sees* x is good when that belief is brought to full awareness under normal conditions. (Values, then, are hybrids of belief and desire. They have both of Anscombe's directions of fit. If I value X and I find out not X, I am going to continue valuing X. In this sense, values are propositional attitudes with which the world must fit. On the other hand, if I believe the proposition **P** that X is good and I find out not **P**, I should change my belief. If I do, this will change what I value. So values are both responsive to evidence and motivational.) Our values, then, are theories of the good that, when formed appropriately, are based on our perceptions of the good. Values, then, are an *excellent* – perhaps, the best – source of evidence for what is really good in the world. The goal of this essay is to explain why we value what we do. The not entirely trivial answer, given (**EC**), is that we value what we do because what we value is, generally, valuable.

---

sophical intuition. 'Murder is bad' is probably analytically true. We do not discover this through our desires, but by an analysis of the word murder. 'Murder' means bad killing. We must, however, use our perceptions of value to decide whether a case of killing is a case of murder or not, to decide whether it is bad or not.

1.2.2 The Fallibility of our Value Perceptions

One might worry that desires are too fickle an entity to count as good evidence of objective value in the world. Not only do our desires for things change, but one person's desires often conflict with others' desires. Harry and I rarely (if ever) disagree on the color of objects. We often disagree, on the other hand, about what objects are desirable. Even worse, some of my own desires change from day to day, or minute to minute. I rarely change my mind about the color of my shirt. But I desired to eat the cheesecake, I ate some, and, then, I no longer desired to eat the cheesecake. Which desire should we trust? Is eating cheesecake good or not?

In response, I suggest that as with normal perceptions, desires can fail to be good evidence. Perceptions do not always give rise to true beliefs about the world. There are a number of reasons this can happen, and, for the most part, those reasons don't make us doubt the evidentiary force of perceptions as a class. As long as, on the whole, there are principled ways to distinguish between good perceptions and bad, we have no reason to doubt that under normal conditions our perceptions – in this case, our desires – give us evidence of the world. As Harold Osbourne puts it,

> "We find no difficulty in maintaining belief in the objective reference of normal sense perception because some men, after a prolonged course of alcoholic training, see pink rabbits where no rabbits are, or because other men, born blind, see no rabbits where rabbits manifestly are. Differences which are explainable are automatically discounted."[15]

Here I survey the conditions under which normal *sensory* perception can fail and argue that those same conditions are conditions under which our perceptions of value can fail.

---

15 [Osborne, 1952 #5: 86]

Insufficient Perceptual Evidence. We can fail to draw the proper conclusions or form the proper beliefs from otherwise accurate perceptions. (a) I see a shape standing on a hill in the distance. I think it is a woman watching the sunset. I *see*, in some sense, a woman watching a sunset. It happens to be a dead tree. In this case, my sense data is not inaccurate; it is just insufficiently detailed for me to draw the conclusion I've drawn or to generate the seeming I have. (B) I sit next to a lady in a coffee shop and I smell vanilla. I conclude that the woman *smells like vanilla*. In fact, the barista is brewing French Vanilla espresso. Again, the evidence of my sensations is insufficient to draw the conclusion I've drawn. This can clearly happen with desires as well. (C) I am eating ice cream on a Lake Michigan beach just off Lake Shore Drive. I am having an extremely pleasant experience; I could sit here all day. I *desire* to continue sitting there eating the ice cream. The perception of good in the experience is largely due to the fact that the taste of the ice cream is subconsciously reminding me of a time I was eating ice cream in Greece with my lover (a good time, of course). Not recognizing this, I conclude, wrongly, that the ice cream is especially good ice cream.

Internally Caused Perceptions. Hallucinations are the best example of what I will call *internally caused perceptions*, that is, a perception not caused by the apparent object of the perception, but by something internal to the perceiver. (a) I stand up too fast and everything turns red. The redness is not due to the external world, not due to a sudden reddening of all the physical objects in my field of view, but due to internal shifting of my biology. If a perception is caused internally, it is not reliable. (B) I'm on LSD and I see spiders crawling over my hands where there are no spiders. Again, nothing about the external world is causing me to see spiders; it is the disordered functioning of my brain. This can happen with desires. For example, (C) sufficient hunger can make even eating cardboard seem desirable. In Chapter 4, I suggest that many of our pleasure and pain-oriented desires are hallucinations of this sort; they are caused, at least partially, by our own internal urgings, rather than by the actual features of the apparent object of our perception. Hunger, thirst, sexual longing are powerful examples. One bit of evidence that these might be hallucinatory is that before and after hunger, one and the same object can seem both desirable and not desirable. Once you give me a cracker, I no longer want to eat cardboard. In Chapter 3, I discuss how a number of our emotional states are similarly hallucinatory. It's dark and I am scared and suddenly I see beasts coming from out behind the trees. Or I am insecure and I experience your offhand comment about my teeth as cruel.

Bias. The deductions we draw from our perceptions can also be twisted by our preexisting desires. (a) Tristan and Harry are watching a baseball game. They are rooting for separate teams. Harry's team's first baseman slides into home. The call is close. Tristan is sure that he sees him as out, and Harry is sure that he sees him as safe. Neither is *lying*. They are both certain of what they saw. So, our desires, our bias for certain outcomes can twist our perceptions (or the conclusions we draw from our perceptions). Another example, (**B**) Tristan is terrified that Harry and Juliet are seeing each other romantically. He walks around a corner and sees them together. Frightened, he jumps back around the corner. In his mind, he is sure he saw them holding hands, but they were not. His fear twisted his perception. Clearly this can happen with our desires as well. (**C**) Tristan really wants to fall in love. He finds Juliet much more lovely (desirable) than if he were indifferent on the matter of falling in love. Or I've been waiting months and months to see the new Matrix movie. I really want to like it. Despite its mediocrity my bias leads me to find it desirable.

Different Perspectives. Graham Oddie suggests that much of the apparent intersubjective conflict in our desires is merely due to the fact that we each perceive value from our own perspective.[16] Just as our physical perceptions are bound by the perspective from which we perceive things, so our value perceptions are bound by our perspective on the world. (a) Standing on different sides of a room, you

---

16[Oddie, 2003: 135-157] Also Dewitt Parker [Parker, 1968] "There are differences and oppositions among the currents of desire; yet even when I stand in one and you stand in another, I can imaginatively place myself where you are and perceive that what you seek is, generically, what I seek."

and I will have differing sets of perceptions. There will be things that you see that I cannot; and things I see that you cannot. If we never move from our respective positions, the conclusions we each draw from our perceptions will be incomplete, and if we have no communication, we will have different beliefs about the room. So too with our desires. We have wants that have a lot to do with who we are and what we know. (**B**) I have never studied **M** and so I don't desire to listen to **M**. My friend has studied **M** and so desires to listen to **M**. We have different evidentiary perspectives on **M**'s music. Furthermore – and this may account for most disagreement about the good – we each have significantly greater access to our own psychologies than we do to anyone else's. There are things I desire that it is entirely appropriate for me to desire for myself that it would not be appropriate for you to desire for yourself given our differing histories, talents, and situations. I really desire to play the piano right now. You don't know *how* to play the piano. My perspective on the world gives me a different, but still accurate, perception of the value of playing the piano.

Differing Abilities. Some persons are born deaf. It doesn't give us reason to doubt that hearing in normal persons is evidentiary. Some persons are born color blind. Some of us lose our hearing. My grandparents have lost their sense of smell. Sometimes the loss of one sense increases the sensitivity of the remaining ones. The ability to sense the world is not an absolute one: we don't all have it to the same degree. The five senses differ across the population in accuracy and breadth of application. Why shouldn't we expect the same with our perceptions of value? There is some evidence that psychopaths and/or sociopaths have lost the ability to see the good. A trained painter has an increased ability to use their visual perceptions to model the world *and* an increased ability to see the good in a difficult painting. We can train our perceptual faculties to be more acute. Why shouldn't we be able to do the same with our desires? Are there not people whom we consider aesthetic experts (like my friend who suggested **M**)? Are there not people we look up to us moral experts? One explanation for such an attitude toward experts is that they have demonstrably better perceptual faculties with respect to the good, either because they were born with better faculties or their faculties are better trained.

Habit Judgments. Harold Osborne suggests some of the judgments that appear to be based on our perceptions are actually what he calls 'habit judgments.' I have learned to distinguish between x and y by the fact that x has always in my experience had feature **P**. I have come to make the habitual judgment that whenever I see **P**, I am seeing x. But it so happens that x need not always have **P**. And, so, my perceptual claims that 'I have *seen* x' are often false. This is common with our moral judgments. You are told from a young age that stealing is bad (and even perhaps recognize some of its badness for yourself). On hearing that Harry stole some bread, you automatically draw the conclusion that that act was bad, whether or not you had a real perception of that badness. Perhaps, Harry stole the bread from a wealthy and evil merchant in order to feed his starving child. Perhaps you'd never considered such a case.

Just as with normal perceptions, we can guard against these failures. With respect to (1) Insufficient Evidence and (6) Habit Judgments, we should be careful to draw conclusions from our perceptions that are commensurate with the amount of perceptual evidence we've obtained. I should claim that there is a shape on the hill that *looks* like a woman (or that has a certain geometrical shape or is a certain color), rather than conclude it is a woman. I should conclude that *something* smells of vanilla, rather than claim the woman next to me smells of vanilla. Likewise, I should conclude that there is *something* good about my experience of the ice cream and the beach, though I can't put my finger on it.

With respect to (2) Internally Caused Perceptions, we should be careful about drawing conclusions from our sensory perceptions when we are in states likely to lead to hallucinations. If I am on psychedelic drugs, severely dehydrated etc.... I should be careful about trusting my perceptions. If there are reasons to suspect that our desires are driven by internal needs (or malfunctions) – i.e. hunger, thirst, addiction, lust etc.... – I should be careful about taking my desires as objective. We should do something similar with respect to (3) Bias. If I have strong second-order desires with respect to desires of type **P**, I should be careful about assuming that my desires of type **P** are really caused by the good of **P**. I will discuss both (2) and (3) in further detail in Chapter 4. Finally, we should take (4) Different Perspectives into account. It is important for us to try to see things from others' perspectives if we want to get a full accounting of value. I will discuss this a bit more in Chapter 3.

In conclusion, the experience conjecture is an elegant solution to two outstanding problems in meta-ethics: the problem of moral motivation and the problem of value perception. If desires are just perceptions of value, then we have a simple explanation of how the good motivates us. In addition, we can explain the gap between our knowledge of value and our motivations; *and* we can explain the gap between the value in the world and our perception of it. And if desires are just perceptions of value, then we also have a more or less mundane explanation of how we can *see* value.

Finally, I want to note that none of what follows *requires* (**EC**). Nonetheless, as with most good theories, (**EC**) is useful. It makes the conclusions I draw and the arguments that lead to those conclusions significantly more elegant. Even so, if you accept the fairly uncontroversial claims that we use our desires and preferences as evidence of value and that to desire something is to, at least, temporarily, feel there is something good in that something, then you need not accept (**EC**) to see the force of the following arguments.[17]

---

17 See [Oddie, 2003] for a further and deeper defense of (**EC**).

1.3 Monism vs. Pluralism

[*Note For The Reader:* If you would like to move on to the meat of the argument for richness, you are welcome to skip or skim this section and move on to **Chapter 2**. The following argument is fairly extensive and, though it is independently interesting and lends support to the general approach of the book, it is not necessary for following the general argument. In this section, I will argue that we should be looking for monistic theories of the good, that is theories that claim only *one* thing is good. In the rest of the book, starting with **Chapter 2**, I lay out an argument for a particular monistic theory, namely that only *richness* is good.]

Value pluralism is the thesis that there are many basic (non-reducible), intrinsically valuable properties in the world. Value monism is the thesis that there is only one intrinsically valuable property. Pluralistic theories of value have strong advantages over existing monistic theories because they more easily capture the value evidence. On the face of it, there are many things that are valued; we love people and paintings; we like foods and generosity; we care about flowers and physics; we value autonomy and pleasure. We treat many of these things as ends in themselves. If all of these things are intrinsically valuable, the monist must show that they all share some single property and that it is this property that accounts for their degree of value. This is a serious obligation, and one that most would admit has yet to be met by any monistic theory. And, so, there are evidentiary reasons to be a pluralist.

There are two types of pluralist to consider. Call them the 'radical pluralist' and the 'moderate pluralist.' The radical pluralist claims that there are many (at least two, though usually many more) different values and that these values are incommensurable. The moderate pluralist claims that all values are commensurable but not reducible. I argue that radical pluralism is impossible, and that, all things being equal, monism is far preferable to moderate pluralism.

The radical pluralist claims that not only are there many irreducible values, but that at least some of these values cannot be compared. This is called value incommensurability.[18] Two values are incommensurable when it doesn't make sense to compare them, that is, when it doesn't make sense to claim that one value is greater than, lesser than *or* equal to the other. Temperature and IQ are incommensurable. It would be silly to compare (literally, though not metaphorically) something's temperature to its IQ. Many committed pluralists claim that some values are just as incomparable as intelligence is to heat.[19] If some two values are incommensurable, monism must be false. I argue that we have good reason to doubt that values *could* be incommensurable, and no good reasons to believe that they must. I argue, first, that given a common understanding of the good's connection to desire, values cannot be incommensurable. Then I look at the common reasons put forward by radical pluralists for incommensurability – most importantly, the common experience of value conflict – and show that these are not evidence for what the radical pluralist claims they are. In the end, I claim that the radical pluralist is not really trying to capture something about meta-value, but something about value, namely the value of variety, a value happily incorporated by the present theory.

1.3.1 Against Radical Pluralism: Argument from the Merit Connection[20]

It is a commonplace worry for the radical pluralist that his position entails that practical rationality is necessarily incomplete: there are times when our rational decision-making process must fail. If two incommensurable values conflict, and no other value is present, there can be no rational justification for choosing one over the other.

---

18 Some pluralists use incommensurability to mean, merely, that there are plural values that are not reducible to one single measure of value. We are not using the word in this sense. That is what I am calling moderate pluralism.

19 [Kekes, 1993], [Nussbaum, 1990], [Raz, 1999; Raz, 1986]

20 The argument of this section was published in Philosophical Studies (2008)

This, on its own, I find rather implausible. Take incommensurable values **A** and **B**. Given their incommensurability and assuming that neither are instrumental to creating some other, commensurable values, it is impossible to have any rational justification for choosing between **A** and **B**. Now, imagine gradually increasing the amount of **A** and decreasing the amount of **B**. Since **A** is a valuable thing, more of it *should* be more reason for choosing it. Nonetheless, though our reason for choosing **A** increases, it can never outweigh **B**. Indeed, imagine we increase the amount of **A** until there are gobs and gobs of **A** and only minimal amounts of **B**. Won't we, at some point in this process, have good reasons to choose **A** over **B**? Peter Schaber gives us a specific example: imagine giving up your autonomy for the remainder of your life in exchange for a small amount of pleasure now.[21] Surely, it is not only permissible for you to choose the autonomy; it is also *justified*. If pleasure and autonomy are incommensurable values, though, the radical pluralist is forced to claim the opposite: no matter how much I increase the amount of autonomy, I will never have any reason to choose autonomy over any amount of pleasure.

I suggest that this type of counterexample can be transformed into a conclusive argument against incommensurability. Call it the Argument from the Merit Connection.

I. The Merit Connection

As discussed in the last section, it is widely accepted that there is a tight connection between the value of a state-of-affairs and the appropriateness of having certain pro-attitudes toward that state-of-affairs.[22] Something about the good 'requires' that we think well of it, that we feel or act positively toward it. There are many ways of capturing this requirement, but I think the most fundamental – call

---

21 [Schaber, 1999: 75-6]

22 [Brentano, 1969: 18], [Ross, 1939: 279], [Ewing, 1948: Ch. 5], [Osborne, 1933] [Chisholm, 1986: Ch. 5], [Lemos, 1994, Ch. 1], [Zimmerman, 1999: 656], [Broad, 1967], [Oddie, 2004: 30-31]

it the *Merit Connection* – goes as follows:

> **(MC)** State-of-affairs **S** merits a desire with a strength propor-
> tional to the value of state-of-affairs **S**. [23]

(MC) is an attempt to capture some basic intuitions about value. It should be noted that **(MC)** follows fairly easily from **(EC)** the
Experience Conjecture: if desires are perceptions of value then the
strength of 'good' desires, of accurate perceptions of value, will map
proportionally to the actual value of the states-of-affairs desired.

Denying **(EC)**, though, will not get you out of **(MC)**, and the
following argument against radical pluralism is in no way dependent
on **(EC)**. One claim that everyone accepts about the good is that,
under the right circumstances, it must be able to motivate us. Mackie puts it well in his famous anti-realist argument:

> "An objective good would be sought by anyone ac-
> quainted with it, not because of any contingent fact
> that this person, or every person, is so constituted
> that he desires this end, but just because the end has
> to-be-pursuedness built into it."[24]

As I discussed in §1.2, the problem of moral motivation – the
problem of the *has-to-be-pursuedness* of the good – is one of the most
persistent in the history of value theory (and I will discuss it in even
more detail in Chapter 4). This problem is nothing other than the
difficulty of explaining the fact that the good can move us. Mackie
thinks this property of the good is so fundamental that the lack of
it in the world is good reason on its own to doubt that there is any
such thing as real value. Whatever their disagreements, all sides of
the moral motivation debate agree on one thing: a state is not good
if it does not move an adequately informed or aware rational agent.

This basic feature of the good gets us half-way to **(MC)**. All that

---

23 This eponym is from [Oddie, 2004: 31].
24 [Mackie, 1977]

remains to show is that there is a tight connection between the proper strength of motivation and the degree of value. But this is uncontroversial. Surely, the better a good is the more it should motivate us. As the amount of autonomy to be gained increases, it is appropriate for me to increasingly desire it. Another way of putting this: we should, if we have adequate understanding, be moved more by the better of two options. When we aren't, this is called weakness of will. Weakness of will is considered a failing precisely because it violates injunctions derivable from (MC). So, the better a good is, the more it should motivate us. The worse a good is, the less it should motivate us. This is nothing other than the Merit Connection. The good merits a motivation whose strength is proportional to the value of that good.

(It should be noted that I have used the word 'desire' in (MC) in place of 'motivation,' and this is because I'm a Humean about motivation for the reasons given in §1.2.[25] If you think things other than our desires can motivates us – beliefs about the good or perceptions of value, for instance – than leave 'motivation' in (MC) in the place of 'desire.' It will not affect the overall argument.)

That desire is *merited* by x does not entail that one should take actions to bring x about. A child is dying of leukemia. This child merits saving. Nonetheless, medical technology has not developed to the point where anyone is capable of saving the child. As no one *can* save the child, no one *should* save the child. My neighbor told our postman to stop stuffing junk mail in our boxes. This was a great a service. It merited a 'thank you.' Unfortunately, my neighbor never told me he did this. Given that I don't know he performed this service, I cannot be blamed for failing to provide a 'thank you.' To merit x is to be worthy of x. Merit, worth and the like are such that if other conditions are met, they impose obligations upon us. If those conditions are not met, though — if, for instance, you don't know what is merited, or you are incapable of fulfilling the obligation that normally would be merited — merit does not impose any obligations.

---

25 Humeanism is the thesis that we can only be motivated by our desires. Earlier, I argues for a version of Humeanism that, I believe, is non-threatening to the Rationalist.

So, the merit connection does not say that you should desire (or be averse to) all possible states of affairs with a strength proportional to those states actual value. Rather, given the limited nature of the human mind, you should appropriately desire those things of which you have adequate knowledge.

Some think that if a state is completely beyond your control, completely unresponsive to any action you might take, that you should have no desires with respect to it. It would be good if the president vetoed the bill in ten minutes. Should you desire the veto, given that you have no earthly way of affecting his choice? I tend to think the answer is 'yes;' I would be reluctant to call people irrational for *hoping* for things they have no power over. Nonetheless, I could see an argument in the other direction. What if the ten minutes pass and the president did not veto the bill? Should you continue to desire his vetoing it? I want to say 'yes' again; this is because I think desires have more purpose than motivating us; they can also tell us about what is good or not. Still, it sounds a bit unhealthy to continue hoping for something that *cannot* happen. Indeed, there are those who think desires with respect to the past are impossible. Anyway, by my tone, you can tell that this is not an issue I wish to resolve here. Why? Because I don't have to. If you wish, set 'practicality' as another constraint on the relation between merit and should. If something that is worthy of desire has fallen into the past or, is in some other way, entirely outside of your control, then you should no longer desire it. This will not affect the arguments to come because no value is essentially 'impractical.' Those events in the past were at one time something someone, somewhere could have had power over. The merited desire at that time would determine the value. [26]

Further notes on (**MC**):

---

26 Perhaps, a reply goes, there are values that are *essentially* impracticable. If this were true, we could not ask how we should desire them if they *were* practicable. This is a strange defense for the radical pluralist because it does nothing to show the incommensurability of important values like pleasure, friendship, autonomy, knowledge and so on. This will greatly weaken the power of the radical pluralist's claims, especially because essentially impracticable values will likely be, for the most part, values that will not alter any of the decisions we make. After all, our decisions will never affect these values in any way. Let's consider this possibility, anyway. By way of an example, suppose universals

i. Some have put forth that some variation on (**MC**) could yield a definition of 'good.' This is not my intention here; and indeed, I have serious worries about definitions of good in terms of 'merit' (or any of the options given by other formulations of (**MC**): 'fittingness' or 'correctness' or 'appropriateness' or 'oughtnesss'). Merit is a value term and, as such, is likely to be analyzed in terms of good. If it is analyzed as such, then (**MC**)-type definitions would be circular.

ii. Neither am I restricting the application of (**MC**) to intrinsic value, as some have done.[27] A state that is instrumentally good merits desires as well, a desire proportional to the degree of that state's instrumental value.

iii. Finally, by a desire for **S**, I mean nothing more than a motivation to bring about **S** (or to maintain **S**). What state-of-affairs **S** is, though, is unrestricted. We can desire a state-of-affairs in which we take a certain action; we can desire a state of affairs which consists of us experiencing or 'having' some other state-of-affairs; or we can desire states-of-affairs that have nothing to do with our experiences or actions.

---

necessarily exist and their existence is valuable (a la Plato). The existence of universals is necessarily impracticable because they have to exist. But just because we have no effect on their existing does not mean that they do not move us. Indeed, they *must* be capable of moving us if they are really values. Remember Mackie. This is what values do. So, how do they move us? Plato thought we should strive to know them, to contemplate them, to appreciate them. This seems plausible. There are many valuable things that we have little practical effect on. Consider the *Mona Lisa*. Practically speaking, my actions are irrelevant to its continued existence. Nonetheless, it still merits my appreciation. As I noted in response to Elizabeth Anderson, though, appreciation must be partly constituted by a desire. You are not really appreciating good X if you are not *moved* by it in some way. But then we *should* have desires with respect to essentially impracticable values. If this is still not completely convincing, imagine a situation where all values are impracticable; you can do nothing to bring any of them about. You can only contemplate them. Surely you still should appreciate them, and, surely, you should appreciate more the better values, and less the worse. The strength of the desire associated with these ideal appreciations gives us a measure of all value.

27 [Zimmerman, 1999], [Ewing, 1948]

II. The Argument

If (**MC**) is true, there is a tight connection between value and desire. This connection allows us to use ideal desires to tell us something significant about the structure of value. This is because the strength of desires merited by a good is a direct *measure* of the value of that good. Furthermore, there is only one relevant measure of desire-strength; therefore, desire strengths are all commensurable. This means that there is one measure for all goods: merited desire strengths. If there is a single measure for a given set of magnitudes, those magnitudes are commensurable. Hence, all values are commensurable.

The argument, more explicitly, is as follows:

I. Desire strengths are commensurable.

II. (**MC**) State-of-affairs **S** merits a desire with a strength proportional to the value of **S**.

III. Therefore, the strength of merited desire is a measure of any and all values.

IV. Therefore, all values are commensurable.

Note what this argument is not. It is not the following rather common objection to incommensurability: we make choices between values; therefore, value must be commensurable. Defenders of value incommensurability rightly reject such arguments. We can make choices for many reasons, most of which do not count as *justification* for those choices. It is not impossible to *make* choices in a world of incommensurable values – we could always flip a coin. How we actually make choices is irrelevant to the present argument. The present concern is with how ideal desirers make choices. Ideal desirers desire with a strength proportional to the actual value of their options. And the strength of these ideal desires gives us a common measure of all value.

III. Objections

In this section, I consider a handful of objections to the argument, beginning with worries about premise **I** and then moving on to prospective counterexamples to (**MC**).

A₁. Perhaps not all desire strengths are commensurable; perhaps the strengths of desires for incommensurable values are themselves incommensurable.

This is not at all plausible. Even if it were true that the values of pleasure and autonomy were incommensurable values, we would still be forced to admit that a strong desire for pleasure can outweigh a desire for autonomy (witness drug addiction) and *vice versa* (witness rehabilitation). The pleasure-desire can be *stronger* than the autonomy desire, its desire-strength *greater*. If so, the strength of a desire for pleasure is commensurable to the strength of a desire for autonomy even if those two values are incommensurable. But because we are all capable of the most blatant irrationalities, a desire for *anything* can become strong enough to trump the desire for anything else. The desires for a friend, for money, for sex, for pleasure, for autonomy, for beauty, or for bagels are all desires that one could imagine overpowering – or being overpowered by – other conflicting desires.

Another way of putting this: the *object* of a desire does not change the basic functioning of that desire in our psychology. To desire **S** is to be motivated to bring **S** about. The more we desire **S**, the more we are willing to do to bring it about; this is true of the desire for **S** *regardless* of what **S** is, regardless of what we are desiring. So even if values x and y are incommensurable, the strengths of desires for states that exhibit values x and y will not be incommensurable.

A₂. One might reply that, yes, the strengths of all *irrational* desires are commensurable, but there are rational desires that are incommensurable, namely, those rational desires that are desires for incommensurable values.

But, I argue, the commensurability of irrational desires, coupled with the fact that irrational desires can be stronger (or weaker) than rational ones, entails that all rational desires are commensurable as well. Consider some *irrational* desire with strength **B**, say a desire for beer. Suppose that **B** is significantly stronger than two other *rational* desires, say, the desire to act dignified and the desire to lose weight, desires with strengths **A** and **C** respectively. Surely this is possible, and because **B** is stronger than **A** and **C**, it is commensurable to **A** and **C**. But if **B** is commensurable to **A** and **C**, **A** and **C** must be commensurable to each other. To see this, consider lowering the strength of desire **B** gradually. Slowly, the beer becomes less and less attractive. At some point, desire **B** is no longer stronger than at least one of **A** or **C**. If **B** is no longer stronger than **A** *and* **C**, **A** and **C** are equal. If **B** is equal to **A**, but still stronger than **C**, then **A** is stronger than **C**. If **B** is equal to **C**, but still stronger than **A**, then **C** is stronger than **A**. And so, if desire-strengths **A** and **C** are commensurable to desire-strength **B**, **A** and **C** are also commensurable to each other. This could be done with any two rational desires for supposed incommensurable values. And, so, desire strengths are commensurable, even if – *per impossible* – the values they are desires for are incommensurable.

B. So, the first premise is sound. The defender of value incommensurability has to attack the second premise: **(MC)**. Elizabeth Anderson puts forward an argument that could be turned into such an objection. She agrees that the good obligates certain attitudes from us. Anderson claims, though, that different types of value merit different types of attitude and not merely desire.[28] "Beautiful things are worthy of appreciation," she says, "rational beings of respect, sentient beings of consideration, virtuous ones of admiration, convenient things of use." She thinks this plurality of pro-attitudes entails that there is a plurality of non-reducible values. And so perhaps the good doesn't merit desire: perhaps different goods merit different, incommensurable attitudes.

---

28 [Anderson, 1993: 44-59]. Also, Stocker mentions something similar [Stocker, 1990: 171-2]

First, the mere fact that we have a plurality of appropriate pro-attitudes toward good things does not entail that there are many values. Consider Anderson's list. Shouldn't beautiful things also be admired? Shouldn't sentient beings also be respected? Shouldn't virtuous beings also be appreciated? Respect, hope, desire and appreciation *are* different concepts and, therefore, have different necessary and sufficient conditions, but those conditions are not on the *type* of value being considered; you can appreciate or hope for any type of value. Perhaps, I shouldn't hope for something I already have because it is part of what it is to hope that you desire something in the future. But this isn't because a future value is a different *type* of value from an already existing value. Beauty is one and only one value; we should hope for it when we don't have it; we should appreciate it when we do. To see this more clearly, consider a situation in which *none* of the values on Anderson's list have come into being yet. There is no beauty, no rational beings, no sentient beings. Certainly, under these conditions, the pro-attitude we should have with respect to all of these values is the desire that they come about. The strength of the desires each of these values merit gives us a measure of their value.

(Moreover, even if different values do call for different attitudes, it is not clear that one is forced to deny the Merit Connection. This is because pro-attitudes, by their motivating nature, must be partly constituted by desires. Whatever the full analyses of these attitudes, one thing these attitudes must do is *move* us in some way. If you appreciate something, you desire (perhaps) to continue experiencing it. If you respect something, you desire to honor it or protect it. If you hope for something, you desire that it come about. Some part of the pro-attitudes' 'pro-ness' is grounded in some pro-*desire*. But as all desire strengths are commensurable, the strength of the desire entailed by hope and the strength of the desire entailed by appreciation are commensurable. And the strength of desire merited by value counts as a measure of value; so, again, all value is commensurable.)

C. Now consider the objection that the merit connection is false because one should value one and only one thing at any given moment: that action which is the best. On this view the ideal desirer has, at any given moment, desires only for the best option and nothing less. There seems to be something right about this: if I have decided that x is the best option of x, y, and z, why should any desires remain with respect to y and z? If this is true, then (MC) is false.

The obvious remark to make here is that this view assumes commensurability. There is no best option if incommensurable values are involved because there is no way to order the values of incommensurable options in the better-than relation. So, revise the objection to the claim that only the best option should be desired *except* when incommensurable values conflict as there is, in that case, no best option. What to desire when incommensurable values conflict? I see two plausible options. Either, nothing merits desire, or each incommensurate value merits equal desire.

In either case, the proposal is not plausible. At any given moment, many things merit my desire, not just options available to me now. Suppose action **A** has the greatest expected value at t_1; it is appropriate for me to desire **A** at t_1. What should I desire for t_2 and t_3 and a time two years from now? It is clear that I should not wait for those moments to arrive before I have any desires with respect to them. Planning is sometimes a good idea and planning must consider many of my desires for the future (or many future values). If that's true then the objection as stated is false. Furthermore, it is clear that some of the multiple desires we have for the future at any moment are more important than others and should be stronger. It is perfectly rational for me to want to fall in love at some point in the future; it is also rational for me to want to finally taste tomato-fried orzo. And it is rational for me to desire the former more than the latter. This is presumably because the former is more valuable.

In addition, a consequence of this view is that there is no rational justification for having desires of different intensity nor is there any rational justification for having desires of any *specific* intensity. As far as this view is concerned, moving about with one continually minimally strong desire, with a Spock-like nonattachment to outcomes, would be ideal. There would be no rational justification for my having an intense desire to save my love from a fire at one moment and a weak desire for tomato-fried orzo at some other moment. Of course, there is such justification, that justification being that the former is so much more valuable than the latter.

D. One might reply to (**MC**) by suggesting that neither desire strengths nor value could have the connection I suggest because both (or one or the other) come only in vague magnitudes. Yes, a very strong desire is clearly greater than some very weak desire. Yes, a very large value is greater than some very small value. Neither, though is greater by any determinate amount, and when magnitudes of desire–strength or magnitudes of value become similar in degree there is no fact of the matter about when they are equal. Value and/ or desire strengths, one might say, are vague measures. Just as you cannot say for some two clouds of similar size that one is greater, lesser or precisely equal to the other in volume, neither can you say for some two values of similar size that one is greater, lesser or precisely equal to the other.

Though, this sounds like incommensurability, it isn't. It doesn't make sense to compare incommensurable magnitudes. It makes perfect sense, though, to compare the sizes of clouds or other vague measures. What might not make sense is to attempt an entirely precise measure of a cloud. This, though, entails none of the problems normally associated with incommensurability. As both meteorologists and physicists know well, uncertainty in the object does not preclude measurement, nor prediction, nor explanation, nor comparison.[29] In the end, the proportionality requirement in (**MC**) does not require either desire-strengths or values to be of precisely determinate magnitudes.

E. One might be worried that assuming the merit connection holds commits one to some form of value realism. Now, for the pur-

---

29 Ruth Chang makes the point that magnitudes that are "roughly on par with each other" are commensurable. *Incommensurability, Incomparability, and Practical Reason*, 4–5, 24–27

poses of this book, I have also assumed value realism. Nonetheless, I don't believe antirealism is a problem for the argument. This argument deals with the essential meaning of the term, independently of whether it actually refers. Defending the merit connection, no more commits me to realism than it did Mackie, a well–known anti–realist. If there is anything that is good, it will have the property that it merits desire. If nothing in the world has that property, nothing is good.

Let's just see how the discussion might go with respect to one version of anti–realism — the most likely to look like incommensurability, I think — just to make sure there are no difficulties. A relativist about value would claim that 'O is valuable to degree d' in which 'valuable' is understood non–relatively as meaningless or false. On the other hand, the relativist would accept that 'O is valuable to degree d *relative to frame* T' could be true; and "O is valuable to degree e *relative to frame* U" might simultaneously be true even if d ≠ e. One might think that the claim that many different claims about the value of a particular property or object or state can all be simultaneously true would make nonsense of all value comparisons. And indeed, one of relativism's well accepted consequences is that morality across reference frames fails to be comparable in an important sense.

None of this causes any problems for the view I've been defending here. If there is no absolute good, then the merit connection stated absolutely entails that nothing merits any desire in an absolute sense. As merit is a value term, though, the relativist would assign it relativized meanings as well and so the following version of the merit connection is also true.

(**MC-relative-to-frame-T**) For all **S** such that **S** is a state of affairs, **S** merits *relative to reference frame* **T** a desire with a strength proportional to the value *relative to reference frame* **T** of **S**.

So even if relativism is true, no values will be incommensurable. No absolute values are incommensurable because there are none.

All values–relative–to–frame–T, that is, all values within a frame, are commensurable to each other because for each reference frame there is a corresponding merit connection relative to that frame. What about the values across frames? These are also commensurable because desire–strength, being a natural property, is not relativised. Value of degree d relative to frame **T** will be greater than, less than or equal to the value of degree e relative to frame **U**. One could determine their comparable values by the strength of the desire merited within the relevant frames. To make clear how this works, compare to the case of Einsteinian relativity. Although there is no privileged or absolute velocity for any object, each object does have determinate velocities relative to different frames. Moreover, because there is a specific meaning to velocity, velocity across frames is commensurable. "Are you moving faster relative to the Sun or the Earth?" is a good question. So is "Is sacrificing the young better relative to the Aztec moral code or the American moral code?" So, even across relative frames, the commensurability of all value is maintained.

IV. Conclusion

There is a fundamental connection between value and desire, one widely accepted, that has been neglected in the debate over incommensurable values. Whatever the reason for the neglect, it is clear that any account of rational desire must take **(MC)** into account. Value merits desire and, at least under most conditions, we should desire according to that merit. The strength of desire merited is directly proportional to the degree of value. This gives us a measuring stick that we can hold up to any value. We can, in principle, measure the value of friendship against the value of pleasure against the value of autonomy against the value of knowledge. All we need ask: how much would the ideal desirer desire this value? The answer to this question for every value gives us a ranking of all values. There are many reasons something might seem desirable to us, and many of these reasons are irrational. To be genuinely desirable is neither to be desired, nor to be capable of being desired, nor to seem desirable – almost anything could fit those bills – but to be worthy of desire, to merit it. And for something to be truly desirable, and not just seem so, it has to be truly valuable; it has to be good. There is a serious independent question about whether there are any real values in the world. If there are, though, 1) they create obligations and 2) help determine our ideal desires. The defender of incommensurability must deny one of these two claims. A denial of the first is a denial that value is value. And a denial of the second, it turns out, is a denial that we should desire the good, and that we should desire the better more strongly than the worse. Neither of these positions is tenable. And so, if there are any such things as values, all of them will be commensurable.

1.3.2 Value Conflict

One might now legitimately wonder what the radical pluralist was thinking.[30] The view conflicts with some of our most basic meta-ethical and moral psychological requirements. The evidence most often cited for incommensurability is the common occurrence of value conflict. Kekes puts the pluralist point forcefully:

> It may be that these [value] conflicts are not due to the incompatibility and incommensurability of values, but why should we think that? What reason is there for distrusting appearances in this case? Why should we reject the thoughtful testimony of millions of apparently reasonable people, including ourselves, that they, and we, often want to realize two values but the nature of these values is such that they cannot be realized together? Why should we doubt this evidence that comes from the contexts of radically different societies separated by vast historical, cultural, environmental and psychological differences? There does not appear to be a

---

30 Hurka supplies and refutes one tongue-in-cheek defense of radical pluralism: "Much modern philosophy reads as if it were inspired by the following argument: 'Utilitarianism is a false moral theory; therefore, the more unlike utilitarianism a moral view is, the more likely it is to be true....' But, obviously, often the best replacement for a theory corrects it at only some points and leaves others of its claims standing." [Hurka, 1996: 575]

convincing answer.[31]

It has always been a bit surprising to me that defenders of in-commensurability cite everyday value conflict as strong evidence for their view. I suggest, rather, that the most common responses to apparent value conflict are strong evidence *against* incommensurability. The fact that we *feel* conflicted, and, more importantly, that we deliberate about what to do during value conflicts suggests that we think values *are* comparable. [32] It is, of course, possible that we are confused, that it is inappropriate for us to be deliberating. But the 'appearances,' as Kekes puts it, strongly suggest that we think there *is* a common measure of the apparently conflicting values. If we really did believe that values were incommensurable, and that there were conflicts due to incommensurate values, we would just throw our hands up at certain conflicts. Why would we try to *get it right*? There is no getting it right in cases of conflict between incommensurable values. But this isn't what happens. When values conflict, we strug-gle, we fret, we make lists, we weigh options, we seek out evidence, we make arguments, and so on. These are the things people do when they are seeking an *answer*. This suggests that conflict is not about the *in*comparability of two values, but the *close* comparability of two values, and that value conflict is about uncertainty in measuring, not impossibility of measuring.

So conflict does not on its own entail that values are incommen-surable. Indeed, it doesn't even entail pluralism. Even a eudaimonis-tic utilitarian can account for at least some situations where agents feel conflict. All I care about is your happiness. Both a concert and a stand-up comic would make you happy. But I can't take you to both, and I am not sure which will make you the happiest. I feel conflicted. Which should I do? In a world of uncertainty, we are often enough unsure which action is the best action, which action will produce the most happiness. And this can leave us feeling conflicted, feeling as if

---

31 [Kekes, 1993 #2: 65-66]

32 On the other hand, it is clear that Kekes is right that some values are contingently *incompatible*. But, as he himself notes (60-61), this does not entail that they are *incom-mensurable*.

we wish we could do both.

So, the pluralist must point to some fact about the *way* we deal with conflict as evidence that we perceive values as incommensurable. Raz, for instance, claims that it is not just conflict that is evidence for incommensurability, but the fact that there are value conflicts in which we *refuse* to compare two options. Take, for example, comparing the value of money to the value of friendship. "It is typical, where options of this kind are involved, for agents to regard the very thought that they may be comparable abhorrent."[33] But does abhorrence at comparing two things indicate that they are incomparable? Do I feel abhorrence at someone comparing (non-metaphorically) my intelligence to the heat of a Miami day? Not at all. Personally, I would find it humorous. If two things are incomparable, it doesn't *make sense* to compare them. We reserve our abhorrence for bad things, not for meaningless things. Raz is right on this, though: it is, generally, abhorrent for Harry to give up an important friendship with Tristan for $10. But why is it abhorrent? Clearly because it is a *bad* choice, it is the wrong thing to do. Harry destroys something valuable for no good reason. That type of action is, plausibly, abhorrent. But we don't find the reverse abhorrent, do we? Surely Harry should be willing to give up $10 to keep Tristan as a friend. But this suggests that the value of the friendship is 'incomparably' *greater* than that amount of money, and not incomparable simpliciter. If Raz is right about our abhorrence, it may entail that the value of friendship is *lexically prior* to the value of money, that friendship is always more valuable than any amount of money, but it clearly does not entail incommensurability.

(Though, on a side note, I don't think this is true either. Suppose I owe money to seven friends. These friendships are all valuable to me, but all of these friendships have one weakness: if I don't pay the money back, I will lose the friendship. Suppose I owe one of the friends, f, as much as I owe all the others combined. I have only enough money to pay the one friend or to pay the six. It seems to me that I am willing to sacrifice the friendship with f so that I can have

---

33 [Raz, 1986: 346]

amount x of money, so that I can pay back my other friends. And, so, I am willing to lose a friend over a certain amount of money. This seems rational. One cannot reply that I am comparing the value of different friendships and not the value of friendship and money. It is in the nature of instrumental values like money that they (somehow) take on the value of what they are bringing about. Money has no value if it is not bringing about other valuable things. And, so, there are times when the value of money and the value of a friend are comparable, namely, at the very least, those times that money is instrumental for creating or keeping a greater amount of friendship.)

1.3.3 Regret

Many radical pluralists point to the fact that we feel loss when we resolve a conflict between values, that we regret the not-having of a particular value, as evidence for incommensurability.[34] If I make a choice between the concert and a stand-up comedy based solely on the pleasure they will bring, the argument goes, then why should I feel any loss when I choose the concert because it will give me more pleasure? All I care about is pleasure and the concert will give me more of what I care about. I am, after all, not *really* losing anything. The pleasure I would have had from the stand-up comic is more than made up for by the concert. Consider this example from Nussbaum: there are two plates, one plate with one bagel, one plate with two. All three of the bagels are more or less the same. All we want, suppose, is greater amounts of bagelness. We are bagel-hungry. Being rational, we choose the two bagels. Wouldn't it be silly, she asks, if we regretted the loss of the third bagel? After all, she claims, we didn't really *lose* anything; we only gained. If all choices, then, are just choices between bagels and bagels, or pleasure and pleasure, or, even, value and value, we should never feel regret. Yet we do feel regret. Hence, there is more than one single value and they are not commensurable.

---

34 [Williams, 1973: 172-75], [Stocker, 1990: 241-77], [Kekes, 1993: 57-58], [Nussbaum, 2001: 106-117],

To evaluate the radical pluralist's claims here, we need to make a distinction between two types of regret. First, one cannot rationally regret the *making* of a certain choice if one rationally concludes that that choice is the rational one. I will only regret making a choice if I feel that that choice was the wrong one. When you regret a choice, it is because you wish you had done other than you had. Call this choice regret.

There is another form of regret, though. We can regret a *situation* because it forces some choice on us.[35] Suppose Juliet foregoes some pleasure to give Harry a ride to see his mother in the hospital. She might rationally regret being put in a situation that causes her to lose that pleasure, even if she thinks that she did the right thing. She doesn't regret her *choice*; she would choose similarly if she could use hindsight to choose again. What she regrets is the situation in which she has to give up some pleasure that, otherwise, she could have had.

The radical pluralist can't point to choice regret to establish his point. I can't and don't regret my *choice* if the relevant values are incommensurable because this would entail that I think I made the *wrong* choice. But there is no wrong way to choose between incommensurable values.[36] If forced to choose between incommensurable values, I will never choose the wrong one.

The radical pluralist is left with situation regret, but situation regret entails neither incommensurability nor pluralism. Commensurable pluralism can easily account for situation regret. The value Juliet places on pleasure and the value she places on taking her friend to the hospital need not be incommensurable for her to regret the situation. It would be nice to be able to satisfy both values, but circumstances don't allow it, so she regrets those circumstances.

Even monism can capture situation regret. Suppose I have an opportunity to earn a $1000 honorarium for a speaking engagement, but another university offers me $2000 to speak at the same time.

---

35 I borrow this excellent distinction from Peter Schaber [Schaber, 1999: 72-3].

36 This is too strong, really. It would be wrong for me to choose between incommensurable **A** and **B** because I thought that **A** was *better* than **B**. This is wrong, though, in the sense that I am choosing according to nonexistent criteria not because I am choosing the worse option.

Stipulate that, being a purely mercenary philosopher, all I care about is the money, and as I am a mere assistant professor, both engagements' offers are significant (and unusual). I will clearly choose the $2000 speaking engagement over the $1000. Clearly, there will never be any reason for me to regret that *choice*. Nonetheless, I might still regret the loss of $1000. Wouldn't it have been nice to have both? It's not often I get $1000 to speak. Wasn't it an unfortunate situation that required both engagements to arrive at the same time? But if this is true, then we can rationally regret situations in which we believe we made the right choice even if there is only one type of value.[37] What one truly regrets, then, is the loss of a situation, a situation that was never really available, a situation where both values (or amounts of value) could have been had.

When we feel regret in this sense, it is because we want *both* of two things that are not compatible (I would rather have $3000 than $2000). To see that this is right, note that when we *don't* want both, we don't feel regret. Say I have a choice between going home by route **A**, which takes 10 minutes, or route **B**, which takes 20 minutes. If my only consideration is the time it takes, I clearly cannot regret the loss of **B** when I take **A**. This is because, I suggest, I don't really want *both* options even though both options do have *value*. Both options do have some good: they get me home in time for dinner. But I only want one or the other, and, so, if I make a choice I think right, I will have no reason to feel regret of any kind.

---

37 The same reply is available with respect to Nussbaum's bagel example. Maybe I *can* regret the loss of the bagel, if what I am regretting is the fact that I couldn't enjoy three bagels, instead of two. This has often happened to the poorer of us when presented with a complimentary buffet, "Look at all the free food; too bad I can't eat it all."

1.3.4 The Repeated Choice Argument

It is a bit of a struggle to see what the radical pluralist is thinking. Let's try one more time. Isn't there some difference between the loss I feel when I choose the $2000 over the $1000 and the loss I feel when I choose my autonomy over some particular pleasure? To see what the radical pluralist might be pointing to, turn the regret objection around. If we regret some choice, it suggests that if we had the opportunity again, we might make a different choice. So, suppose I have a choice between x and y. As far as I can tell, x and y are equivalently valuable or they are incommensurable. I choose x. Awhile later, a situation more or less identical arises. Again, I have to choose between x and y. This time I choose y. What is my reasoning? I don't choose y because I think I made a mistake in choosing x the first time. I choose it merely because I *didn't* choose y the first time; some part of me regretted the loss of y the first time. And this seems rational even if I don't think there is an intrinsic value difference between x and y.

How could this be if there is only one thing of value? If both x and y are choice-worthy only because they have the same degree d of property **P**, then what could justify my preferring, in the second case, y to x? No matter how many times I was offered the choice between the $2000 honorarium and the $1000, I would never have *any* reason to choose the $1000 over the $2000. But the same is true even if I receive $1000 for *each* speaking engagement. *If money is all that matters*, I have no reason to choose the speaking engagement I forewent the first time over the one I actually chose; the money amounts, are, after all, equal. If I choose my friend's pleasure over my father's pleasure this time, and *pleasure is all that matters*, there is no reason that, given the choice a second time, I should favor my father this time. (This is *contra* Hurka's response to the argument from regret. He claims that it is rational to regret the loss of a value even if there is only one value, as long as the values are what he calls intrinsically distinct. My father's pleasure is intrinsically distinct from my friend's pleasure; they are clearly different things. Hurka thinks it is rational to give my father the pleasure the second time merely because it is my father's pleasure and not my friend's and that my friend's pleasure was satisfied the first time through. But if the 'intrinsic distinctness' between x and y makes no value difference, then how could it *justify* my choosing y over x? If pleasure is, by stipulation, the only thing that *matters*, it cannot matter *whose* pleasure it is.[38]) Each time I get to make choices of this kind, I should do the equivalent of flipping a coin, and should feel no loss if chance leads me to always choosing x rather than y.

Moreover, the same is true even if there are plural but commensurable values. If the only thing that makes x and y choice-worthy is their degree of *value*, and x and y both have the same degree of value, there can be no justification for preferring y to x in either the first or the second case. So, if it is rational for me to choose y over x in the second case, value can't be commensurable. **Q.E.D.**

But does the radical pluralist have a better reply available? How does he explain the rationality of choosing y over x? He will say something like the following: we choose y not because it is better than x in any way but just because it is its own unique value that deserves to be pursued. But this is not sufficient. Certainly, y deserves to be pursued; it's a good. But the radical pluralist needs to explain why it needs to be pursued in place of x; x is good as well and also deserves to be pursued. Well, the radical pluralist might continue, we choose y the second time because it is good to have as many values realized in a particular life (or world) as we can. But this, though it seems true under some interpretations, is a *value* claim. Our lives are better, it is claimed, the world is better, when a variety of values are instantiated. So why do we choose y over x the second time? Because this time round the realization of y is actually more valuable than the realization of x: realizing y makes our lives more varied than realizing x would. But if we choose y because it is more valuable than x, then x and y are commensurable.

Perhaps, all along the intuition that radical pluralist has been working from has been an intuition of value and not an observation

---

38 [Hurka, 1996: 563-65]

about our attitudes toward value. He sees a world with only one value as a bleak world. But he knows that this is not a bleak world. *He* values so many different things; so, there must be a variety of values.

But if variety is valuable, then it is yet another bit of value evidence that the monist must explain; it is not on its own, an objection to monism (or moderate pluralism). (The fact that variety is valuable, of course, is no reason – in the absence of a good God – to think there *must* be a variety of non-reducible valuable properties.) If a monist claims that property **P** is the only thing of value *and* **P** can account for the value of variety, then the monist has an explanation for how we can rationally choose y over x, an explanation more or less identical to the radical pluralist's. Is there any reason to think that the monist can't capture the value of variety? Not at all. Indeed, if richness is something like unified variety, then the theory we are presenting in this essay easily captures the value of variety.

In the end, the radical pluralist has an extremely weak position. The Argument from the Merit Connection showed that it is incompatible with a basic understanding of the relation between value and desire. Furthermore, the radical pluralist's most cited evidence, value conflict, actually seems to be evidence *for* commensurability. The argument from regret turns on an equivocation between choice regret and situation regret. Choice regret seems to assume commensurability, and commensurable value theories can account for situation regret. Finally, the value that may be driving the radical pluralist – and perhaps the pluralist in general – the value of variety, can plausibly be captured by a monistic theory; and is easily explained by the value theory being presented here.

1.3.5 Moderate Pluralism

Looking at the literature, you might think this is the death knell of pluralism. Though many radical pluralists seem to assume that commensurable pluralism is as 'bad' as monism, commensurable pluralism does not obviously *entail* monism. There are strong theoretical reasons, though, to think that monism is preferable to moderate pluralism.

The moderate pluralist asserts that there is an objective, non-reducible, commensurable plurality of values. Because these plural values are commensurable, there must exist a set of proportionality measures between them that preserve the transitivity of value. Suppose x, y, and z are the fundamental values. To make this a complete value theory, we need to add to it something like the following: (**A**) $x=2y$, (**B**) $y=2z$, and (**C**) $x=4z$. So our theory of value is that x, y, and z are valuable and (**A**), (**B**), and (**C**) hold between them.

What explains this complicated set of value facts? What for example is the explanation for (**A**) $x=2y$? It is not an analytic truth. Even supposing goodness is defined in terms of some natural property x, it is not going to be the case that the value of x will be part of the analysis of x. Consider: $Good =_{def} x =_{def} (analysis of x)$. If x is supposed to serve as a naturalistic reductive definition of x, then no value terms can occur in (analysis of x); that is, it cannot be part of the definition of x that x is twice as valuable as y. But this should be unsurprising: does anyone find it plausible that value proportions will be part of the final analyses of life, love, happiness, pleasure, freedom, knowledge, rightness or any of the other prospective values?

But the only other plausible explanation for (**A**) is not available to the pluralist, namely, that x has twice as much of some good property **P** as y. This option is monistic: it reduces the value of x, y, and z to the value of **P**. In the end, the pluralist has stipulated away the only possible explanation for (**A**). And, so, the pluralist is forced to accept a number of, in principle, inexplicable synthetic truths – not just the basic facts that x, y, and z are intrinsic non-reducible goods,[39] but also the facts that the measures between them are what they are. This becomes, clearly, more and more unpalatable the greater the number of values we postulate; so, a theory like Michael Stocker's which posits nearly as many types of value as there are experiencers becomes, on the face of it, little more than description.[40] Most of the facts in such a 'theory' of the good are unexplained facts.

There will, undoubtedly, be something at least partially unexplained in any theory of the world. And if no 'ought' can be derived from an 'is,' any value theory will have some partially unexplained basic fact or facts. But pluralism entails that there are unexplained facts that would otherwise be begging for explanation. What makes the good attach to x exactly twice as much as to y? In general, if two things are commensurable, the explanation for this fact is that they share some property. The reason the temperature of my hand and the temperature of a Miami day can be compared is that they both share a property: heat or kinetic energy. The reason I can compare my weight and the weight of Jupiter is that they both share a property: mass. The reason that we can compare my intelligence and yours is, presumably, that we both share some property: intelligence. If values x, y, and z are all commensurable, we have an immediately good reason to assume that there is some property **P** shared by x, y, and z that makes them valuable to the degree that they are valuable. **P** is an explanation for the commensurability of x, y, and z. But the pluralist is committed to claiming that there is no explanation for their commensurability.

On the face of it, this is a strange claim to make. What reasons in general do philosophers have for giving up on the search for explanations beside the fact that they've found a good one? A monist has a reason to stop seeking explanation. If property **P** is the only good, it must be that the fact that **P** is the good is, at least partially,

---

39 It is, at least, a structurally possible option that you could explain the good of x, y, and z *via* definition, that is, the good *means* (x or y or z). I find this unlikely: it would be worrisome if our basic ethical concept would be an essentially disjunctive one – but whichever way that turns out, it would still not serve as an explanation for (**A**), (**B**), and (**C**).

40 [Stocker, 1990: 267-8]

basic and unexplained; either because **P** is good by definition or by synthetic necessity. The pluralist, on the other hand, is under the obligation to give some similar justification for giving up his exploration of value. The only one forthcoming is that he has tried hard to find a unified value theory and has failed.

But the plausibility of this explanation clearly depends on how hard he has tried. I, of course, think we haven't tried hard enough: the number of monistic theories of the good that have been vigorously explored can probably be counted on one hand, and have focused, for the most part, on properties closely tied to the human psychology: pleasure, desire-satisfaction, reason. Shouldn't we look a bit further afield? If value is, after all, part of the structure of the objective universe, why need it be captured by some obvious, easy to grasp, human-oriented concept? The basic concepts of physics certainly aren't so easily grasped. We have yet to find a unified theory of our physical universe. Are we justified in giving up?

Pluralism is a philosophically unstable theory; it will always leave us with the suspicion that there is something deeper to be discovered. If ever we did come to a good pluralist theory, we would (and should) still be severely tempted to continue looking for the unity underneath those plural values. And, so, without some argument to show that monism is impossible (and none, I hope I've shown, is forthcoming), we have good reason to continue the search. Moreover, if we find a monistic theory that can capture as much evidence as a pluralistic one, the monistic theory is the better one.

1.3.6 The Goal

The claim, then, is that, all other things being equal, the following is the structure of the ideal value theory: there exists a property **P** whose distribution in the world determines the value structure of the world. This is either because the property **P** is identical to the property of being good or because the property **P** is the only thing that has the property of being good.[41]

A monistic theory that can do a reasonably good job capturing the plurality of value evidence will be preferable to any pluralistic theory. As it stands right now, pluralistic theories are more viable (and more useful) because they are more accurate. We value love, life, art, memory and so on…. It is easy for pluralism to capture this, but has been extremely difficult for monism to do so. Because of this difficulty, traditional monistic theories have resorted to what we can call explaining away the evidence rather than explaining it.

Let me make this distinction clear: a thousand people have an experience that seems to be of being abducted by aliens from a saucer-shaped ship over Denver. These experiences are evidence for the way the world is. Among the abductees are several UFOlogists. Certain of the UFOlogists *explain* this evidence by a simple theory: there are aliens looking rather like the aliens that they seemed to experience and these aliens abduct people. Others of the UFOlogists attempt to *explain away* this evidence with a different theory: there are no aliens that abduct people, but there are hypnotists that can make people think that they have been abducted. Determining which UFOlogists are correct would require investigation, but, without further argumentation, the first group is clearly being more faithful to the evidence. They genuinely want to explain *what they saw*. The second group, on the other hand, dismisses the evidence and attempts to explain it away. They want to explain a different fact: *why they think they saw what they think they saw*. All other things being equal,[42] the first group's theory is preferable: we have no immediate reason to believe in the hypnotism described, but we do have immediate reason – namely the abductees' experiences – to believe in alien abduction.

---

41 These two options correspond to what has been called respectively ethical naturalism and ethical intuitionism. I do not want to decide, here, between them. I will talk often as if good and richness are identical; this is for ease of usage. It may be that richness is just the only thing that has the property of being good.

42 Now, of course, all things aren't equal in the case of UFOs. Most accounts of UFOs conflict with our best scientific understanding of the universe. Leave that to the side, for the moment.

Value theorists are in the same position as the UFOlogists, and the reason that pluralism has some advantage over monism is because it takes our evidence seriously and attempts to explain it, rather than explain it away. Monistic theories like early utilitarianism almost invariably attempt to explain away much of our value evidence. Suppose we are eudaimonistic utilitarians. Our general method of explaining away is to claim that any intuition we have that some **V** other than happiness is valuable is due to the fact that **V** is normally instrumental to creating happiness, that there is some strong, but contingent connection, between **V** and happiness. Our intuitions that life, integrity, honesty, not-killing, beauty, knowledge etc… are valuable are all explained away in this manner. Not surprisingly, many of the strong objections to utilitarianism claim that it fails to take seriously our intuitions that things other than happiness are valuable.

In the rest of this essay, I attempt to *explain* the plurality of things we intuit as valuable (the plurality of things we desire). I claim that life, persons, love, and beauty *are* intrinsically valuable, and they are valuable because they are examples of richness. In this way, I hope to deflect the strongest form of pluralist objection to monism.[43] If I am successful in that task, then, given the arguments of this section, we have strong reasons to suspect that if there is any satisfactory value theory, it is monistic.

---

43 There is one set of value perceptions that the theory will need to explain away, a subset of our intuitions about pleasure and pain. I will deal with this in Chapter 4.

2
THE VALUE WORLD

The world is overflowing with the objects of our desire, replete with things we value. Just as an adequate theory of physics needs explain the physical properties we observe, an adequate theory of value should explain our observations of value properties. Those observations, I have argued, are our desires and values. I attempt, in this chapter, to make reasonable the claim that the many things we truly value, we value for their richness. I am forced by the sheer abundance of the topic to move fairly quickly over a wide territory. This means, of course, that I can do no more here than touch on each of the prospective values. A full defense of the reducibility of all value to richness requires full analyses of properties like knowledge, consciousness, life, freedom, and persons: analyses that are difficult and controversial. Nonetheless, the chapter serves to motivate the impressive potential explanatory power of the present thesis and, hopefully, to leave one with the sense that this is a neglected program of study in need of further investigation.

There are many metaphors for richness out there, many ways for latching onto the tension between unity and variety. Call it simplicity and complexity, call it intelligibility and interestingness, call it harmony and conflict or use any of a dozen other antinomies to capture it. One way of framing the determination of this chapter is as a pilgrimage through and to these metaphors, a journey to see them for what they are, in all the places that they reside. How likely is it that the parsimony of the physicist is related to the harmony of the pianist is related to the union of an intimate human relationship? The connections seem nothing more than poetic initially. I begin now the attempt to thicken these connotative connections into something more robust, to bind together through richness the values of artistic appreciation and knowledge, desire-satisfaction and experience, scientific theorizing and freedom, life and community. There is much speculative philosophy here, I freely admit, but it is, I hope, unified speculation, unified by plausibility, first, and richness, second. The way the several speculations hang together is as important as the success of each postulation on its own.

On a personal note, I hope this chapter stirs in the reader at least a bit of the amazement I felt and still feel at the recognition of richness in the things we love. The effects of this recognition on me were not only intellectual but practical as well. I found and find myself enjoying things I have not been able to enjoy before. I find myself understanding more of my previous enjoyment. I find myself understanding and sharing in more of the enjoyment of others. None of these personal experiences can be made into forceful arguments here. Nonetheless, these practical effects of adopting, at least provisionally, the viewpoint that richness is the one thing of value are important evidence of the accuracy of that viewpoint. Good theories are, generally, useful; and the usefulness of a theory is, in general, a sign that it has got something right. I have the expectation that this book and this chapter will, no matter what one's intellectual commitments turn out to be, affect how one experiences value. The reader's experiences and the sharing of these experiences are a type of evidence unavailable to me now, but will, I suspect, be an important source of corroboration for what follows.

2.1 Isomorphism

I begin in what might seem an odd place, with the unifying power of isomorphism. Though it does not immediately come to mind as a recognizable source of value (or, even, of richness), isomorphism unifies, I suggest, many of the rich wholes we most appreciate. We find isomorphism in the value of mental representation, in artwork, in desire-satisfaction, in love, in the value of species, and many other places.

2.1.1 Isomorphism and Unity

Two states (or objects, structures, systems, sets) are isomorphic when the states can be mapped onto one another in such a way that for each individual (member or 'part') in one state there is a corresponding individual in the other state that plays a corresponding functional role (or exhibits corresponding relational properties) in that state. Examples of isomorphism of varying degrees are the livers of healthy adult mammals, photographs and their objects, the vocalizations of the word 'isomorphism' as uttered by all English speakers and so on. Isomorphism as described is evident in many of the things we most value and, I suggest, it serves as a richness-creating unification that can explain, at least in part, the value of those things.

I begin with an example to demonstrate that isomorphism is unifying. Consider the formal system 'pq' created by Douglas Hofstadter. Recall that a formal system consists of a language, grammatical rules for creating well-formed formulas, axioms, and rules of inference. The pq-system has three symbols in its language: 'p,' 'q' and '-.' There are infinite axioms in pq, all of the following form: xp-qx- in which the variable x stands for some number of –'s. So, ---p-q----, -p-q--, and ------p-q------- are all among the set of axioms.

System pq has only one inference rule.

"RULE: suppose x,y, and z all stand for particular strings containing only hyphens . And suppose that xpyqz is known to be a theorem. Then xpy-qz- is a theorem."

So if ---p---q- is a theorem, you can validly deduce that ---p----q-- is as well, and if -p---q---- is a theorem, then -p----q----- is a theorem.

I invite you to play with this system for a few moments before going on. Create some axioms. Deduce some theorems. Pay attention to the patterns. Can you develop the ability to quickly recognize a theorem?

If you did develop the ability, I suspect you noticed that pq is extremely similar to another more familiar system, namely, addition. To see this, map p onto '+,' q onto '=,' and use the dashes as a representation of the natural numbers. With this mapping, ---p-q---- is equivalent to 3 + 1= 4 and ------p-q------- is equivalent to 6 +1= 7. As there is a mapping of the language of pq to the language of addition that preserves truth values and validity, pq and addition are isomorphic.

Note, more importantly, the intuitive unity of addition and the pq-system. (Indeed, there is an inkling – because they are both abstract systems – that they are the same system.) The pq-system and addition belong together. Further evidence of their unification comes from the strong and legitimate suspicion that pq was created as a representation of addition, that it was designed to be considered hand in hand with addition.

Isomorphic states are unified by their isomorphism. Moreover, they are unified in precisely the manner required by the definition given in §1.1. To see this, recall that a state is unified if there is a set of somewhat simple, complete, and deterministic law-like rules that could serve as an explanation for the state. Well, there is a simple law-like rule that can explain the structural similarity of pq and addition. Namely,

(ISO) m+n = s is a theorem of the addition system iff m'pn'qs' (where m', n', and s' denote strings of m, n and s hyphens in length) is a theorem in the pq-system.

(ISO) is a complete explanation of the unity of pq and addition. Because it is simple, deterministic and complete, the rule tightly unifies addition and the pq-system. Moreover, and more importantly for my purposes, (ISO) or something like it is the reason that we intuitively see addition and the pq-system as unified. It is because there is this simple mapping between the two that we recognize them as belonging together.

This generalizes. The unity of any two isomorphic states-of-affairs is explicable through simple rules such as (ISO). Suppose states-of-affairs **S** and **T** are completely isomorphic. Then for every part s in **S**, there will be a corresponding part t in **T**, and for every relation **Rs** that holds between s and (s1, s2 .... sn) there is a corresponding relation **Rt** that holds between t and (t1, t2....tn). The unity of **S** and **T** is captured by something like:

(GISO) Rs(s, s1, s2,...sn) is true iff Rt(t, t1, t2,... tn) is true.

Rules that fit the form of (GISO) properly explain the tight unity of isomorphic states-of-affairs.

2.1.2 Partial and Indeterminate Isomorphism

As we saw in Chapter 1, unity comes in degrees. The same is true of isomorphism. Two states that are completely and deterministically isomorphic are tightly unified. States less completely isomorphic are less tightly unified.

Partial Isomorphism

S and T are partially isomorphic when some but not all parts of S are isomorphic to part of T. Call this partial isomorphism. If S and T are partially isomorphic, they are unified in proportion to the greatness of the isomorphism that governs them. For example, the image of Harry in a mirror is isomorphic to the visible surface qualities of roughly half of Harry.

The mirror image is not isomorphic to all of Harry. You cannot map Harry's back onto any of the points on the mirror's surface. Neither does it capture any of his interior biology, nor, of course, does it capture any of the intricacies of his psychology. Nonetheless, a mirror is still isomorphic to a restricted subset of Harry's properties and, therefore, is somewhat unified with Harry. The greater portion of Harry the mirror mirrored, the more unified the mirror image would be with Harry. An equally representative statue of Harry at time t, for instance, is even more tightly unified with Harry than the mirror at t because the statue captures the three-dimensional Harry.

Territory maps are another good example of partial isomorphism. Maps and what they are maps of are isomorphic. But maps leave much of the structure of the real world out. Some maps leave out more than others. Maps with more fine-grained scale-ratios have a higher degree of isomorphism to the territory that they map than those with less fine-grained scale-ratios. Intuitively, the more detailed the map is the more unified it is with the territory it maps. A perfect map would be indistinguishable from the territory it mapped.

Indeterministic Isomorphism

An isomorphism between two states can be grounded by an indeterministic mapping relation as well. In Hofstadter's system the deterministic mapping is as follows:

pq   addition

P $\leftrightarrow$ +
Q $\leftrightarrow$ =

- ↔ 1
-- ↔ 2 etc...

For each symbol in pq there is a single corresponding symbol in addition and vice versa.

Consider, though, altering the rules of the pq system into a system, call it pqxy, such that the rules of pqxy give us the following mapping:

pqxy   addition

p or x ↔ +

q or y ↔ =

- ↔ 1 etc...

In the pqxy system then, -p-q-- is still a theorem, but -x-y-- is a theorem as well and so are -p-y-- and -x-q--. Addition and pqxy are related by a disjunctive or indeterministic mapping.

The aggregate of the formal systems pqxy and addition are clearly unified by the mapping given (or, more precisely, the rules that generate the mapping). But the aggregate of pqxy and addition is not as unified by isomorphism as the aggregate of pq and addition. System pqxy has an overabundance of symbols; there is an important sense in that it looks less like addition than pq does. This fact is explained nicely by the characterization of unity given in §1.1. The unifying rule for pqxy and addition is indeterministic while the unifying rule for pq and addition is deterministic. Indeterministic rules are, all other things equal, less unifying than deterministic ones. In general, then, indeterministic mappings will be unifying, but the degree of their unifying power will be correlated with their degree of determinacy.

Call an isomorphism 'tight' when it is both complete and deterministic. Isomorphic states are unified to a degree proportional to the degree of the tightness of this isomorphism.

2.1.3 Isomorphism and Richness

An aggregate of isomorphic states is not necessarily rich. An aggregate is rich if it is varied *and* properly unified. Isomorphism is, I have shown, a proper form of unification. The richness due to isomorphism in a whole consisting of two (or more) isomorphic states depends, therefore, on the tightness of the isomorphism between the two states (the degree of unity) and the degree of variety between the states. Consequently, an aggregate of isomorphic states is not rich if **(A)** the states have little to no richness individually or **(B)** the states are (more or less) identical, such that there is little to no variety between them. The first type of failure is one you should be familiar with from our discussion earlier. Intrinsically simple things, though unified, are not rich because they lack variety. The aggregate of arrows 1 and 2 is an example of a failure of type **(A)**.

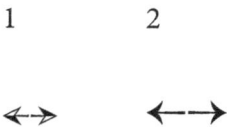

1   2

↔   ←—→

1 and 2 are different and isomorphic. Their aggregate does not create (much) richness, though, because there is little variety between them, and so there is little variety in the aggregate.

More complicated are failures of type **(B)**. Consider, again, the booklet of three hundred identical Rembrandt reproductions. The first reproduction is of *Portrait of the Artist at His Easel*, as is the second, and the third and the three-hundredth. There is no identifiable difference between any of the reproductions other than their placement in the booklet. Suppose for the moment that a reproduction of Portrait of the Artist at His Easel is valuable in virtue of it being rich (see §2.3 for some defense of the claim that aesthetic value is due to richness). The intrinsic value (and richness) of a single Rembrandt reproduction is **V**, say. What is intuitively obvious but a bit puzzling in theory is that the entire booklet of Rembrandt reproductions is not as one might expect 300**V**. Each of the 300 reproductions is worth **V**, but, apparently, when considered together much of that value disappears. Where does the value go?

This evaporation of value is explicable by the present theory. Though there is a tight unification between the Rembrandts, no Rembrandt after the first adds any significant variety to the booklet. As you add reproductions the unity stays, more or less, constant, and the variety stays, more or less, constant; and, therefore, the richness stays, more or less, constant. There is little richness in the booklet above and beyond the richness of a single reproduction of *Portrait of the Artist at His Easel*. When and if isomorphism unifies several rich objects that are not in any important way different, the isomorphism does not bring any extra richness into the world.

There are times though when isomorphism is a source of great value. Those times are when isomorphism unifies objects that are rich in different ways. To see this, first consider other cases in which we unify things that are already intrinsically rich, for instance, a case where we create a booklet of 300 different Rembrandt reproductions. There is no value evaporation in this case. None of the richness in the paintings is lost as we place them side by side (unless Rembrandt himself started – as many artists do – repeating himself). The unification of unique rich objects is protected from the diminution of value described above. Moreover, and this is key for much that follows, significant richness over and above the original richness is often be created. This is because this new unification creates a new whole that did not exist before, a whole that is significantly more varied than any of the unique rich objects that make it up. The booklet of three hundred unique Rembrandts is much more varied than a single Rembrandt. So not only is there no loss of value, there is an important augmentation of value.

This augmentation is evident in many unifications of rich objects. Animals and plants are rich, but the complex ecosystems that unify them are a new richness above and beyond the beings that live there. Two humans are rich, a fully unified relationship between two humans even richer. Each of the pages of Ulysses is rich, the aggregation of them all much richer than the addition of all their individual values. Most of the lines in Hamlet are rich; the entire play performed makes those same lines that much richer. When rich objects are unified, a host of new relations are formed between the varieties of each object that do not exist when considering the objects alone.

The richness of the unification of independent richnesses depends on how much of the variety of the constituent richnesses is being unified. Two human beings standing next to each other are unified by place and structure. Two humans working together to move a couch are also unified by purpose and movement. Two humans working as a team in doubles tennis are further unified and two lovers who have known each other their whole lives are even more unified. In each case, there are rich human beings being unified. But clearly, the latter cases are more valuable than the former. This is because more of the richness of each person, more of their variety, is being unified in the latter cases. Standing next to a person is not as valuable as being in love and being loved. The lovers must bring more of their richness to the collaboration than the couch-movers, and so their relationship is richer.

One more example along these lines. Imagine I put eight rich statues in a circle, ordering them arbitrarily. The statues are now unified by being in a circle (and being statues). This is not a particularly special situation because nothing else about the statues is being unified. I might as well have made the circle out of marbles and considered the statues on their own. Now I place them in order of their height in a circle. Better: now their size is unified as well. Now imagine that I put the two wood statues across from each other and the two stone statues across from each other and so on.... and place them on the circle according to the average height of the facing statues. Better still: now size and material is taken into account. And so on. The more that my ordering of the statues takes into account about the statues the better. The more of the variety that is captured by the unity, the richer the circle of statues.

Unities of unique richnesses are richer than the richnesses on their own proportional to the amount of each richness that is unified. We will see this again and again as we move through the rest of this book, so it is important to fix it in mind now. The unification of multiple rich things is an added richness above and beyond the richness of the constituent richnesses. How much richer is determined by how much of each richness is considered in the unification.

Isomorphism is a particularly impressive form of unification, and so richnesses unified by isomorphism will be a particularly impressive form of richness. When appropriately unique and rich objects are unified by isomorphism, little to none of the original richness is lost, but significant richness over and above the original richness is added. The isomorphism creates a new whole, one significantly more varied than any of the constituent rich wholes. I will be looking at many examples of value-inducing isomorphism in the following sections, most importantly, mental representation, artistic representation, and desire-satisfaction.

I want to finish here by noting that there are many of us that value isomorphism as isomorphism. This is especially true of those who call themselves truth-seekers: scientists, philosophers, artists, and the like. Einstein said, "It is a magnificent feeling to recognize the unity of a complex of phenomena which appear to be things quite apart from the direct visible truth."

Who can deny the appeal of seeing the golden ratio repeated throughout nature? Or delight at the thought that a galaxy looks like a hurricane? Or be fascinated by the fact that the embryos of all mammals look almost identical? Or that the equations that govern ocean waves ended up governing electrons as well? Or that the fall of an apple from a tree is identical in important ways to the orbit of the Moon around the Earth?

The revealed isomorphisms of science, mathematics and philosophy are widely valued, and not merely for the instrumental power gained by knowing the isomorphism of rich states-of-affairs. As Einstein suggested, it is the recognition of unity in diversity, the recognition of richness itself, that is the source of wonder.

2.2 Mental Representation, Knowledge and Experience

> "The brain—is wider than the sky—
> for—put them side by side
> the one the other will contain
> with ease—and you—beside—"
>
> Emily Dickinson

A representation is, by its nature, isomorphic with the state it represents. The unification of representations and the represented is a clear example of isomorphic unity. Call this representational unity. Many things we like or value, representational art (paintings, novels, movies), scientific models, topographical maps, data graphs, and so on, are representations. Most of what we value them for, I suggest, is that they are representational unities. The richness of one state representing another rich state **R** is richer than **R** is on its own. This is due, I have argued, to the richness of the representation itself (which is more or less equivalent to the richness of **R**), and to the richness created by unifying the representation and the represented through isomorphism. The more that is represented by the representation and the tighter the isomorphism between the representation and the represented, the richer the unification of the two, the richer the state of representing.

This dual standard that is the measure of richness explains why the most important and remarkable representations, by far, are those of the mind. No other representations that we know of can match the quantity (variety) of states that the mind can represent or the incredible accuracy with which it accomplishes such representations. The mind is a representational gourmand, 'wider than the sky' in an important sense, wider than anything perhaps. A listing of the things represented by any single mind at any time would stretch well beyond the length of this whole essay (imagine, for instance, an autobiography including everything you remember). Even a listing of things occupying one's present consciousness is outsized.

The mind is the most marvelous of mirrors: perpetually generating representations of the world here and now in three dimensions, in five senses, with shadings of value and desire and fear, in real-time, with both abstract and concrete facts captured, both rich and simple states modeled. Furthermore, this mirror remembers non-trivial portions of those conscious representations and unifies them within the larger representation that is the continuously updated model we all have of the world in which we live. On top of this, the mind is a kind of meetinghouse for the universe's richnesses. It is a place where otherwise disparate richnesses can be brought together. When I pay close attention to the *Mona Lisa*, it joins in my mind a community of other painting representations. I can compare and contrast it with cave paintings and my five-year-old's paintings and Picasso's and Breughel's. I can use it to increase my understanding of movies and novels (and vice versa). It can leave me with thoughts about women or smiles, or psychological states or mountains or some rustic place where I once lived. Through imagination, through reason, through emotional and metaphorical resonance, each of the richnesses in my mind can be unified with others within other rich thoughts. These new thoughts are a further richness above and beyond the richness of the representations themselves.

The richness of the mind, of the psychological, is not too surprising once you look at the tremendous power of the biological basis (or biological cohort) of the mind. The brain contains over 100 billion neurons. The number of possible connections between them is greater than the number of atoms in the universe. The brain is certainly the most complex biological object available for study and it seems likely that biological objects are the most complex, the richest, natural objects in the universe (see §2.5.1). We have some good reason, then, to think that a properly directed and ordered mind is one of the greatest sources of richness in existence. This aligns nicely with the high value we attach to such a mind.

There are two aspects of mental representation that I want to focus on in a bit more detail because of the uncontroversial nature of their value and the incredible importance they have in our lives: knowledge and experience.

2.2.1 Two Types of Mental Representation

Intuitively, the mind represents the world in (at least) two fundamentally different ways. Looking at the square below, I believe several things about it.

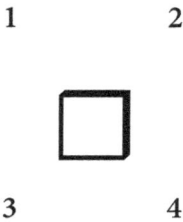

1   2

□

3   4

I believe it has vertices at **1, 2, 3, 4**. I believe it is on the page. I believe it is relatively small. I believe it is bounded by black lines and so on. I also see the square. If I close my eyes, I can remember or visualize the square. Both my beliefs and my visualization are commonly accepted ways of representing the square mentally.

There are important differences between these two types of mental representation, differences important for determining the value of these representations. Call the class of mental representations that are like belief 'concept representations.' Examples of concept representations are knowledge, the remembering of facts, thinking, non-sensual imagining-that p and the like. Call, on the other hand, the class of mental representations that are like perception or visualization 'sense representations.' Examples of sense representations are imagining (sensually), visualizing, perceiving in all five senses, remembering (sensually), the sensory elements of dreams, hallucinating and so on. Concept representation is non-qualitative, abstract and 'cold.' Sense representation is qualitative, detailed, and 'warm.'

There is good *prima facie* reason, I suggest, to think that these are fundamentally different types of representation. The important difference between the two is that accurate concept representations are not necessarily isomorphic to the things that they represent, but accurate sense representations necessarily are. Given the discussion of isomorphism and richness, we should expect this to lead to value differences between the two types of representation.

Visualize the above square. This visualization is a sense representation. If the square is fully imagined, the following facts are all true of this representation: the four angles of the represented square add to 360 degrees. Side 12 is parallel to side 43. The area of the square is equal to the square of each of the sides and so on. One's visualization of the square has these properties because the square has these properties. In virtue of visualizing the square, you have a representation with all the (necessary) geometric properties of a square.

On the other hand, the fact that you have a mental representation of the geometric properties of the square, does not entail you have any beliefs about the geometric properties of the square. Your visualization has the property that its area is equivalent to the square of its sides, but it is certainly possible that you don't believe that the area of the square is equal to the square of the sides. A child can visualize a square with next to no knowledge of its geometric properties. One's visualization represents facts about the square that my beliefs don't. And, so, beliefs and visualizations are different types of representation. As there is nothing special here about visualizations, we can conclude that concept representations are fundamentally different from sense representations.

One might reply that you do have beliefs about the area of the square, it is just that you are not conscious of those beliefs. This can't be right, though. The four-year-old doesn't have any conscious or unconscious beliefs about the area of the square or the rightness of its angles – indeed, they probably don't even have the concepts – but four-year-old's can certainly see squares. Nonetheless, even if it is granted that, a la Plato, one has unconscious beliefs about all of the geometric properties of the square (yet to be remembered), beliefs and imaginings still must be different mental representations. This is because one's visualization is conscious. You do have a conscious mental representation of those geometric properties. As the assumption of the objection entails that those conscious representations cannot be beliefs, that representation cannot be a belief. Therefore, sense representations and concept representations are different types of representation.

Another objection one might raise is that I am not really representing the geometric properties of the square; my representation has the properties of the square, but does not represent them. Whether you think this last is true, note that it opens up a parallel line of argument that reaches the same conclusion. The visualization has the properties of the square, but my belief representation does not. By Leibniz's law, these must be different types of representation independently of whether the imagined square represents the geometrical properties of the square.

In any case, I don't think it is true that your visualization does not represent the geometric properties. The imagined square must represent the geometrical properties of the square. A drawing of a square represents a square because it represents its geometrical properties. This is also true of a visualization. A square is nothing but its geometrical properties, most of which are necessary properties of the square. (Geometric properties that are not necessary: size, width of the sides etc...)[1] If the drawing or the visualization failed to have the properties of the square, it would fail to represent the square.

There is much more to say here, but it is a little far a field for the present topic. I wanted to give a little argumentative support to the general feeling that we 'think' about the world in two different representational ways. This will be helpful for discussing the relative values of knowledge and experience. The quick way of capturing the difference between these types of mental representation is by the tightness of the isomorphism they share with the things they rep-

---

[1] I am not arguing, by the way, that there are non-propositional mental representations. It is possible that sense representations are propositional in some way. I am merely suggesting that they can't be concept representations. They are different from beliefs and from knowledge. It is, of course, possible (epistemically) that this entails that they aren't

resent. Sense representations have a high degree of isomorphism to the thing they are picturing – at least with respect to the properties that are captured by the representing sense. Beliefs, on the other hand, need have little to no isomorphic relation to the thing they represent.[2] A belief that the square is on the page need not be square-like in any way (nor page-like).

2.2.2 Knowledge

"All men, by nature, desire knowledge." Aristotle

The desire for knowledge for knowledge's sake should be familiar to most philosophers. Sometimes it seems good to know, independently of whether the knowledge is useful. I remember as a child intensely wondering whether there were planets around other stars – not for any power that knowing would give, not to tell others – just for the sake of knowing. The fact that, apparently, one can be frivolously curious suggests that knowledge is intrinsically valuable.[3] What we want when we want knowledge is to unify our mind, as much as we can, with the richness of reality. We want to 'have' the world, in the only way we can really have anything in this world, with our minds. This unification is valuable because it creates rich states of affairs. The unification creates richness in two, by now, straightforward ways: first, by creating a unity of two rich states, those two states being the mental structure that is our knowledge and some portion of the world being represented by that knowledge; and second, by adding a rich entity, namely, the knowledge representation

---

propositional. This is irrelevant to my present concerns.

2 There is much debate about the structure of beliefs and the structure of the propositions that we believe. It seems likely to me that propositions and beliefs have structure. We can after all see the similarity of certain propositions and can understand, more importantly, the logical relations between those propositions. Nonetheless, one supposes that propositions and beliefs about a square don't have to be square-like.

3 Clearly, another important reason that knowledge is valuable is that, by its nature, it gives us information about the world, and this is extremely useful. Knowledge has, without question, tremendous instrumental value.

itself, to the already rich structure of the mind.

(There are really two types of knowing that correspond to the two types of mental representation; here I deal with concept representation knowledge. In the next section, I will deal with experiential knowing.)

Knowledge and Isomorphism

Consider the state of affairs that consists of Harry having full knowledge of some further state of affairs **S**. To know everything about **S** is to be unified with the **S**-part of the world. This state of affairs is unified in virtue of a tight connection between mind and fact. This is not to say that individual beliefs have any isomorphism to the things they are beliefs about. A single belief about squares is not itself square-like. On the other hand, a complete set of beliefs about the location of a square will be square-like in one important sense. Call the set of beliefs about the square **B**, and call the set of location facts about the square **S**. The isomorphism between **B** and **S** is governed by this RULE: If s is a fact in **S**, then there is a belief that s in **B**. This rule generates the following mapping.

S	B
There is a point on the square at p1. ↔	I believe there is a point on the square at p1
There is a point on the square at p2. ↔	I believe there is a point on the square at p2…
…	
There is a point on the square at pn. ↔	I believe there is a point on the square at pn.

The rule and the derivative mapping tightly unify the objects of set **B** with the objects of **S**. This is, by its nature, a tight isomorphism: it is simple, largely complete, and, given **S**, deterministic.

A legitimate worry here is that we rarely have complete sets of belief about any robust real-world states of affairs. Though I know a lot about my house, I don't know everything about my house. Though **B** is isomorphic to the square, it is, because it is infinite, an impossible set of beliefs for a finite mind to have. We don't usually have belief sets that are completely isomorphic to the world.

This is true, of course, but not problematic. For one, partial isomorphisms are unifying and we often know a lot about some state of affairs. Set **B** is an example of a complete set of beliefs about something; it is an ideal that we rarely reach. Nonetheless, it is often an important ideal towards which to reach. When I'm trying to deduce what's wrong with my PC's operating system, it is important for me to acquire a more and more detailed belief representation of the state of my operating system. Those beliefs need to be available to me for ratiocination if I am to work out what is wrong with my operating system. And so it is in many areas of our life. Concept representations are useful in a way that sense representations are not because we can reason with them. Qualia cannot be the premises of an argument. Beliefs can. Sometimes we need to reason with a wide number of propositions. These times we develop detailed belief sets, belief sets that are largely isomorphic to some portion of the external world. The more we know about a particular state of affairs the richer the state of affairs that exists between knowledge and world, and this accords with our intuitive ascriptions of value. This state of reasoning, this way of being aware of the world is a rich state of affairs, a rich way of being connected with the world, and it is rich in part because of its isomorphism to the external world.

Furthermore, some partial sets of beliefs 'encode' complete sets of beliefs. This, indeed, may be the ultimate purpose and value of concept representations. Harry believes that there is a point everywhere on the line between 1 and 2. This belief all by itself allows Harry, through reason and intelligence, to generate an infinite set of beliefs about side 12 as they are needed. Belief sets such as these are 'pseudo-complete.' Such sets function very much like a complete set of beliefs because they allow us to quickly generate any particular belief from what would be the complete set. Generally, our belief systems are a mixture of the general and the specific. The general beliefs are a type of zipping mechanism for the mind, a method for compressing vast quantities of information. This is necessary, efficient and useful. So, knowledge that is 'pseudo-complete' is instrumentally valuable to creating genuinely complete belief sets. (I should add to this that most beliefs, specific and general, are zipped forms of experiences.

There is a point everywhere on the line between 1 and 2 immediately brings to mind, at least for me, a sense representation of a line.)

Knowledge and the Structure of Belief

Knowledge is also rich in virtue of the rich structure of beliefs. That belief structures can be rich is entailed by the fact that we can know rich things. When we know rich things well, our belief sets are intrinsically rich in virtue of being isomorphic to those rich things. If true belief structures can be rich there is no reason to think that false ones can't be rich as well.

The most obviously rich belief structures are good scientific and philosophical theories. It is widely accepted that the measure of how good a scientific theory is is two-fold. The best theories explain (1) the widest variety of evidence by (2) the most unified explanation.[4] A theory improves if you hold the simplicity of its rules constant and increase the variety of data it explains or a theory improves if you hold the variety of the data it explains constant and increase the simplicity of its explanatory rules. Another way of putting this: we like wide theories and deep theories. We like theories that explain lots of particular facts about the world and we like theories that explain deep unifying features of our world. A theory of the animal kingdom that does no more than list all the animals according to their species and family is a wide theory covering the full diversity of the animal world, but it is also a shallow theory, explaining very little of the diversity of the animal kingdom; it only loosely unifies the animals. Quantum mechanics is an even wider theory. Moreover, it is also a deep theory, explaining and unifying most of the evidence of our lives, applicable to animals and chemistry and physics.

We measure all knowledge in the same twofold manner. One can know a lot in a shallow way or one can know a lot in a deep way. I have a cousin who can name all the Presidents' votes on war-related matters. This in itself is quite a bit of knowledge along one dimen-

---

4Robert Nozick argues good theories are examples of richness as well, "A good theory is one that tightly unifies (in explanatory fashion) diverse and apparently disparate data or phenomena, via its tightly unifying relationships." Pg 417

sion, the wide dimension. It is not very deep knowledge. That same cousin also has generated a theory about why Presidents of certain religious faith win elections when they do. If true, this is deeper knowledge. These two ways of gaining knowledge, the wide way and the deep way, can plausibly be captured by the oft-quoted Archilochus dichotomy between the way the hedgehog knows and the way the fox knows, "The fox knows many little things. The hedgehog knows one big thing." Though it is plausible that these are two different ways of getting knowledge, there is no reason to think they are incompatible. A person who knows the theory of the animal kingdom given above knows quite a bit along the wide dimension. A person who knows the basic rules of quantum mechanics knows quite a bit along the deep dimension. A person who knows the basic rules of quantum mechanics and all of its consequences has deep and wide knowledge. Each of these three is knowledgeable, but clearly the third is the most knowledgeable. God the omniscient would be neither hedgehog nor fox, but a combination of both: one who knows all the little things and all the big things (or, assuming a unified universe, the one big thing). And this would be, by definition, the greatest knowledge.

The greatest knowledge is rich, then, because it unifies us with the world, and because it itself is a unified variety. Indeed, what this discussion seems to show is that richness is the measure of knowledge: knowledge increases the more you increase the deep knowledge without reducing the wide knowledge and vice versa, knowledge increases the more you increase the unity of the beliefs while holding the variety constant or the more you increase the variety of the beliefs while holding the unity constant. The richer your true justified beliefs, the more you know.

One last thought about concept representation. A singular statement of the form **A** is **P** is a recognition of the unity of **A** with all things **P**. If I know Ed is a horse, I know that Ed is unified with all other horses. This is a feature that one doesn't get through mere conscious awareness of Ed. Awareness of Ed may generate a representation of all of Ed's horse-like properties in the mind, but it does not represent the unity of Ed with other horse-like objects. This is one of the reasons that concept representations are so useful. Through abstraction, we can make deductions about things of which we have no present awareness. Indeed, we can make deductions about things we've never had nor could ever have awareness of. It allows us to connect and model further richness in the world beyond what we experience. The ability to categorize is the ability to see the unity of the world, an ability necessary for seeing richness.

2.2.3 Knowledge vs. True Belief

Is knowledge intrinsically better than mere true belief? True belief that is not knowledge is lacking in justification (at least). Justification is a procedure or set of procedures that if applied to the forming of a belief makes it likely that that belief is true. The justificatory procedures, I suggest, are rich in their own right. Most think, for instance, that perception and reasoning from properly obtained evidence count as justification. But both instances of accurate perceptual consciousness and reasoning from premises are rich. I make both of these claims plausible in the next couple of sections. Moreover, when our beliefs are justified, the beliefs are unified with the justificatory procedure. If my belief is justified by a certain perception then that belief is unified with that perception (and all the physical and psychological elements that go into making-up that perception). Likewise, if a certain line of reasoning justifies my belief, the belief is unified with that reasoning.

Two more important value differences between knowledge and unjustified true belief: (1) Grant that when we believe something we generally also believe we have justification for believing it. Then if we do not have justification for our beliefs, we believe something false, namely that we do have justification. This breaks the unity of mind and world, and so our total mental state is not as rich in mere true belief as it is in knowledge. (2) True unjustified belief is, generally, less useful than knowledge. If my beliefs are not justifiably true, their truth is unreliable. There is no reason to think that will go on being true. But if my beliefs are justified, there is a good chance that they will more reliably vary in conjunction with reality. Mere true belief is like a face and a photograph of the face. Knowledge is, generally, more like a face before a mirror.

2.2.4 Experience and Consciousness

There is another type of 'knowing.' Harry knows Juliet. He does not believe Juliet; he is acquainted with Juliet, he has experienced her. The two types of knowing are intimately connected. Sometimes, learning new things about Juliet, believing knew things about her, helps Harry to experience her, to perceive her more accurately, and, likewise, his experiences of her lead him to have new beliefs about her. And it is this type of knowing, I suggest, that fills our lives with the most richness. Better than merely learning the fact that there were planets around other stars would have been to see them myself, to experience them first hand.

I've argued that the isomorphisms due to sense representations are generally tighter than those due to concept representations. Thusly, accurate sense representations are generally more tightly unified with the world than true belief. Here are some important and relatively uncontroversial (though not exhaustive) features of experience (that is, perceptual, phenomenal, or qualitative consciousness): it is 1) sense representational, 2) multi-sensual, 3) continuous, 4) affective, and 5) unified. All of these aspects add to its richness, the first and fifth in virtue of adding to the unity of our experiences and the second, third, and fourth in virtue of adding to the variety of our experiences.

One scan of the visual field is enough to establish the wide variety of detail that comprises experience. Right now, before me, is the computer screen, with all its complexities, the words I'm writing on the screen and all the icons of the word processing program I use; intricate patterns of light are coming through the blinds, the table spread is ornamented in red and yellow; there is a pen, two cd cases, two postcards, my silver watch, the dark mahogany walls and so on and so on. Similar variety is available to most of our senses most every waking moment. I feel the seat underneath me. I'm wearing shorts and the sensation is different where my skin touches the chair. There is an air vent beneath me and I feel the cool air blowing across a section of my calf; I feel the chair against my back and shirt on my skin and so on. Moreover, the sensory variety in consciousness is greater than just the – manifestly incredible – variety of occurrent sensations. When I look down at my desktop, part of my model of the desktop is that it feels smooth even though I am not touching it; part of my experience of the window is that will feel warm because it is in the sun, this though I cannot directly sense that warmth. To the physical senses, add our evaluative sense (desiring). Part of my present awareness might contain the feeling that some red flowers would look nice on the corner of the desk or that it would feel good to scratch my arm. Moreover, more complex emotions, memories, and the connotative aspects of objects are commonly, if not always, a part of present awareness. Instantly, one captures through isomorphism the full variety of large swaths of the world. And all of this is immediately unified, brought together in a single experience.

If this description is more or less accurate, then experience is on the whole far richer aspect of our lives than (concept) knowledge. The theory being put forward here makes a value prediction, then: all things equal, we should value knowledge by experience over concept representation knowledge. It is difficult to easily test the prediction because of the philosophical complexities surrounding concept and sense representation: whether they are fundamentally different, whether one is necessary for the other and vice versa. Nonetheless, it is quite plausible that we – even us philosophers – intrinsically value knowledge by acquaintance, the experience of the world, more than we value conceptual knowledge of the world. On the whole, I would rather experience the distant planets than know – even quite a bit – about them. Barring extraordinary circumstances, no one would give up one's perceptual capabilities, one's ability to directly experience the world, for any amount of knowledge, no matter how great. This I suggest is because it is in experience that most of the richness of our life resides. It is through experience that we most directly come to 'have' the richnesses of the outer world, to be unified with the rich universe, and it is in experience where much of our intrinsic richness resides.

Another way of distinguishing between the value of knowledge and sense representation is that one of the great values of knowledge is that it is instrumental to generating sense representations of the world. Given a detailed list of facts about distant planets, one would, if they cared at all, immediately attempt to imagine them, to 'experience' them through visualization. This is because sense-representations, even imagined ones, are generally more detailed, more likely to match the world, and richer than concept representations. To have detailed knowledge of my PC or my house or the solar system is to have a method for generating a rich sensory model of any of these.

In the end, there is something artificial about the dichotomy I've been pushing, merely because all these types of representation are so tightly linked. Perceptions, as Strawson put it, "are soaked with, infused with, animated by, irradiated by," beliefs.[5] And beliefs are immediately generated out of and immediately generate imaginative, perceptual representations. Both types of representation are available to consciousness. Whether the totality of consciousness is something above and beyond qualitative experience or not, I do not know (perhaps, for instance, we 'perceive' our beliefs via belief qualia). Whatever consciousness turns out to be, it is at least as varied as experiential awareness.

Consciousness 'contains' perceptions and other sense representations and contains both belief-like states – representations of what is – and desire-like states – representations of what is a good. Moreover, this variety is fully and immediately unified by consciousness, by being brought into a working, consistent model of the world.[6] Consciousness is not only unified in the moment but over time.

5"Imagination and Perception" pg 41;
6Leibniz seemed to think that consciousness is the only truly unified thing. This is why consciousnesses (monads) are the building blocks for all other things in his ontology

Consciousness concertedly keeps my notion – my full notion, its perceptual, emotional, possible properties – of the world consistent, moment after moment, even as each moment brings an onslaught of new variety. Whatever else consciousness is and whatever other value it might have, it is, at the very least, extraordinarily valuable in virtue of being this inimitable rich representational structure. The three-dimensional, multi-sensual, dynamic, emotionally detailed quality of consciousness makes it orders of magnitude more complex than any other non-mental representation. Though I think it is a mistake to think that only conscious states are valuable, it should be no surprise, given the present understanding of value, that so often in the history of value theory, we have mistaken the value of consciousness for all the value there is. It is both incredibly valuable and the value with which we are most intimately connected.

2.2.5 Reason and Consistency

The rules of logic, the acceptable deductive and inductive rules are all law-like. As such, the rules of logic can serve as good nomic explanations for the structure of a reasoned set of beliefs. A valid one hundred-step proof of **P** from two assumptions **Q** and **R** is a unified set of propositions. The rules of deductive logic are a good explanation for the beliefs and their relations. Of course, logic allows for an infinite number of claims to follow from any two premises, so the rules have a great amount of indeterminacy. On the other hand, logic plus some hard to define rule about elegance can reduce that indeterminacy greatly. Well-structured proofs are such that each step in the proof seems that it has to be precisely where it is (much, as we shall see, like good art). A set of propositions that all follow logically from some smaller set of propositions is more unified, all things being equal, than a set of propositions that isn't logically related in this fashion.

[Leibniz, 1925].

Reason is also instrumentally valuable. Reason is what allows reasoners to recognize unity (and, therefore, richness) in the world. Richnesses are varieties that exhibit certain regularities. These regularities are such that they require explanation. It is in virtue of being reasoning creatures that we can uncover the unifying explanations that underlie the variety in things. Perhaps, the greatest example of this is in the sciences: the central place of reasoning in science is uncontroversial. But in addition, we wouldn't recognize the unity in poems, or movies, or persons, or mammals without the ability to reason both inductively and deductively. Awareness of richness is itself rich. Reason greatly increases our ability for such awareness. Non-reasoning creatures cannot see the unity of an apple falling from a tree with the moon orbiting the earth, and so are incapable of experiencing the full value of the world.

Under certain conditions, consistency is also a good indication of unity. If a collection of propositions or beliefs is consistent when it would seem highly unlikely that they would be consistent, it suggests that those propositions or beliefs are unified. Consider a set of twenty thousand apparently random specific testable claims about my actions in the last five seconds. Any truly random set of this many claims that purports to be about my actions in the last five seconds is extremely likely to contain many contradictions. One claim might be that I was dancing in a garage while another might be that I was asleep. Suppose, though, that on examining all twenty thousand claims, we find that they paint a consistent picture of the world. Under such conditions, we are justified in concluding that the collection of claims is not random, that there is some explanation for the compossibility of the claims. There are a number of unifying explanations for the consistency of a set of claims: the set might be a set of logically equivalent claims; it might be a set of claims all part of a deductive proof; it might be that they are all true claims (it being a nice feature of true claims that they are all mutually consistent).[7] Whatever the unity ends up consisting of, the consistency itself of these types of proposition sets is a good indicator of unity. All

---

7As I mentioned earlier, present consciousness contains an amazing amount of 'claims.'

things being equal then, we have an explanation for why a consistent set of beliefs is better than an inconsistent set of beliefs, even if both sets are false.

2.3 Aesthetics

Aesthetics is, as Nozick put it, "the area that speaks most frequently and articulately about value."[8] It is also the field that has most obviously and repeatedly appealed to the concept of richness and its synonyms. Without some explanation for why so many philosophers of beauty have been misled, this in itself is some evidence that richness occupies an important place in the value realm. And, if richness is valuable in art, then we should suspect it will be valuable wherever we find it, whether in art or not. I want to spend some time here looking at how others tried to frame the concept of richness with respect to art. This will serve to deepen the understanding of richness given here and help to recognize it in other, not obviously aesthetic objects.

Many aestheticians have attempted to reduce the value of beauty to the value of the experience of beauty, to reduce it to the value of the pleasure beauty gives. Many have argued that beauty is nothing other than the property of being the object of an aesthetic experience. This is tightly connected to a broader effort to reduce all value to psychological states and/or relations to psychological states. This broader project should seem unlikely given the basic assumptions of this essay. If value is real, it is real in the way that electrons are

---

The fact that consciousness, for the most part, manages to continually produce a, more or less, consistent picture of the world suggests that the many elements that make up consciousness are governed by rules. What this unity consists in is not immediately obvious, but it seems clear that it has something to do with model-making in a spatio-temporal world. There must be rules governing our conscious model of the world, for instance, about overlapping objects (both in time and in space). Our conscious mind takes the evidence of the world – both past and present – and 'attempts' to create a consistent model of that information.

8[Nozick, 1989: 415]

real and stars and the Big Bang; we have no good reason, a priori, to think that all value is psychology centered. Electrons and stars and the Big Bang existed before we did; why not value? It may, of course, be contended that value is an objective feature of humans alone (or of consciousness alone, or of desiring things alone) and that it came into being when humans came into being (many objective properties are like this: for instance, being a human liver). If the experience conjecture is right, though, if it is plausible that being the object of our desires is a reason for thinking something good, then it is highly implausible that the only things that are good are psychological states. We desire intrinsically many things other than psychological states. This can be seen most clearly when we look at the things we love. Juliet cannot love Harry merely because of Harry's instrumental value in creating certain psychological states (this will be elaborated further in Chapters 3 and 4). It is not truly love if all you care about is how the other affects your pleasure. But we love many things, people and paintings, victories and valleys. This suggests that more than just psychological states are valuable. It suggests that when we call a painting good because it is beautiful, we are claiming exactly what it seems like we are claiming – that the painting itself has intrinsic value. It is imperative, then, for a theory of the good that purports to capture all value to explain both the value of beautiful objects in themselves and the value of the experience or appreciation of those objects. In this section, I hope to show that degree of richness is a plausible measure of the value of both. In addition, I argue that this theory of the good can straightforwardly explain the apparent subjectivity of aesthetics, the central place of representational art in aesthetics, and the value of originality.

2.3.1 Making Art

I have spent some time, strangely enough, working as an actor. One common commandment a beginning actor hears repeatedly is "Make choices, as many as one can." Go to a creative writing class, or a painting class or a film class and you are likely to hear a similar injunction. It sounds an odd imperative on its own. Doesn't it matter if the choices are good choices? Surely, making a slew of bad choices isn't going to create good art, no matter how many you make.

In the end, of course, an actor does want to learn to make 'good' choices, but first she has to learn how to make choices at all, how to keep her focus and broaden her awareness so that her entire performance is under her control, all vocal inflections, all facial expressions, her posture and gestures, everything. Only once this has been understood and mastered can the actor truly perform her entire part; if the actor does not make all the choices she can, if she does things without reason or out of habit, some of the performance is, in a sense, being performed without her. Some of her facial expressions, her intonations, some of the character she communicates to the audience is out of her control. There is no guarantee, under those conditions, that the things she does will be good.[9]

Making music is similar to making a novel to making a painting to creating a character as an actor in that the artist must in some sense be present in the whole creation. An artistic creation begins as an idea, however vaguely established, in the mind of the artist (hence, that most common – and, therefore, annoying – of questions for the artist: where do you get your ideas?). This idea might be structural or emotional. It might be centered on a plot idea in a certain genre or by a feeling of how a single eight bar theme could be expanded into a symphony. The making of the artwork consists in a series of choices made in conformity with that idea, choices that will

---

9This, of course, does not mean that the actor or the pianist is *deliberating* about each element *during* the performance. This is likely to be impossible. Nonetheless, some sense of the overall impact desired must always be guiding the performer. It is also true that much deliberation can be done *before* a performance, and this is what rehearsal and practice are for.

best achieve the idea, choices of word, of color, of vocal intonation, of note, of inflection, of instrument, of gesture, of paint, of canvas, of perspective, of theme, of expression. The sum of these choices gives rise to the final (usually) complex product. And, yet, if the artist has done well, this final complex product will be unified. The thing will be colored through and through by the original idea. It will be one thing. Everything will belong there. The complete idea serves as the set of unifying rules for the final product.[10]

This most generalized sketch of artistic creation suggests that the best art is the art that brings the most variety ('the maximum of re-alities') together under one idea ('simplest of hypotheses'). The best art is the art where every single part is 'chosen' by the unifying idea.[11] Every word, sound, meaning, character, plot element, allusion, rhyme, rhythm and theme. And this art, art full of unified choices, is just the richest art, isn't it? We are told, then, as beginning artists, to make the maximum choices so that we can design a unification of the maximum of realities. Take the microscope to the artwork: when you find, no matter how deep you look, unified choice, that is beauty, that is richness.

10Dewey calls this set of rules a 'sieve' [Dewey, 1958]. The artist throws his options into the sieve, and the sieve allows only those things through that are in conformity with the original idea. The sieve, the artist's overall conception, is the unifier. Note that the sieve need not be a fixed and passive object. It is a creation of the artist and it can be, and usu-ally will be and should be, altered in the process. *The best art is that which allows as much variety as possible through an otherwise fine-grained sieve.*
11Some ideas reduce the amount of choices one makes – for instance, I could have an idea of a painting that is just a blank canvas. This type of idea removes the need to make choices just as much as it removes the variety. The final product is less impressive for both reasons.

2.3.2 Organic Unity: Richness?

It should be no surprise, then, that theories of aesthetics with richness-like concepts at the center of aesthetic value have a long tradition. I do not to imply that it is a universally accepted or, even, presently popular theory of aesthetic value. Nonetheless, great aestheticians from every philosophical epoch have returned to the idea. I believe the work done in Chapter 1 goes a long way on its own to remedy the most common problems with such theories. First, many characterizations of richness have been binary: something has it or it doesn't. Aristotle's definition seems to be an example of this. But perfect richness is probably impossible; even perfect unity is highly unlikely in anything as complex as art. Any aesthetic theory that has the consequence that nothing is valuable is problematic. Moreover, an aesthetic theory should account for the fact that beauty comes in degrees; some things are more beautiful than others. Again, a binary account of richness would fail this test. The definition given earlier, though, allows for degrees of richness while also capturing the notion of ideal richness. Other richness-like accounts of aesthetic beauty have the reverse problem; namely, they are so vague as to allow almost anything to count as richness. I hope the definition in Chapter 1 has also remedied this problem. Although, most things will be rich to some degree by the definition; there are clear predictions about which things will be richer. I want to look now, in a cursory, way at the many characterizations of richness and make plausible that we are all talking about the same thing.

Aestheticians have most commonly referred to richness as organic unity or organic form, but something like it has gone by many other names: esemplastic unity or coadunative unity (Coleridge); intensive manifold (T.E. Hulme); synoptic configuration (Harold Osborne); principle of integration (G. N. G. Orsini); unity in multiplicity (George Santayana). Orsini suggests also: "synthetic unity, total unity, integral unity or integrated unity, complex unity, intrinsic unity etc..."[12] The plurality of names for richness is matched by a plurality of (closely related) attempts to characterize it. One might worry that this variety is due to the fact that there is no single concept unifying these characterizations.[13] I suggest, though, that richness as I've defined it can unify these many depictions of organic unity.[14]

The concept of organic unity originated by noting the similarity between good art and living creatures. Plato said of rhetoric that

> 'all the parts should be in keeping with each other and with the whole like a living being, with a body of its own, so as not to be headless or footless, but so as to have middle and members, composed in keeping with each other and with the whole.'[15]

The organic metaphor has been in use ever since. As artists, we try to create things as natural and surprising as the multifarious living world. There are many features of living beings to which the organic metaphor might be pointing. First look at the property of having tightly interdependent parts. "Men call beautiful the things in which the parts fully answer to each other..."[16] said Dante. The functioning of most of the parts of a living body depends on the further functioning of most of the other parts. A human being needs its liver to survive and the liver needs the heart to survive and the heart needs the lungs to survive and the lungs need the liver. This is also true of the best art. In living beings, the parts must answer to each other. What the heart asks for, the liver gives; what the liver gives the heart takes; what the liver asks for, the heart gives; what the heart gives, the liver takes. Likewise, in the best art, no part is placed without respect for the effect it will have on the other parts or without an understanding of how it itself will change in the context of the other

12[Orsini, 1969: 29-30]
13John Fisher (conversation, 2003) has suggested to me that there are no good objections to the view that organic unity is beauty because there are no sufficiently precise elucidations of the view. I have tried to remedy that here by moving toward a rigorous definition of richness.
14For excellent histories of the concept of organic unity in art, see [Orsini, 1969; Orsini, 1973]. I am greatly indebted to these two overviews.
15[Plato, 1995: 264c]
16[Dante, 1964: Iv3-15 trans. G.N.G. Orsini]

parts. Consider, by way of an example, the following epigram at the beginning of Vladimir Nabokov's novel, *The Gift*.

> An oak is a tree. A rose is a flower. A deer is an animal. Russia is our fatherland. Death is inevitable.
>
> P. Smirnovski A Textbook of Russian Grammar

'An oak is a tree,' is a simple, obvious and rather boring sentence on its own. But it has a different force in the context of 'Russia is our fatherland. Death is inevitable.' Moreover, 'Death is inevitable,' is equally trite and uninteresting on its own, but when placed beside such simple and uncontroversial truths such as 'An oak is a tree. A rose is a flower,' it gains some of the terrifying force it should have. Our experience of the whole passage changes again on reading the citation that this is from a grammar book (and, of course, the citation of a grammar book would have little interest without the passage above it). When one considers the passage as a whole, one is touched by an image of a school and a child, of a particular culture; and most importantly of a deep aspect of the universe's nature in which some Russian, and all the rest of us, developed and will die. All the impact of this opening epigram must then, of course, be answered by the opening passages of the novel and in a great novel, by the closing passages as well and everything in between.

A number of attempts have been made to capture this notion of interdependence philosophically. Aristotle said of tragedy that it is a whole,

> "the structural union of the parts being such that, if any one of them is displaced or removed, the whole will be disjointed and disturbed. For a thing whose presence or absence makes no visible difference, is not an organic part of the whole."[17]

John Hospers put it:

> "In the unified object, everything that is necessary is there,

---

17[Aristotle, 1968: VIII.51A 32-35]

and nothing that is not necessary is there... in a work of art, if a certain yellow patch were not in a painting, its entire character would be altered, and so would a play if a particular scene were not in it, in just the place where it is."[18]

Dewitt Parker claims that 'the ancient law of organic unity' is "the fact that each element in a work of art is necessary to its value, that it contains no elements that are not thus necessary, and that all that are needful are there."[19] And Harold Osborne put it,

> "The theory of organic unity claims that any subtraction or addition would diminish the value of the work (of art) as a whole, changing also the character of all the parts... [20]"

These characterizations all suggest the following principle of organic unity.

Principle P: **"O is an organic unity only if p is a part in O if and only if p is necessary to the value of O."**

If an organic unity is a richness, I can explain principle **P**. If the value of **O** is determined by its richness, then it is partly determined by how unified **O** is. If **O** is perfectly unified, then there are rules that govern **O** such that every single part p of **O** must be exactly where and how it is. This is because unified rules are deterministic and complete. If, as Aristotle says, the loss or addition of a part makes no 'visible difference' in the whole, then that part cannot be required by the explanatory rules and so is not unified with the other parts by those rules.[21] At worst, these extra 'parts' are like gaudy frames on subtle paintings; at best, they are useless. Furthermore, if

---

18[Hospers, 1967: 43-44]
19[Parker, 1968: 36]
20[Lord, 1964: 263]
21Many aestheticians of this ilk sometimes seem to claim that interdependence is the *definition* of art and not just a measure of art's beauty. Though I find this slightly ridiculous – it is, after all, a rather stringent requirement – it is a claim to the side of the present exploration: I don't care what art is, but what makes art, or anything else, beautiful when it *is* beautiful.

a part is not there that the rules suggest should be there, the explanatory force and, therefore, the unifying force of the rules is destroyed, thereby 'disjointing and disturbing' all of the other parts or, thereby changing 'the character of all the parts.'[22]

Few if any artistic works meet this ideal of unity, of course. If I change the epigram above to read "A dear is a mammal," instead of "A deer is an animal," almost all, if not all, of the force the novel will still remain. (Although I do not want to deny important differences between those two phrases. 'Mammal' is a more scientific term than 'animal' and may seem less likely in a grammar book, or it may reduce some the sense that the first sentences are uncontroversial and obvious. Notice also that mammal doesn't fit the rhythmic development of the phrase as well. Consider the predicates in order: tree, flower, animal, fatherland, inevitable. Notice that as the concepts move from the concrete to the abstract the number of syllables grows. Furthermore, note that at the important transition from 'A deer is an animal' to 'Russia is our Fatherland' both animal and fatherland are dactyls, thereby strengthening the connection between the two halves of the epigram.) Even the greatest works have filler words and passages that could have been replaced with other words and passages without causing harm to the work. These are not counterexamples to my definition. They are examples of the obvious truth that perfection is nearly impossible to achieve. What Dante and Aristotle and the others are pointing to is the ideal artistic work. All art, they are saying, strives to be an organic unity. What I've tried to do, with my definition of richness, is give us some way of measuring

---

22Also Kant, "In painting, sculpture, and in fact in all the formative arts, in architecture and horticulture, so far as fine arts, the design is what is essential. Here it is not what gratifies in sensation but merely what pleases by its form that is the fundamental prerequisite for taste. The colors which give brilliancy to the sketch are part of the charm. They may no doubt, in their own way, enliven the object for sensation, but make it really worth looking at and beautiful they cannot. Indeed, more often than not the requirements of the beautiful form restrict them to a very narrow compass, and, even where charm is admitted, it is only this form that gives them a place of honor.... Thus it is with the frames of pictures or the drapery on statues, or the colonnades of palaces. But if the ornamentation does not itself enter into the composition of the beautiful form-if it is introduced like a gold frame merely to win approval for the picture by means of its charm-it is then called finery and takes away from the genuine beauty."[Kant, 1964]

how closely a work has neared that ideal.

Aristotle goes beyond **Principle P** in The Politics; he claims that in the good society "The whole is prior to the parts." Coleridge generalizes this claim, "Depend on it, in whatever is grand, whatever is truly organic and living, the whole is prior to its parts."[23] [24] [25]

What could this mysterious phrase mean? How could a whole be prior to its parts? A whole consists of its parts! If the whole exists, so do its parts, of course. Clearly, we must understand this metaphorically to understand it at all. I suggest the metaphor be read as follows: understand, quite naturally, 'the whole' to mean the unity of the parts and 'the parts' to mean the variety that is unified into the whole. The priority of the whole to the parts, then, is captured by the fact that the unity of rich things is a nomic explanation for the variety. Explanations are, by their nature, prior to the facts that they explain. I had the reasons why I wrote this sentence before I wrote this sentence. The Laws of the Universe existed before the apple fell on Newton. The artist has an intention before he has his artwork. If the unity of a whole comes 'after' the parts, if it feels like something that we add to the parts, if it is ad hoc, the unity does not serve as an explanation for those parts, and so those parts are not really unified, are not really part of a whole.

Coleridge gives us an example. He compares Shakespeare to the playwrights Beaumont and Fletcher,

> "The plays of Beaumont and Fletcher are mere aggregations without unity: in the Shakespearean drama there is a vitality which grows and evolves from within – a keynote which guides and controls their harmonies throughout…."

23I shouldn't rush by so quickly as to ignore that Coleridge is, more or less, not just making an aesthetic assertion, but claiming the thesis of the present essay [Coleridge, 1949: 196].

24This is clearly related to Plato's, "the all is not the whole," that is, the sum of the parts – the all – is not the same as the whole made of those parts. [Plato, 1992: 204 B]

25Also [Osborne, 1952]: "a configuration such that the configuration itself is prior in awareness to its component parts and is not explicable by a summation of its parts and their relations according to additive and discursive principles."

Beaumont's and Fletcher's plays are made, on the other hand,

> "Just like a man might put together a quarter of an orange, a quarter of an apple, and the like of a lemon and a pomegranate, and make it look like one round diverse fruit."[26]

Clearly aggregations are unified in some sense of the word; they are after all together. But why are they aggregated as such? Is the peach-ness explained, the pomegranate-ness? In richness, the 'key note' must come first; it 'guides' and 'controls' the variety throughout; always present. It is impossible to fully understand the worth of any part of a work in isolation from the rest of the work. Take out the quarter of a peach – it is a quarter of a peach – it retains most of its significance and value. On the other hand, take out Ophelia from *Hamlet* – what is she? Her lines create no real Ophelia without the rest of the play. (I have discussed this before: recall the example of Whole **W**, with parts a,b,c and explanations **E** and **F**).

A closely related characterization suggests that in organic unities, the whole is (somehow) in the part. Kant said that in an organism, "every part is reciprocally ends and means."[27] Henry James says that, in each part of the novel, "there must be something of all the other parts."[28] (This should remind many of us of Leibniz's monads in which the entire universe was reflected in each of its atoms.) In a perfectly unified richness, the rules are as deterministic as those of Laplace's *Celestial Mechanics*. This entails that the having of any part necessitates the having of all the others. Hence, each part can be legitimately seen as both the result of any of the other parts or the cause of the other parts. For instance, 'minds' might end the first line because 'finds' ends the third line, but it is equally explanatory to say that 'finds' ends the third line because 'minds' ends the first. For any part p, part p and the rules entails all the other parts. Each part together with the unifying rules, then, has 'something' of all the other parts; it is both ends and means, depending on how you squint

---

26[Coleridge, 1907: 256] *via* [Orsini. 1973]
27[Kant, 1964]
28[James, 1951: 404]

your eyes.

I end this brief survey with a reminder to the reader of the most prevalent characterization of organic unity, that of 'unified variety.' Harold Osborne in his *Theory of Beauty* says,

> "All works of art, even the simplest, are fairly complex for immediate perception and it has been a commonplace of artistic criticism that a good work of art must have a high degree of unity.... The two notions, however vague, suggest that works of art of whatever kind may have in common the formal property of being complex unities."[29]

In the *Ars Poetica*, Horace says that a poem should be a unity of different parts.[30] Coleridge repeated many times "unity in multiplicity," as his formula for aesthetic success.[31] John Hospers has stated that the organically unified object,

> "should contain within itself a large number of diverse elements, each of which in some way contributes to the total integration of the unified whole, so there is no confusion despite the disparate elements."[32]

Santayana cited 'unity in multiplicity' as the key measure of the value in aesthetic form.[33] All of this, of course, is consistent with Nozick's and Hutcheson's definitions of organic unity with which I started the entire investigation.

There are many other common claims made with respect to great art, claims that could plausibly be construed as being about richness.

29[Osborne, 1952 #5: 92]
30[Horace, 1974]
31[Coleridge, 1949]
32Also A.C. Bradley, "To consider separately the action and the characters of a play, and separately the style and versification, is both legitimate and valuable, so long as we remember what we are doing. But the true critic in speaking of those aspects does not really think of them apart: the whole, the poetic experience, of which they are but aspects, is always in his mind; and he is always aiming *at a richer, truer, more intimate repetition of that experience.*" {Italics mine}[Bradley, 1909: 16-17]
33[Santayana, 1988]

It is often claimed that great art seems 'inevitable,' as if it had to be the way that it is. This is plausible if the best art follows from simple powerful rules. Great art is also art that rewards repeated examination. I often judge the quality of a novel by how tempted I am to reread it. The complexity of the artwork is great enough to deserve repeated study. This is plausible if great art encloses a 'maximum of realities.' Reading a great novel is an activity akin to scientific investigation, then, an immersion in the variety of details with the goal of understanding them, of grasping what unifies them. And as I mentioned earlier, great art is art where many choices seem to have been made, where the artist is there all along designing it according to a plan. The importance of choosing every part of an artistic work is clear when we understand in what the unity of artistic works consists. Furthermore, the making of choices allows us to be original, to create something new. I will argue, briefly, in § 2.3.5. that the value of originality is also captured by richness.

It is outside the scope of this book to examine the details of twenty-five hundred years of aesthetic criticism with respect to organic unity. This short review shows, though, that many have identified something tantalizingly similar to richness as central to aesthetic value.

2.3.3 Beauty: In the Eye of the Beholder?

One benefit of the view that aesthetic value supervenes on richness is that one can explain the apparent subjectivity of beauty with an objective theory of value. Harry loves the *Mona Lisa*. Tristan finds it a bore. Harry thinks it is extremely beautiful and, therefore, valuable. Tristan thinks it is intrinsically worthless (despite the tidy sum it would fetch at auction). Who is right? Many have thought that it doesn't make sense to ask the question. It is not, one might say, that one is right and the other wrong. They are both right: beauty is in the eye of the beholder. Tristan doesn't appreciate the *Mona*

Lisa, and so the painting isn't beautiful to him. Harry does appreciate it, and so it is beautiful to him. Is this right?

I argue here that the value of art is objectively fixed by the amount of richness in the art and the amount of richness that art brings into the world. The value it brings into the world may depend on objective features of the person who is appreciating the artwork, and, this, I suggest, is what gives rise to the sense that the value of art is subjective.

There are many sources of richness (and, therefore, value) in our experience of art. First, good art is intrinsically valuable because it itself is rich. It is rich in all the ways that Aristotle and Plato and Dante and Coleridge and Kant and Nozick have pointed out. Second, art is valuable in virtue of being the object of rich appreciations. A skillful, fully aware appreciation of a work of art brings into existence a mental model of the artwork that is largely isomorphic to the work itself. This entails, as earlier noted, the creation of a rich entity in the mind, the creation of rich relation between mind and fact. Finally, art is valuable in virtue of causing rich, non-appreciation experiences in the observer. Art is instrumentally valuable in creating rich mental states that are not representations of the artwork itself. Art, and rich art in particular, brings to mind memories, thoughts, emotions, theories and so on that are not actually in the artwork itself. Rich art invites us to imagine rich situations that are not in the artwork and teaches us important things about human nature and our own emotions that we can use throughout our lives. It is possible, that an object that is less intrinsically rich may provide more richness of this third variety than a more intrinsically rich work.

The value of art appears subjective because for any particular piece of art, there appear to be many competing, and, more importantly, equally valid, experiences of the value of that artwork. I suggest that when we disagree about the value of an aesthetic object, it may be due to any number of things, none of which is strong evidence that there is no objective value in the aesthetic object itself. First, it may be due to the fact that one of us is failing to see properly. This may be due to value hallucinations, artistic inabilities, insufficient knowledge of the artwork, insufficient knowledge of the artwork's context or any of a number of other errors or limitations. Our perceptions of value can fail in many ways and all of those failures are common with respect to aesthetic judgments (see §1.2.2). Moreover, evaluating the richness of artwork is especially difficult. I am a person of above average intelligence who has spent much time becoming sensitive to the value of aesthetic objects, and yet I know that most of the intrinsic richness of a good symphony escapes my ear. For one, I don't have the training for it. Possibly, I don't have the proper mental abilities. If I believe my present enjoyment of a symphony tracks the objective value of the symphony, then I and a more acute person will likely disagree about its value. This is not because the value is subjective, but because I am in an epistemically disadvantageous position compared to the expert. Tristan may not have the education, training, or concentration required for accessing the full value of Ulysses. The novel may deal with situations or concepts with which he has little or no familiarity. As such, it does not fully connect with Tristan's psychology and so the reading experience does not form a rich whole with the book. Most artworks are based on large sets of assumptions, propositions the artwork does not explicitly represent but with which it assumes that the appreciator is familiar.[34] Without knowledge of these assumptions, it is impossible to appreciate the full richness of the work. For this reason, art from other cultures or different historical periods may be, by its nature, partially inaccessible to us. Or we might be too young or old or the wrong gender to understand its basic assumptions.

(On the other hand, it is remarkable how much artwork is appreciated across time and culture. Artworks exist whose basic idea is accessible to persons anywhere. These artworks have a universal 'message,' one that connects with something fundamental to all hu-

---

[34]An interesting question is whether the assumptions are *part* of the artwork or adjuncts to it. I lean toward including them in the artwork. Suppose you read the following sentence opening a novel. "The light turned red, but Dangerfield hit the gas anyway." Clearly, it is part of the novel that Dangerfield is doing something dangerous because of the way red lights and gas pedals operate in the real world. The author need never explicitly say anything about the operation of streetlights, but someone who didn't know about the conventions of streetlights would clearly be missing part of the *actual* novel.

man experience. These are widely revered because they are unified with so much of humanity's experiences and capable of being appreciated by so many.)[35]

All of this means that artworks can have significant intrinsic value and still fail to be appreciated by intelligent appreciators.[36] Some disagreements, then, are due to the inability of one person to see. Part of the novel is hidden from Tristan; he is blind to it. The richest things are the most difficult to see, to bring fully into awareness. Scientists, artists, psychologists, critics require years of training because of the density of the things they study, because of the difficulty in seeing the unity through that density; just as in science or the study of ethical value, there are skills required to see art as it is, to experience its value.

The second reason for our differing experiences of value with respect to art is more important for the present discussion. The reading of a novel brings to mind both the story of the novel and many things not actually in the novel. The experiences the novel generates will vary greatly from person to person, not due to any failure, but merely because people are different. It is this last element of the value of art, I suggest, that gives rise most strongly to the feeling that aesthetic value is in the eye of the beholder. The experiences that a particular artwork bring to mind depend on the mind that is appreciating the artwork. The quality of appreciation, then, is not entirely determined by the intrinsic richness of the artwork appreciated: it is, at least partially, dependent on properties of the observer. A novel may connect with large sets of beliefs, memories, and hopes of Harry while leaving Tristan cold. This may be because Tristan isn't a very good reader, as we've mentioned, isn't good at recognizing richness

---

35But I think it is a mistake to undervalue 'dated' art. It may be that an artwork can no longer connect with a large number of people or a rich chunk of our present experience. This does not mean that in its time, if you knew its basic assumptions, intimately understood its assumed milieu, it could not be the object of great appreciation. It's just that it is an artwork apposite for a specific people in a specific time and place. The value of its place in *that culture* is never lost even if it can no longer be appreciated.

36There is, indeed, a critical bias, toward artworks of this sort. I have little doubt that *Finnegan's Wake* is an amazingly rich novel, but I doubt that anyone other than Joyce could have ever come close to fully appreciating it. Its intrinsic structure gives it value, but its inaccessibility to appreciation puts bounds on how much value it has in the world.

in a novel, isn't good at evoking images or putting himself in the position of others. On the other hand, it may be due to no fault of Tristan's. Their disagreement may because Harry is seeing things that are not really in the artwork at all. A woman named Juliet is a main character in the novel and this reminds him of his wife, Juliet. A set of rich memories about Juliet comes to mind as he reads the novel. He finds this valuable, and it is. Tristan, on the other hand, does not know Juliet so well. He reads the novel without this added richness and so it finds it less valuable. Harry is genuinely accessing value, namely, his memory of Juliet, it is just not value that is in the novel; it is not value that is there for others to find.

That beauty is partly in the eye of the beholder is not surprising if background knowledge is necessary to access the beauty of many things, or if background knowledge can add value to a person's appreciation. This is not just true with respect to artwork. Scientists describe deadly viruses, fungal outbreaks, proofs, quantum fluctuations and the molecular structure of certain rocks as beautiful. Most of these things are not beautiful to the average person's immediate perception. Nonetheless, these are, generally, rich things. It is just that seeing the richness requires some study. You need to know the structure of the DNA; you need to know the patterns of cellular clumping; you need to understand the molecular symmetries. The beholder who has done that study, that has this proper knowledge, sees beauty that the untrained eye cannot. Moreover, DNA, deadly viruses, and fungal outbreaks mean something very different to these scientists than they mean to an average person. They are connected with large aspects of those scientists' personal lives. They are connected to memories of places and mental states that they are not connected to for others.

Finally, note that the variability in the value of reading experiences is usually circumscribed by the intrinsic richness of the work. Works that exhibit actual richness are the ones that can be richly appreciated.[37] Works that are not rich might cause other rich experiences, of course, but they cannot be richly appreciated. If I see a

------

37Similar phenomena arise in ethics as well. Isn't it better for me to save my mother from

mark on a door jamb, it reminds of my grandmother's house where they would measure my height each spring and it reminds of my grandmother and her pancakes and so on. The mark on the door-knob is not rich; my experiences that are caused by that mark are. Nonetheless, I cannot richly appreciate the mark. It is not the type of thing that can be richly appreciated.

In conclusion, though the value of the reading experience or the experience of DNA or of a play or whatever varies from individual to individual, the value of these experiences is not subjective in any sense important to the debate about value realism. For each reader, the value of reading the novel is objectively fixed – that is, its value is independent of what that reader, or anyone else, thinks of the value – fixed by the objective features of the book and objective features of that person's psychology, fixed by how much richness exists in the book and in the mind experiencing the book.

2.3.4 Art as Representation

"Illusion is the first of all pleasures." Voltaire

A competing theory of what aesthetic objects are and what makes them good is the representational theory of art. Plato, for instance, thought that all art was 'merely' imitation. He claimed that the best art did no more than hold a mirror up to the world.[38] The artist's job, according to this theory, is to reproduce some part of reality as faithfully as possible.

It is clear that not all art is some form of representation. Music

---

the river rather than the stranger? A universalizable ethics seems to deny this intuition. But, I believe, the above considerations can be applied to such cases, to show that, at least, there is a legitimate sense in which your mother is more valuable in your experience, *objectively*, than the stranger. Whether, this leads to an ethic in which we *should* save our mother, I leave to the side here (though it seems natural that we should protect more strongly those things that seem more valuable). This might lead one to the conclusion, not surprisingly, that what you should do is intimately connected with who you are, despite the fact that what is right or wrong in any situation is objectively fixed.
38[Plato, 1974: 596e]

and many abstract paintings are clear and convincing counterexamples. Moreover, even for the representational arts, the measure of good art is not merely how closely it resembles reality. If this were so, photographs and minute-by-minute diaries would be the highest form of art. Most representational art is not even trying to represent something actual; rather it is trying to present something plausibly actual.

Still, a great part of the value of representational art does relate to its correspondence to reality. Raskolnikov is not supposed to be a real person and the murders he commits are not real murders, but he is supposed to act like a real person, and it should be plausible that a person of his character might commit those murders. Moreover, aspects of Raskolnikov are isomorphic to aspects of many people. This is what is scary and tragic about Raskolnikov.

A representation does not need to be of some particular real thing to isomorphically unify with reality. I write a pamphlet on how to use an airport (any airport). My pamphlet does not refer to an actual airport, but rather to an abstract airport that has the general features of most airports. A good pamphlet along these lines will be unified with most airports, through a partial isomorphism with those airports. A bad one will have little correspondence to real airports. Novels in which the characters act inexplicably are generally weaker than ones in which the characters are intelligible. Good representational portraits are rarely attempts to look exactly like the subject; they are not intended to fool us into thinking the person is actually there. Something important about the person's character, mood, place in society, though, should be captured, should be represented. Much good art is trying to communicate something about something, like my pamphlet about airports. All other things being equal, the more of what is communicated that is actually true, the more value that piece of art has. So, one source of value for representative art is its unification with reality. The deeper and truer a representation is, the more of reality with which it is unified. This unification of artwork and world is rich for all the reasons given earlier, and it is this richness that we value.

Moreover, the more 'real' the representations of an artwork are, the more likely that an artwork will connect with large portions of an appreciator's experience. It is because Raskolnikov, no matter how outlandish, is a coherent and realistic character that his actions are frightening and compelling. It is because parts of Raskolnikov remind us of parts of ourselves or parts of others we know, that Raskolnikov is such a rich character, that his story can affect our experience of our lives. The more evocative a representation, the more of our own mental richness will be drawn forth during our appreciation of the artwork. So representational art is rich in virtue of its own intrinsic richness, in virtue of its unification with the things of which it is a representation, and the unification of it and the minds of its appreciators. Furthermore, it is instrumentally rich in virtue of its ability to bring to mind other richness not explicitly in the work itself.

2.3.5 Originality

There are two ways a creation can be original, one contextual and one causal. A work is original contextually if it is something that has not been done before, if it is new to the world. It is original causally if it is generated solely by the artist and not by some form of copying.[39] There is obviously a tight relation between the two. If an object is truly original in the second sense and it is a rich object (therefore, an unlikely one), it is unlikely that it is not original in the first sense. Likewise, if an object is truly new, truly contextually original, it must be (unless it was randomly generated) an instance of causal originality.

The value of contextual originality is easy to capture. If a work is merely a reproduction of a work of art already produced, it does not add variety to the world, and so does not add much value to

---

39This distinction is similar to one made by Margaret Boden. She distinguishes between historical creativity and psychological creativity; historical creativity more or less corresponds to what I have called contextual originality. Psychological creativity is similar to causal originality. [Boden, 1994]

the world except inasmuch as it facilitates the further appreciation of its basic structure by more and varied consciousnesses. Imagine again the booklet of 300 identical Rembrandts. Such a book is not 300 times richer than a single copy of a Rembrandt. The more contextually original an artwork (or an idea, or a machine, or a thought etc….) the more value it brings to the world. The more newness in a work, the more the richness of the world is increased. It is further evidence for the present theory that this is precisely the reason one values most originality: just because it is something new.

Causal originality is also valuable. If an artist merely copies another artist's work, she serves as little more than a mimesis machine. Though there is some value in copying, it is not nearly as rich an act of creation as one that connects with the full variety of the artist's own peculiarities, her own uniqueness. An act of original creation is an attempt to map parts of our own mind onto the materials of the world. Inasmuch as each individual is a unique and rich creature, acts of original creation are unique and rich events. It may happen that, by amazing coincidence, I produce something that has largely been prefigured by other artists, but if I am not just copying these other artists, it is highly unlikely that this particular act of creation, this one that connects up with who I am and what I've seen, is itself identical to acts of creation due to those other artists, even if the created object turns out to be similar. In other words, though the work is not contextually original, the rich relations between my mind and the creation will be; they will be new relations to the world. As such, causal originality is valuable even when it is not a source of contextual originality. This notion of causal originality is tightly bound up with discussions of autonomy and freedom which I will discuss in §2.4.1.

2.3.6 Conclusion

The class of things called art is rather large; the class of things called beautiful even larger. At one level, it is obvious that what makes one artwork beautiful may be very different from what makes another beautiful. Hemingway's novels are stark revelations of human character. Nabokov's novels are intricately stylized philosophy and humor. Rembrandt's portraits are detailed attempts to fix a human emotion. Rothko's paintings are abstract evocations of an eternal landscape. There are different reasons that all of these are beautiful, yes, but this is because there are different reasons each is rich. The human character, the language, the human face, the landscape are all rich things (to name just a modicum of what creates richness in the work of those artists). Some artwork is ordered representationally, some abstractly by elements of form, some conceptually by commenting on other artwork or the history of art. Some is simple in perception and only varied in what it evokes, in what it turns our attention toward. Some artwork has the contrary effect, chaotic in experience, but improbably unified down below. Some artwork is intrinsically 'bad,'[40] and certain people like it for richness in their own psychology; some artwork is intrinsically good and certain people don't like it because it is too difficult or it is unfamiliar or they are untrained. Some artwork's greatest value is its accessibility, its instrumental power in creating richness in many human minds. Some artwork is great for its universality, still powerful in other cultures or different times. Some artwork's very difficulty is a sign of its richness. We must pay close attention to what we value in art if we want to unify aesthetics. What is it we really like about an artwork? I suggest that when you look closely, in all these cases, and the host of others you can generate yourself, you'll find something rich, either in the work itself or in yourself.

40Read: 'less good.' On the view I am presenting, there is no negative value. See Chapter 4, §4.41.

2.4 Freedom, Desire-Satisfaction, and Persons

I will deal in this abbreviated section with three rather large topics, freedom of the will, the value of desire-satisfaction and persons. I consider them together because there is a neat little set of relations between the concepts. 1) A person is free when taking action X when that person is the genuine cause of X. 2) The desires that are most worthy of being satisfied, whose satisfaction has the most intrinsic value are those that make us most free when we act on them. 3) Those same desires are the ones that are most intimately connected with who we are, with what it is to be the unique person we are.

2.4.1 Freedom

There really are only three positions anyone holds about the freedom of the will. **(A)** We are not free because we have no control over anything. Argument: either the world is deterministic or it has some amount of indeterminism. 1) If the world is deterministic, there is one and only one thing that can be done at any moment. Therefore, we don't control our actions because we *have* to do whatever we do. So, if the world is deterministic, no one is free. 2) If the world is partially indeterministic, on the other hand, then there might be times when an actor has more than one option. This does not help, though, because random events, by their nature, are also outside of our control. As determinism and indeterminism are the only two options and both entail we are not in control of our actions, that we are not free, we are not free. Indeed, it is logically impossible that we are free. Call this position the Anti-freedom Position.

(B) One is free at (at least some) time t because at t, there is more than one possible action that one can take. This is the view of the Libertarians. Freedom is possible for the Libertarian because, they say, the world is not entirely deterministic. We can act without external causal influence and (somehow) this gives us freedom. They deny the second half of the argument for Anti–freedom.

Or (**C**) Compatibilism: we are free as long as our actions flow from our person in the proper manner. It does not matter if the world is deterministic. It does not matter that we had to do the action we are doing as long as we, our desires, values, are the proximate cause of our actions, that is, as long as we do what we really want because it is what we really want. If it is genuinely my desires or values that caused my action, then the action is mine and I am free. This is the view of the compatibilist. They deny the first half of the argument for Anti-freedom.

I am going to assert with only a short defense a compatibilist definition of freedom put forward by myself and Rachel G. K. Singpurwalla.[41] I believe that compatibilism is the right view to hold for reasons that I can only briefly go into here. For the present purposes, though, note that (**A**), the first position, the view that it is not possible that we are free, is not relevant to the thesis of this essay. I am concerned with what we value, and it is uncontroversial that we value freedom whether we have it or not (though that we all do value it so highly is some evidence that we can have it). If I am right, we must value freedom, whatever it is, for its richness.

There are two strong arguments against (**B**) Libertarianism. The first is the argument for the Anti-freedom position. The second argument against libertarianism is that the compatibilist can better capture our common sense understanding of freedom. In particular, a compatibilist definition of freedom has the potential, I suggest, to capture the fact that we generally talk about freedom (and the intimately connected concept of moral responsibility) in degrees. Our common sense view holds that we can be more or less free and more or less responsible. The libertarian has difficulty explaining this.

A widely accepted ethical principle is that ought implies can. If an actor can't do **A**, then **A** cannot be morally required. So, if an actor is not free, the actor cannot be morally responsible for her ac-

---

41 [Singpurwalla, 2001]

tions. "Ought implies can" is an instance of a broader, less discussed, moral principle, namely, that moral responsibility (all things being equal) is proportional to freedom. A person is less responsible for actions they have less control over.

Consider: after being convicted of murder, a criminal's defense team is allowed to provide evidence of mitigating circumstances to lessen the weight of punishment. Examples of mitigating facts: that it was a crime of passion, the criminal's horrible childhood, that the person was addicted or on some drug. Each and every one of these things is an attempt to show that the criminal was not as responsible as he would have been otherwise. Why do these things show him to be less responsible? Because they show he had less control over his actions than he would otherwise would have. His animal emotions, his environment, or his addiction turn out to be better explanations of his action than he is.

We commonly talk about freedom and responsibility in this manner, in terms of less and more. The libertarian definition of freedom, though, does not allow for degrees of freedom. Either we have more than one possible option or we do not. For the libertarian, we are free if we do, not free if we don't. There is no more libertarian story to tell. It is not clear why we would ever need a mitigation phase of a trial with respect to dessert if the Libertarian view was the right one. But the mitigation phase *is* about dessert. This suggests, though, that the Libertarian is not really talking about freedom, at least not what most of us mean by freedom. More importantly, this gives us reason to think that the Libertarian might have failed to capture what it is that we value about freedom.

Freedom, for the compatibilist, on the other hand, only requires the proper causal connection between people and their actions. The compatibilist accepts that we cannot entirely create ourselves. By the time we make our first choice, we are already made, and so that first choice will be due to something outside of our control, namely us. This doesn't matter, though. What matters is that it is genuinely us that makes that action happen, *whomever us* has turned out to be. But our actions can be more or less connected to us; our actions can be more or less *ours*. And so the compatibilist can capture that freedom comes in degrees.

So we need an account of what it means to be the cause of your action. Singpurwalla and I put forth the following suggestion: you are free when you act on values that you formed on the basis of a rational evaluation of all the evidence of your life. The more evidence you take into account in forming your values and the more your actions are consistent with those values, the freer you are.

We consider three competing compatibilist views: Harry Frankfurt's view that we are free when we act consistently with our second-order desires,[42] Gary Watson's view that we are free when we act according to our values[43] and Susan Wolf's (rather complicated) view that you are free when you can do the (objectively) Right action for the (objectively) Right reasons.[44] The Right reasons for Wolf are a) you believe your action is Right and 2) you believe it is Right because of rational deliberation about the action.

In response to Watson and Frankfurt, we argue that both second-order desires and values may not be properly ours. Both our second-order desires and our values could be due to brainwashing, for instance. If we are brainwashed by a cult into valuing praying to a tree ten times a day, that value is not properly ours. When we act from that value, we are not fully free. The brainwasher is more in control of that action than we are. Susan Wolf makes a similar response to Watson.[45]

Wolf's view, on the other hand, that we are free when doing the Right action for the Right reasons leaves us no explanation for freedom in the non-moral realm. Here's how Singpurwalla and I framed

---

42Harry Frankfurt, "Freedom of the Will and the Concept of a Person," in his *The Importance of What We Care About* (Cambridge: Cambridge University Press, 1988), p. 11-25.
43Watson, "Free Agency," in *Free Will*, ed., G. Watson, (Oxford: Oxford University Press, 1982), p. 96-110.
44S. Wolf, *Freedom Within Reason* (Oxford: Oxford University Press, 1990)
45As Singpurwalla and I put it: "Take for example the brainwashing of Winston Smith in George Orwell's *1984*. By the end of the book, after he has been brainwashed by O'Brian and the rats in Room 101, large portions of his values have been altered. Winston spends the rest of his life acting according to these new values. According to Watson's theory, Winston is as free as he can be. But do we consider his acts of allegiance to the fascist state as free as O'Brian's acts of allegiance? Would we hold him as responsible? In a similar

the objection to Wolf:

Say that the True moral theory says that in circumstances **C**, Action **D** and Action **E** are morally equivalent and that either one would be the best action that James could take. James decides, then, on the basis of Reason, that he will do **D** or **E**. Morality has nothing more to say about the matter and so, according to Wolf, it is irrelevant to his freedom how he decides to do one or the other. But imagine now that James has been hypnotized such that if he were ever faced with a choice between **D** and **E**, he would choose **D**.[46]

Wolf claims we're free when we can do the right thing for the right reasons. Here, James not only can do the right thing, he actually does the right thing. But the intuition is strong that choosing **D** because you were hypnotized to choose **D** is not as free as if you chose **D** for some other, personal, non-moral reason. The point of this objection is that when we reach that place where the Good has nothing more to say, there can still be choices to be made. These choices, like all other choices, can be more or less free.

But the overarching failure of all three of these alternatives is the failure to recognize that freedom and moral responsibility come in degrees. Consider the following five cases:

> "1) A kleptomaniac steals her roommate's billfold.
>
> 2) A weak-willed and flat-broke person is overcome by her strong desire for cocaine, and although she thinks it is wrong, she steals her roommate's billfold to buy cocaine.
>
> 3) To feed his starving child, an out-of-work Christian who deeply believes in the ten-commandments steals his roommate's billfold.
>
> 4) Jenny, a small-time crook who values getting something for nothing, but who has never reflected upon this value,

---

vein, consider values that are the result of a serious prolonged mental illness, say, a deep chemical imbalance. Are the misanthropic actions of the paranoid schizophrenic free? Is he responsible for his actions? Even though that misanthropy is the central feature of his character? And finally, if you acted on values that you had due to a childhood trauma, say a hatred of all women due to an abusive mother, would you be free? It seems obvious that the person who acts from their values in all of these cases is not as free as a person whose values were not 'implanted' in them in one of these ways."
46[Singpurwalla, 2001, 8]

steals her roommate's billfold.

5) Jimmy, a small-time crook who values getting something for nothing, and who has reflected upon and endorsed this value, steals his roommate's billfold."

I suggest that these cases are ordered from least free to most free and least responsible to most responsible. The kleptomaniac acts according to a compulsion that is almost entirely out of her control. The drug addict is, likewise acting from a strong desire out of her control, but it is not a compulsion (at least not a compulsion to steal). We do not think that the addict absolutely had to steal. We would be more angry with her than the kleptomaniac. (By the way, be careful to evaluate the addict merely for stealing the wallet and not for the addiction itself). The Christian has been put in a moral dilemma; and although it is certainly his choice to steal, he is forced to it by the demands of the circumstances. Though there is not any compulsion forcing the Christian to steal, we understand that he doesn't really want to steal. We blame him less than Jenny who enjoys stealing. If asked, Jenny would say that it is exactly what she wants to do. Jenny, though she sees nothing wrong with stealing, has been raised without knowing any other way of acting. She is less free than Jimmy because she is acting according to a sort of peer pressure, a kind of social determinism. If she were forced to sit down and think about stealing and other things she cares about, she might not steal the wallet. Jimmy, on the other hand, is doing what he really wants to do.

Neither the Libertarian nor the three other compatibilist views can capture this ordering of the actions. Singpurwalla and I agree with Watson that it is important that we act from our values rather than passing or shallow desires. The drug addict and the kleptomaniac are acting contrary, we suspect, to their values. What we really want is tightly associated with what we think is good. But Wolf is also right that it matters how you come to your values. Sometimes, your thoughts about what is good are not really yours. They could be formed to rationalize certain unhealthy desires, or are really the values of your parents, or are brainwashed or habitual or completely unevaluated or contradictory. We agree with Wolf that we are most free when our actions have been rationally evaluated, when the values that drive our actions have been rationally formed. But I have already established what a rationally formed value will look like; it will be a value that takes into account all of the value evidence, that is all your desires, your perceptions of the good, and forms the best theory about what is good based on that evidence. Singpurwalla and I suggest that one is most free when one acts from what we call one's *values-of-one's-own*:

> A value is a *value-of-one's-own* in as much as the value was formed through rational reflection on the totality of evidence of one's own experience and inasmuch as it is not inconsistent with rational reflection on the totality of one's experience.[47]

Think of values-of-one's-own as inferences to the best explanation from the evidence of our life experiences. They are our best theories of the good given the unique evidence of our life. And what could we be more closely identified with than our experiences and values (our wants, hopes, loves, goals, plans etc...)? Values-of-one's own capture both of these central aspects.

Our view of freedom, then, is as follows:

The Life-Experiences View: an agent is free in doing action x in circumstance C in as much as that agent is acting from values-of-her-own and not contrary to values-of-her-own.[48]

To be free is to act from values that are most your own, not values of your mother or values of someone holding a gun to your head, not the values of the brainwasher, or the values of your social group, not a compulsion or an addiction. It is to act not according to transitory desires, but according to values that capture your full life experience, according to values that are somehow yours and yours alone. Sing-

---

47[Singpurwalla, 2001, 10]
48[Singpurwalla, 2001, 11]

purwalla and I address the five cases above:

1) The kleptomaniac is not free because she doesn't act from any value-of-her-own, and indeed, we suspect she is acting contrary to values-of-her-own. Kleptomania is indpendent of rational evaluation of ones's experience. 2) The smoker is more free because she does see something good about the cigarettes, but this value is due to a temporary physiological urge, and not to the conclusions she has drawn from her life experiences, and thus is not a central value for her; in addition, she is acting contrary to other more rational values of hers such as health and not stealing from friends. 3) The Christian, on the other hand, is acting from a clear value-of-his own, his love for his child, even though his action is contrary to another value-of-his-own, his value to obey the commands of God. Thus, he is freer than the smoker or the kleptomaniac since he is acting from deep values-of-his-own. Because he is acting contrary to deep values-of-his-own, however, he is not as free as Jenny. 4) Jenny does exactly what she really wants to do. But Jenny has not arrived at her values by evaluating her life-experiences; she just accepted them uncritically from her environment. Thus, she is less free than Jimmy. 5) Jimmy steals from a value that is really his own, a value that he came to through thinking about (at least a partial set) of the evidence in his life.[49]

The most rational beliefs to hold are, generally, those that take all available evidence and draw reasoned conclusions from that evidence. A theory which explains all of the evidence is a better explanation than one that explains less. And a theory that explains most of our evidence and isn't contradicted by any of the evidence is better than a theory that explains an equivalent amount of evidence, but is contradicted by some evidence. Likewise, the most rational value beliefs to hold are those that take the full variety of one's perceptions of value and unify that evidence using reason. The most rational values to have are those that are the best theories of what is good. The best theories, as I've already discussed are the richest (see §2.2.2), the simplest ones that capture the most varied evidence.

49[Singpurwalla, 2001, 12]

And, so, our values-of-one's-own are our richest values. What does this say about the value of freedom? A compatibilist considers actions *thickly* rather than *thinly*: actions are partly constituted by the intentions that led to those actions, as opposed to being merely the physical (or mental) movement that completed the act. In all five cases above, the thin action is the stealing of a wallet. But the freedom of the stealing act depends on the intentions behind the act; the freedom of the action depends on what the thick action is. On the life-experiences view the freest actions are ones that are partly constituted by a value-of-one's own. And these actions are, all other things equal, the richest actions.[50] Another way of putting this: given that freedom and responsibility come in degrees, we need a measure of both. On our view, the measure will be the same measure one would use to evaluate the adequacy of any theory. I have argued that that measure is richness.[51]

(I am in position, now, to lend some extra weight to the claim that causal originality is rich. When we create something that is truly our own, in which it is genuinely us that made the thing happened, it is an instance of causal originality. But the more causally original an action, the more it arises from values-of-one's-own. Therefore, we should expect acts of causal originality to be intrinsically rich.)

Two final comments: 1) The view entails that no one is maximally free. One can never fully rationally evaluate all the evidence of one's life for two reasons: the quantity of evidence is enormous and

---

[50]In addition, recall that it is not sufficient that I believe x is good for x to motivate me; I must perceive x as good for x to motivate. For a value belief to motivate, it must generate a perception of value. But since a value of one's own is a rich theory of what is good based on the richness of one's experience, the desire this value gives rise to is a desire due to a perception of the richness of one's life. When I believe that 'Honesty is good' because of repeated experiences of the value of honesty in my life, that value has the power to motivate me in a way that my other less evidenced value beliefs do not. When the belief that 'Honesty is good' comes to mind, so does, at least implicitly, a host of examples of that fact. These examples, these memories allow me to *see* the good in honesty. When I truly act from the *full* evidence that formed the value of my own, I am acting from as rich a perception of value as I can have. Desires such as these, the most rational, the most rich, are the ones it is good to satisfy.

[51]Another benefit of compatibilism, and our view especially, is that it *explains* the connection between freedom and moral responsibility. Free actions are the ones you are responsible for because they are the ones that are yours.

it is continuously coming in. This is not problematic, though. None of us is maximally beautiful, but we don't despair. We are beautiful to a degree and some to a great degree. None of us is maximally intelligent. This is no disaster. We are all intelligent to some degree. The same is true of freedom. None of us are perfectly free, but we all are free to a degree.

2) Even if Libertarianism is right and compatibilism is wrong, what we have described above is a deeply important source of value in human lives. If you think it is the wrong account of freedom of the will, we can call it something else. The version of compatibilism put forward is often considered synonymous with autonomy, and autonomy is highly-valued. We all agree that there are serious value differences between actions taken due to brainwashing, addiction, compulsion, social coercion, out of ignorance and actions taken rationally, from our values, for the things we love. The life-experiences view does a good job of explaining those value differences, and showing how they are differences due to differences in the richness of those action states.

2.4.2 Desire-satisfaction

A popular form of consequentialism claims the only thing of intrinsic value is the satisfaction of desires (or preferences), and that one should maximize the amount of desire-satisfaction.[52] The intrinsic value of satisfying desires can be captured by the present value theory.[53] Desires, I have argued, are a form of representation. They represent the way the world should be. So, when the world

---

[52]If we take seriously the experience conjecture, we have good reason to deny such theories. It is clear that we, in general, desire more than desire-satisfaction; in fact, most of our desires are not for desire-satisfaction, but for some mind-independent state in the world. Juliet desires Ralph Nader to be president. This is some evidence that there is something good about Ralph Nader being president, *independently of whether she desired it.*

[53]Desire-satisfaction is also *instrumentally* valuable. I have argued that, in general, desires are good evidence for what is good in the world. Therefore, satisfying desires, generally, brings good things into the world. Satisfying desires also seems to make people happy. If happiness is a good, then desire-satisfaction is instrumentally valuable for that reason as

aligns with desire, when desire is satisfied, an isomorphic relationship is created between our mental state and the state of the world, a unification of desire states and facts. This is good for precisely the same reason that accurate perception or awareness is good, because it unifies rich states of affairs, creating a further richness.

This explanation of the value of desire-satisfaction allows us to avoid some of the difficulties normally associated with views that ascribe intrinsic value to desire-satisfaction. The difficulties arise because it is highly implausible that all desire-satisfaction is equally valuable. Surely, satisfying fleeting, meaningless desires is not as important as satisfying deeply thought-out, life-long desires. Harry, impulsively, on walking into the candy shop, wants a bon-bon. Juliet has dreamed her whole life of having a farm where she can breed horses. Assuming that there are no other important consequences due to satisfying either desire, and I can satisfy only one of them, surely, I should satisfy Juliet's desire. If desire-satisfaction were all that were good, though, the satisfaction of the two desires would be equivalently valuable: one satisfaction point for each. As they are not equivalently valuable, we can conclude that certain desires are

---

well. I consider this further in Chapter 4. Also, it is important not to conflate the value of desire-satisfaction with the possible value of the pleasure we take in desire-satisfaction. If desire-satisfaction is only good because it creates pleasure, then it is not intrinsically good. To see that there is value in desire-satisfaction, on its own, suppose that Harry has a fleeting, but intense desire *for someone else* to eat a bon-bon. Suppose Juliet has a strong, long-standing desire for a certain type of person to be president. I can satisfy one and only one desire, but *whichever desire I satisfy, neither Juliet nor Harry will know.* I have less reason to satisfy Harry's desire than Juliet's. Some people respond differently to this type of example. They consider this a counterexample to the claim that desire-satisfaction is intrinsically valuable. But consider the following case. Juliet's father worked his whole life carving a freestanding carousel. His final quixotic goal was to top it with gold and then burn it to the ground. Juliet's father died before he could finish his strange project and he left no instructions requiring its completion. Nonetheless, Juliet, understanding nothing about his reasons for building and burning, feels that, if she can, she should finish the project, burning and all. It was her father's lifework, after all. What could explain (rather than explain away) such a feeling of obligation? One simple explanation is that desire-satisfactions of some sort are good, even if the desire no longer exists, even if no one is going to get pleasure from the desire. This can explain, I suggest, Aristotle's odd claim that the happiness of a person can be affected by events that happen after that person's death. If happiness (*eudaimonia*) is just a measure of the good in a life, and events that occur after the life can add to that life's richness, then post-mortem events can affect the happiness of a life.

more important to satisfy than other desires. Some desire-satisfaction is better than other desire-satisfaction.

A number of solutions to this problem come to mind. (1) One might think that satisfying Juliet satisfies more desires than satisfying Harry. She desires several aspects of the horse farm while Harry only desires the bon-bon. It needn't be the case, though, that deeply thought out desires are always associated with more desires than shallow ones. One can have a host of trivial and unimportant desires associated with bon-bons or any other trivial object. Even were this the case, satisfying Harry's collection of bon-bon desires would not be as valuable as satisfying Juliet's horse farm desires. (2) Or one might think we should satisfy Juliet's desire because it is more intense than Harry's. Harry, though, could easily have a sudden intense desire for a bon-bon; and Juliet's desire for the horse-farm may be strong but less fiery. Meaningless, bad, and fleeting desires can all be intense. (3) Or perhaps we can explain the greater importance of Juliet's desire by claiming that we should satisfy the most long-standing desires. Imagine, though, that Harry has had a weak hypnosis-induced desire for bon-bons since he was three years old, one that immediately returns after eating a bon-bon. Surely, it will not outweigh Juliet's desire, even if she formed it only, say, two years ago. In all the above cases, it is not only that Harry desires something small and relatively valueless, but also that he doesn't desire it for the right reasons.

The tack that most theorists tend to take here is that one should satisfy the most rational desires. This is most obvious intra-subjectively. If Harry is on his way to the most important job interview of his life, one that he deeply cares about, then perhaps he should continue on to that interview rather than missing the interview to satisfy his fleeting desire for a bon-bon. Suppose one should most satisfy the desires that it is most rational for one to have.[54] Which desires are those? Presumably, the most rational desires to have are the ones that reason, given all available evidence, suggests are the best to have.

---

54 I think this is right but notice that it is a difficulty for a theory of value that claims *only* desire-satisfaction is good. What makes a desire the best one to have? Presumably, it is a desire for creating the maximal (or appropriate) amount of value in the world. But on

Return to Harry and Juliet: Harry's desire for a bon-bon, we assume, does not connect with the full evidence of his experience. Whatever the intensity of his actual desire for the bon-bon, it only deserves a light intensity; it is only rational for him to want it to a small degree given the evidence of his life. Juliet, on the other hand, has thought long and rationally about her desire for a horse-farm, it connects with rational values about natural beauty, about the caring for others, about riding through the countryside. These values became her values because they capture the evidence of her experiences, of times when she has been out in the fields or woods, times with her pets, her horses, and the many times she's ridden, when she learned to ride, when she's competed or watched other competitions and so on.

So, the best desires to satisfy are those desires that are the most rationally arrived at, and, I'm sure you have noticed, these are just the desires that arise from values-of-one's own. It is plausible that these are the richest motivational states one can have.

I argued that the richest awareness is awareness of richness because such awareness creates an isomorphic unity between two rich states. Likewise, the richest desire-satisfaction is the satisfaction of the richest desires because this creates an isomorphism between two rich states. [55]

(One last thing: values-of-one's-own are also those values most directly connected to what have been called 'life-plans' or life-proj-

---

this view, the world with maximal value is the world in which the most best desires are satisfied. But which desires are those? Just those that have the most best desires satisfied. This monism gets caught in a vicious regress.

55One might reply that one can desire simple things for rich reasons, that a value-of-one's-own can motivate one to want something intrinsically valueless. If this were true than satisfying the richest desires might not always unify two rich states. Generally, I don't think this is true. If richness is the one thing of value, then rational values will most often motivate one to desire rich things. Values-of-one's own, by their nature will generally attach to rich objects. It is no surprise that Juliet's horse farm is a much richer thing than Harry's bon-bon. (This is something I will discuss more in the next chapter where I argue that rich things are the only appropriate objects of love.) Values-of-one's can, of course, motivate you to desire simple things that are merely instrumentally valuable, that is, merely instrumental to the bringing into existence the thing you *really* value. Juliet may desire to fill out a loan form so she can get a loan so she can get her farm. This desire follows from a value-of-one's-own, but the state of the world created by satisfying that desire is, presumably, not that rich. This is not problematic, though, because intuitively we don't think satisfying the desire to fill out the loan-form is as valuable as satisfying the desire

ects.'[56] The most valuable desires to satisfy, all other things being equal, are those that fulfill life-long, repeatedly evaluated and modified values that connect with large portions of a person's experience. If a value has survived rational reevaluation over a period of many years and in the face of numerous experiences, if much of one's life and energy has gone into satisfying this desire, and through all that, the desire remains, there is good evidence that this is a value-of-one's-own, that it is a rich value, one most worthy of satisfaction.)[57]

2.4.3 Persons

People are valuable because they are reasoners and knowers and experiencers. People are valuable because they are creators of art and other rich objects. People are valuable because they are desire-holders and desire-satisfiers. People are valuable because they are rich biological creatures (see below: §2.5.1). All of this, and for reasons of richness, adds to the value of a person.

We also clearly value particular people, unique people, not just because they are organized DNA and have consciousness but because they are the unique people that they are. What makes a person unique is largely captured by her values-of-one's-own. These are

---

for the horse-farm. This is because the filling out of the loan form is less isomorphic to the motivational structure of Juliet's mind. The filled-out loan paper is only partially isomorphic to the picture of the world her values create; the horse farm is almost entirely isomorphic to that picture. Desires to bring into existence the very thing you most value, and most rationally value, will generally bring rich things into existence (check examples from your own life if you don't believe me) and the satisfaction of that desire will create the unification of two rich objects *via* isomorphism, which is itself a further rich state of affairs.

56[Williams, 1973]

57By the by, an ethical theory designed around satisfaction of these desires must turn out to be an excellent approximation, under most conditions, to the correct moral theory (see §4.4) If the desires we are supposed to satisfy are those that are motivated by the *best* theories of what is valuable, the ones with the most evidence supporting them, then, by satisfying those desires, we will create, to the best of our knowledge, the world with the most value (or – not wanting to assume maximizing theories – the most proper distribution of value). The theory that richness is the good can capture why these are the desires that merit satisfaction.

the things we value in the unique person: her likes and dislikes, her hopes and fears, the ways she's decided it is best for her to interact with the world, and the unique experiences that brought her to see the world in such a way. If the uniqueness of a person is due to her unique perspective and her unique perspective is best captured by her values-of-one's-own, as I've suggested, then the uniqueness of a person is due to a particular rich feature of who she is, namely, her unifying theories of the good based on the full variety of her experience. And, so, persons, unique individuals, are instances of richness, and this is what we value them as. Some evidence of this has been given already. If the view of freedom put forward is close to correct, then each person's values-of-one's-own is in some fashion that person. I will be discuss this in greater detail in chapter 3 (in particular §3.1.3).

2.4.4 Societies

Persons are rich. Societies are unifications of persons; so, we should not be surprised that societies are rich. Social institutions – legal, cultural, and historical – unify the complexities of human affairs. The richness of a society depends on the tightness of this unification and how much of each individual citizen's richness is brought into that unification. It is plausible that our highest social ideal is one where all the members of the society are able to best be themselves or deliver their abilities to the whole while not destroying the unity of the whole.

It is widely accepted that the difficulty in forming good social structures is due to the tension between the desire for a stable society and the desire to give the citizens a measure of autonomy. We want most a peaceful society where individuals are able to add their full unique flavor to the whole. Plato argues in The Republic that the best city will be the most unified city. He goes on to describes a society in which each citizen performs the tasks for which they are best suited and all the actions of the state are governed by the most rational persons such that all actions add to the good of the whole. Those whose nature lends them to carpentry will carpenter, those whose nature lends them to soldiering will soldier and so on… In this way we form a state where everyone's skills are maximized, everyone's true nature is brought out, the entire variety of the society is expressed. Aristotle objected to Plato's overemphasis on unity, claiming, "that as the city goes further and further in the direction of unity, it will not even be a city." A completely unified city, Aristotle may fear, would consist of a single individual, for clearly a single individual will be more unified than any two individuals. "The parts of a city," he says, "must differ in kind." Aristotle thinks Plato's unity is excessive: he thinks for instance, we need to allow for people to change professions. This debate is echoed throughout the history of political philosophy. No one other than true violent anarchists deny that a certain amount of harmony is good, nor that a certain amount of individuality is good. The debate, then, is over how to balance the two, to balance the unity of the society with its variety. The debate, I suggest, is about how to make a society the richest.[58]

(Permit a Plato-inspired speculation. Plato thought that there was a tight relation between the best-ordering of an individual psychology and the best-ordering of a society. Both, Plato thought, required all the parts to be unified by reason. Note, though, if we apply this symmetry principle to our understanding of the richest psychol-

---

[58]Look, for instance, at the main theories of social justice. They range from claims that society's one and only legitimate purpose is to protect individual rights to views that say the public good itself is all that really matters. The libertarian social philosophy is focused on protecting the individual good, in protecting the freedom of people to be any way they want, protecting, for the most part, the full variety of visions of the good life. Nonetheless, their vision of variety is not without limit; they generally believe a society can be unified by the market (and protective forces, police and army). They want a society in which individual producers freely respond in unique and varied ways to the unique and varied desires of individual consumers in which this leads to communal choices. On the other end of the social justice spectrum are communitarians who think that the highest good is the public good, is the *community* itself. This community is defined by its shared values, traditions and history. But even the communitarians argue that the autonomy of the individual is important; it is just that they argue that outside of the context of community, such autonomy is meaningless. The difference between the two is the difference between a jazz quartet and a string quartet. Which is better, I will not say, but what is clear is that they are competing visions not just of how a society should be formed, but how a society will be richest.

ogies, it would suggest that the richest society would be one that rationally evaluated all the evidence of the good available to it through the experiences of its individual members and made its decisions according to those values. The best society would act according to the values-of-its-own. And isn't this what true capitalism and representative democracy – the present winners in social organization – are attempting to achieve? Isn't the goal of democracy a society where everybody's understanding of the good is considered by the actions of the state? Isn't the goal of capitalism, an economic system where everyone's preferences have weight?)

This applies to collaborations at every level. In corporations, sports teams, artistic collaborations, families, conversations, scientific investigations and every other collaboration one important measure of the value is how well the collaborative effort balances the tension between the need for unity and the expression of individuality. The ideal is to collaborate in such a way that each member of the collaboration can express themselves fully and uniquely in a way that contributes to the overall functioning of the whole collaboration. In other words, the ideal collaboration is the richest.

2.5 Environmental Ethics and Evolution

2.5.1 Environmental Ethics[59]

Environmental ethics is a relatively new field of study, but it is built on ancient intuitions about the value of natural objects, the value of life, the value of natural beauty, and the value of the re- markable interdependence of nature. During the industrialization of the Western world, these old intuitions have clearly been neglected both in the culture at large as well as in the predominant academ- ic ethics. There is little place for those intuitions in the traditional person-centered ethics that have dominated Western philosophy over the past several centuries. These ethics have sought to maxi- mize human well-being in the form of pleasure or happiness or pref- erence-satisfaction. Alternatively, they have sought to protect the rights of human beings: the right to life, property, well-being, and so on. The development of these theories has run parallel to a general growth in the well-being of the Western citizen. These theories cer- tainly arose, at least in part, as a response to the socio-political chal- lenges of the past few centuries. Many of these challenges have less- ened in the Western world, and new challenges have arisen — chief among them is a rapidly worsening environmental crisis. Unfortu- nately, the ethics that arose to improve human lives are ill-suited to capture the intuitions mentioned above. Ecosystems have no feel- ings. The oceans do not (obviously) have rights. Some animals most certainly do suffer and feel versions of pleasure and happiness, but can we naturally extend some notion of rights to them? And once we do, how do we still account for the strong intuition that a human life counts for more than that of a mouse, for instance? The general response is that natural objects are only instrumentally valuable, but this is deeply unsatisfying to many of us. Surely, there is something good-in-itself in a rainforest: its beauty, its richness, the depth of its species, etc. The rainforest's existence makes for a better world, all

---

59I provide a similar argument based on this section in [Kelly, 2014].

other things being equal, and this is so independently of whether the forest does any good to humans at all.

I argue here that the present theory can resolve many of these puzzles.[60]

Let us look to three areas of trouble for the environmental ethicist. Anthropocentric theories have trouble capturing the appropriate value of non-human animals, the value of ecosystems, and the value of (untouched) wilderness.

Non-human Animals

> "The prodigious diversity of macroscopic structures of living beings rests in fact on a profound and no less remarkable unity of microscopic makeup" [italics mine] Jacques Monod.142

> "Life is a paradoxical phenomenon. *It is enormously varied* – with creatures ranging from one thousandth of a millimeter to dozens of meters in length, having life-spans from hours to thousands of years, and with some species that spread over the whole globe, while others stay in their tiny ecological niche. *And still, life is extremely uniform.* All cells are built according to the same principles from the same molecular building blocks, no matter whether they are free-living microbes or a tiny part of a huge organism, and regardless of their position in the big family tree of life," [italics mine] [Gross, 1998: 1].

Living organisms are the prototypical examples of richness. The variety of functioning structures in a full-grown animal is a true wonder. There are over two hundred different cell types in the human body. Each living cell has a variety of different structures within it. A 'typical' plant cell, for instance, contains, at least, the following sub-structures: Golgi apparatus, endoplasmic reticulum, vacuole, vesicle, ribosome, cell wall, chloroplast, cell membrane, nucleus, mitochondrion, cyclosol, middle lamella. And complex clumps of

---

60These challenges led Peter Miller to create his "Value as Richness" theory in 1982, twenty years before I wrote this book. And the usefulness of Richness Theory in environmental ethics as it's come to be called, is further defended by [Mikkelson 2011] and most recently in [Mikkelson, In Press].

cells form bigger structures, such as tissues and organ systems. More fundamentally, there are twenty amino acids that regulate the functioning of each cell. These amino acids link together in uncountable combinations to compose the larger proteins that form the basic structures of the cell and, in turn, of the organism as a whole. The way in which the amino acids link together determines how they function; the order of the amino acids and the shape of the final protein distinguish the proteins from each other. It is estimated that there are 5,000 different proteins expressed in each cell. One could go on: the structure of DNA, the variety of life-states an organism undergoes over time, the behavioral responses to the multitude of stimuli an organism can receive.

And yet life is unified to a great degree. The unity is made apparent by each organism's consistent structure over time, its set of regular behaviours, and the fact that each organism contains similar underlying biological 'instructions'—the DNA—that appear in and govern every living cell. We can identify a single organism through time just by following it; it occupies a unique shape in space-time. We can also identify a single individual by its peculiarities of behavior. And each living organism has a unique set of DNA that governs its everyday functioning and overall development; the fact that all the events that make up living a history can be explained, at least partially, by a single set of instructions suggests remarkable unity.

The structures and behaviors of living creatures are largely determined by their usefulness in the continuance of that organism's genes. The incredible variety of functions in each living creature all work together so that nearly all aspects of the creature can be understood as leading toward the end goal of healthy reproduction. This suggests that some rule like **S**: "**P** is in organism **O** if **P** contributes to reproduction and overall survival of **O** in environment **E**."

This is not as simple a rule as it looks, of course. **S** masks the hidden complexity in the rules that govern **E**, the laws of physics and chemistry. Nonetheless, given a set of rules governing a specific environment, one can expect a nomic explanation for why most of the parts of a living organism function the way they do. These rules are determined by the 'purpose' of survival and the regularities of the environment from which the creature evolved and in which it lives. An animal will breathe on a regular basis as long as the air is not noxious. This breathing requires the regular functioning of multiple organs and muscle groups, which in turn requires the proper functioning of countless cells. All of this is intelligible as part of a method for maintaining the energy required to do other things necessary for survival, such as gathering food, avoiding predators, and so on. The entire structure, more or less, of a living organism is intelligible in this way. It is an incredibly complex and incredibly harmonious thing—and, therefore, incredibly rich.

Richness can account for the value we generally give living beings. Does this help with the animal rights question?

Most of us have strong intuitions that non-human animals deserve some moral respect. Indeed, the intuitions are strong enough that anthropocentric theories have been somewhat successful in stretching their notions of value to include non-human animals. Rights-oriented theories have first reduced rights to having interests and then argued that animals have interests. Somewhat more plausibly, in my opinion, maximizers of preference or eudemonia have argued that animals have preferences and/or suffer pain and must therefore be accounted for in the maximizing calculations.

The theory that richness is the good certainly can explain the intuition that non-human animals are intrinsically valuable and, therefore, intrinsically deserving of moral respect. But our intuitions of the value of animals are more specific than the simple proposition "animals have intrinsic value." It is not just that we think animals matter, it is that we think certain animals matter more than others and that humans matter the most.[61] Only the most extreme of us would rate the rights, suffering, and life of a mouse as highly as those of a human. But the individualist theories of animal rights can't account for this intuition. In fact, they generally attempt to ex-

---

61 We have a way to go in understanding the capabilities of animals. It may be that we vastly underrate the richness of certain creatures, dolphins, parrots and other primates come to mind. But I suggest that would be a value mistake made on factual ignorance not due to faulty value perceptions.

plain away such feelings as speciesism. But accounting for a natural speciesism does not eliminate this intuition. No serious person is considering bringing mice into the benefits of the welfare state, for example. But if a mouse has an interest in being alive, then it has the same (inviolable) right to life as a human. If a mouse can suffer pain, its pain counts just as much as the pain of a human being.

A natural way to capture our intuitive ranking of the value of various species is according to the species' apparent complexity. We value a mineral less than a plant less than a worm less than mouse less than a bear less than a human. Gregory Mikkelson has argued that one good richness proxy in this debate is the number of cell types a species has, cell types being able to stand in for the variety of functions and abilities an animal might have. "This richness proxy affirms that humans are special. Most if not all non-human organisms have fewer cell types than humans," says Mikkelson.[62] This does not mean that animals are not worthy of moral respect, of course, nor that humans will win every conflict between animal interests and human interests. Merely, our intuitive ranking of animal value matches our intuitive ranking of the richness of these animals. This strong correlation is powerful evidence that what we value in living beings qua living beings is their richness.[63] And, importantly, it gives us an account of animal value that does not fall prey to the problems that arise for traditional extensions of anthropocentric ethics.

Ecosystems

One of the deepest divides in environmental ethics is between holists and individualists—those who think that things like ecosystems have intrinsic value versus those who think that any value ecosystems have derives from the individuals affected by that ecosystem. This divide clearly maps onto those who have tried to extend

---

62[Mikkelson, 2011]

63Also [Miller, 1982; 108] Thus, we are reminded of Aristotle's ranking of humans above animals and animals above plants on the grounds that the plant can only assimilate nourishment, grow, and reproduce, whereas an animal can do these and perceive and move around as well, while humans share the basic animal capabilities plus the intellectual life. Humans are richer in the variety of capacities they possess than are animals and plants."

anthropocentric ethics to account for environmental value versus those who feel that such ethics will always be inadequate. For this reason, there have been few, if any, environmental ethics that can establish the intrinsic value of ecosystems and still support the traditional intuitions of human-centered ethics.

The theory that richness underlies all value can bridge this divide. Clearly, an ecosystem possesses richness. Ecosystems are massively complex, somewhat unified systems. In many ways, they mirror the structure of living organisms. Intuitively they are not as tightly unified as individual organisms, but they are unified to a degree. It is meaningful to talk about the harmony of an ecosystem. It is meaningful to talk about the interdependence of an ecosystem, how each part plays its 'role' in an overarching pattern. Ecosystems have some variety that individuals don't, the obvious being the variety of different organisms, each playing a role. Conversely, ecosystems lack some of the richness that individual creatures have, such as conscious awareness of the world and self-awareness, to name a couple of important features.

Again, then, we see that conceding value to ecosystems need not trump all human or individual interests. Likewise, conceding most of the tenets of traditional ethics need not require denying the important intrinsic value of ecosystems.

On a related note, we also value the diversity of life in and of itself. This is easily explained by the value of richness: a functioning (unified) ecosystem with greater diversity is clearly richer than one functioning equally well but with less diversity. The loss of a species is a significant decrease in the variety of the biosphere. This is a natural explanation of the value of biodiversity in our ecosystems.

Wilderness

The value of wilderness can also be captured by richness theory. In general, human intervention in an otherwise wild area disturbs the unity of the area. A soda can in the deep rainforest of Brazil is jarring: it doesn't belong there, just as a Metallica guitar solo doesn't belong in the Ode to Joy. Wilderness ecosystems have their own unified functioning that is almost invariably harmed by human intervention.

Again, none of these considerations are overriding in themselves. A less diverse but more unified ecosystem may be better than one with greater diversity. The value of timber may override the value lost in cutting and replanting (although this becomes less and less likely the more ancient the forests that are destroyed). And there may come a day when we learn to alter ecosystems for their own benefit, a day when we can build homes and lives so well-integrated with the wild that they increase the beauty and value of the area, though this day seems far off for now.

Monism and Environmental Ethics

For some reason, we've become accustomed to the theoretical inelegance of anthropocentric monistic value theories. Those theories often casually discard the intrinsic value of consciousness, knowledge, beauty, love, freedom etc.... Most of those who don't take this casually find themselves in the pluralist camp, but, as we saw above, these theories have their own difficulties.

Taking environmental ethics seriously, though, provides urgency for solving these problems. Anthropocentric theories are not up to the task of protecting the values we associate with the environment. And the pluralistic theories, even if we ignore the theoretical problems, just add the environment to a long list of valuable things. A monistic theory, on the other hand, should attempt to show that the value of the environment is precisely the same value we protect and pursue in other realms. Making this connection is essential, I suggest, to motivating action. When we see that the value we hold most dear (the only value) is present in ecosystems and animals and wilderness, we will, naturally, begin to take it seriously in our calculations.

It is of note that I originally formulated the theory of this book in response to the challenges of environmental ethics just as Peter

Miller did. I don't think this is a coincidence. Environmental ethics forces us to improve our value theories because the values are clear and clearly not captured by our favorite theories. It is not just that the study of the environmental values forces us to 'expand' our value theories and make them more inclusive. It also requires that we deepen them. As Mikkleson says, "Richness Theory (RT) actually explains individual-level intrinsic value better than individualistic theories do."[64] I hope the many arguments of this chapter are a strong defense of that claim. Environmental ethics does not force us to jettison our intuitions of value in the individual, anthropocentric world; it forces us to come to a better understanding of what underlies those intuitions. This is borne out by the theory that richness is the one good. (And, of course, if we expand and deepen our value theories then we make them richer.)

2.5.2 The Progress of Evolution

There are several myths about evolution that are easily dispelled: among them, the sense that the human species is the end of evolution, or that each creature is designed to perfectly fit its environment, or that all parts of biological beings are optimal. Evolution has no 'end' goal and, as far as evolution is concerned, the human, the domestic dog, and *e coli* bacteria are equally successful. Animals do not fit any environment perfectly; they fit their environments well-enough to reproduce. Neither is any being optimal, nor any part of that being optimal for any particular environment; at most, a creature is the best arrangement of parts that have come about, not the best possible.

Nonetheless, it is not easy to dispel the feeling that evolution does have a direction and is not value-neutral. I suggest that this is because the course of evolution has not been value-neutral. Clearly the present biological world is better than the one that existed three

---

64[Mikkelson, In Press; 104]

billion years ago. If we have any value intuitions, we have this one: that a world with nothing but a bacterial scum is not as valuable as one with the eco-systems and complex biologies that are present today. Clearly, this value intuition can be captured by the present theory. Though bacteria are rich, they are orders of magnitude less rich than a mammal, for instance. Evolution has created a more valuable world, then.

There is a stronger claim to make here, though. Given how we've described richness, we would expect evolution (under sufficiently hospitable conditions) to generally create richer and richer objects. One easy way to see this is to consider biological species as genetic collections. Harry is a stamp collector. Juliet is a collector of Star Wars lunch boxes. Tristan collects shells. Collections are rich things whose richness depends on the tightness of the selecting rule and the variety of the resulting collection. The more and more varied shells that Tristan has in his collection, the better the collection. Natural selection is also a form of collector. Each species is a collection of genes, and most of those genes were 'selected' because they enhanced the ability of that species to survive (or more specifically, because they enhanced the ability of some individual in the species to survive). The metaphor of a collection is particularly apt here because collections tend to grow in richness over time. Why? Because in collections, the unity is more or less fixed, while the variety steadily increases. Harry gets more and more types of stamp. Juliet finally finds the pink Boba-Fett lunchbox. Presuming they don't destroy parts of their collection, the collections increase in richness because they increases in variety. The same is roughly true of the collections put together by natural selection. Within the genes that make the human species are genes first used by bacteria and sea creatures and small mammals and 'lower' primates. The species that have survived to this day are all collections that were started with the beginning of life 3 billion years ago and have been more or less collecting variety since then. Given the vast variety that mutating DNA allows for and the amount of time the collector has to work, we should expect natural selection to create collections dense with richness.

This increase in richness due to natural selection is not inevitable or necessary. Natural selection hasn't done much for Mars, after all (we think). Even on our own planet, there have been many periods (we're in one now) of mass extinction where the overall richness of the biosphere dropped dramatically. Nevertheless, if natural selection is allowed to continue selecting and to keep some of its collections together, the richness of the surviving collections should tend to increase. Indeed, moments of mass extinction generally increase the richness of the remaining species by discarding species that are not as unified with the environment and by forcing the remaining collections of genes to adapt, to develop new traits thereby increasing both the unity and variety of the remaining species.[65]

Another useful metaphor for thinking about the richness of evolutionary creation is to recall the model for artistic creation briefly put forward in §2.3.1. Rich objects are those that appear designed. This is because it looks like many choices have been made; it doesn't look as if the object could have happened randomly. Biological creatures clearly look designed (witness the Argument from Design). What does the designing? Natural selection does the designing. Take the microscope to the biological creature: when you find, no matter how deep you look, what looks like unified choice, that is beauty, that is richness. This is true of biological creatures, and this is because biological creatures are the result of 3 billion years of 'choices.'

---

[65]Sometimes, of course, natural selection does go backwards in richness. Blind cavefish lose the richness of their eyes. Our appendix was once a functioning organ, but now it is no longer unified with the functioning human. Nonetheless, usually the most efficient method to evolve is to take previously developed organs and use them in novel ways in the changed environment. Species that adapt in this way or more likely to reproduce.

2.6 Conclusion

> One thing is needful: 'Giving' style to one's character – a great and rare art! It is practiced by those who survey everything that their nature offers in the way of strengths and weaknesses, and then fit them all into an artistic plan, until each thing appears as art and reason, and even the weakness charms the eye. Here a great mass of second nature has been added, there a piece of first nature has been removed – in both cases through long practice and daily work. Here the ugliness that resists removal is hidden, there it has been reinterpreted into the sublime... Finally, when the work is complete, it becomes clear how it was the compulsion of a single taste that was ruling and forming, in things both great and small. Whether the taste was a good or a bad one means less than one thinks—it is enough that it is one taste. Friedrich Nietzsche[66]

Here is Nietzsche's great aesthetic interpretation of the good life: take the full variety of your life and unify it according to a single 'taste.' Nietzsche famously abandoned 'morality' – "whether it is a good or a bad one means less than one thinks" – but he did not abandon telling us how to live. What matters is that we make our life and everything in it one thing. And this, I've argued, is what matters in everything.

We like to see the motley, multiform world harmonized. When we look on desires being satisfied, when we feel our beliefs coming into agreement with reality, when we meet a person whose experiences have been brought together into a story and directed into a life-plan, we see it as good. Nozick notes that the root for the word 'good' is 'ghedh' which means 'to bring together....' It is a crazy, dangerous, divergent world for the most part. This isn't bad really; this is what makes it interesting. But we don't want the world to be dangerous and haphazard, we don't want it to be conflicted and random; we want its wildness to find some accord; we want the fluctuations to find some continuity. We want a world completely and utterly

---

66[Nietzsche, 2001; 290]

its own, completely and utterly unique, but, somewhere deep, completely harmonized. Put to the side pleasure and pain and consider the other things you value: wouldn't it be better if they could keep their basic essence, but were just a bit more interesting, a bit more surprising, a bit more varied? Or alternatively, wouldn't life be better if ▮▮ings you value could keep their variety and abundance, but b▮▮▮ more in harmony, a bit more intelligible, a bit more meaningful? I have tried to develop in this chapter, through example, a way of understanding our interaction with value in the world. The way value finds its way into our lives is as a balance between two opposites, unity and variety, a balance between mystery and understanding, a trade-off between abundance and intelligibility. We want our lives to be as full as possible, yet still one life. We want our lives and everything in them to be rich.

I concede that the preceding chapter is a bit breathless. To be fair, it needs to be evaluated as a whole. Each argument on its own is subject, of course, to quibbles and genuine objections that cannot be fully refuted here. But taken together, I hope, the initial plausibility of each argument on its own lends weight to the plausibility of all the others. There are many things that we value; I have tried to take that appearance seriously. It needs explanation. I've begun, here, the process of capturing all of our value data under a single unified theory of value. Hopefully, the intelligent reader will be able to expand on the arguments I have begun.

In the next two chapters, I want to slow down again and show how a proper evaluation of the values in this chapter might go with respect to a couple of important values: love and pleasure. I choose the first because of an important meta-ethical argument that comes out of it and the second because it appears to be a significant counterexample to my theory.

3
LOVE AND THE GOOD

"If I speak in the tongues of mortals and of angels, but do not have love, I am a noisy gong or a clanging cymbal. And if I have prophetic powers, and understand all mysteries and all knowledge, and if I have all faith, so as to remove mountains, but do not have love, I am nothing...

"Love is patient; love is kind; love is not envious or boastful or arrogant or rude. It does not insist on its own way; it is not irritable or resentful; it does not rejoice in wrongdoing, but rejoices in the truth. It bears all things, believes all things, hopes all things, endures all things. Love never ends....

"When I was a child, I spoke like a child, I thought like a child, I reasoned like a child; when I became an adult, I put an end to childish ways. For now we see in a mirror, dimly, but then we will see face to face. *Now I know only in part; then I will know fully, even as I have been fully known.* And now faith, hope, and love abide, these three; and the greatest of these is love." [italics mine] Corinthians 13: 1-13

Good things are those things that it is appropriate to have positive attitudes toward. We should appreciate good things, desire them, hope for, love, and like them. Call these attitudes the pro-attitudes. The pro-attitudes should be directed at things that are actually good, and good things deserve to be the object of pro-attitudes. It is a mistake to love hateful things, an error to value valueless things. Likewise, it is a mistake to dislike good things, to fail to appreciate valuable things.

Here I exploit these facts in two ways. First, might the pro-attitudes themselves tell us what makes the good their appropriate object? Is there something about desire, love, and value that will tell us why desire, love, and value should be directed at the good? I suggest there is, and the most useful of these pro-attitudes is love because love must be directed at things of intrinsic value. One can desire **X** or hope for **X** for instrumental reasons but one can only properly love something for its intrinsic value. And, so, when we've discovered a proper object of love, we will have discovered something of intrinsic value.

Second, the fact that we should love the good is a value fact like other value facts, a fact that needs explaining.[1] Richard Kraut suggests that "there are least three conditions that make a life a good one: one must love something, what one loves must be worth loving, and one must be related in the right way to what one loves."[2] Whatever the good turns out to be, then, it needs to explain what is good about loving good things (and possibly what is confused or even bad about loving bad or worthless things). More specifically, if value is monistic, the final theory must claim that there is some property **X** for which the act of loving (or valuing or desiring) property **X** also has property **X**. If it turns out there is only one such **X**, then, if there is any good at all, **X** is that good.

So one goal of this chapter is to discover what the appropriate object of love is. I argue that there is a love -- *deep love* -- that is the best love. The proper objects of deep love, it turns out, are rich objects. And as the proper objects of the love are good things, whatever is good is also rich; so richness is a necessary condition for the good. The best explanation for this fact, I argue, is that richness is the good. The second goal of this chapter is to explain why the best love is the deepest love by appealing to the claim that richness is the good. I claim that the loving of rich objects is itself a rich state of affairs, and so if richness is good then loving richness is also good.

1[Nozick, 1981: 428-435]

2[Kraut, 1994: 44]

3.1 True and Deep Love

We love things – roses and books and medallions. We love ideas – theories and arguments and inventions. We love animals and people, most of all, maybe, people – persons, that is – persons in their "vague complexity."[3] We love persons as lovers and as fathers and mothers; we love them as friends and as masters; we can love their biology or their mind. We can love them for moments or years, with passionate intensity or with steady, unswerving care. A perfect stranger's smile or someone else's child crying can inspire a fleeting feeling of love. Love makes us act both heroically and foolishly; love can make us risk our own hopes and well-being for another. We can lose ourselves in love – our tastes, values, behaviors. Temporarily or for the rest of our lives, the good of another (person, thing, idea) can become our own. In the best of love, we desire to have but not to own. In the best of love, we desire to learn and are unafraid what we will find out. In the best of love, we see the other for what the other is, and we see it as good.

I argue there is something common to all loves[4] and that this is apparent when we look at how we measure love and what makes a love the best kind of love. I suggest that there are three central measures of love. Call these measures the *truth*, the *depth*, and the *strength* of love.

3"Love demands in interest in that vague complexity we call another person." [Singer, 1984: 8]

4We can use the term 'love' to refer to nothing more than a strong desire or preference. Real love is more than this. In this other usage 'love' is intended as nothing more than an intensifier. For example, if I mean by, "I love chocolates," nothing more than that I have strong desires to eat chocolates, this is not 'real' love; it is just a strong desire. Nevertheless, this does not entail that there isn't a concept that cuts across most usages of 'love,' (nor that we can't have some form of real love for chocolates).

3.1.1 True Love

> "To be englowed by someone's love, it must be we ourselves who are loved, not a whitewashed version of ourselves, not just a portion. In the complete intimacy of love, a partner knows us as we are, fully." Nozick[5]

> "Love is indignant if any part of the individual is severed or held back." Hegel[6]

> "As wolves consume the lamb so lovers love their love." Plato[7]

In the ideal love, we genuinely have the other; we know the other entirely, as it (he, she) is, its real self. There is nothing held back from us; there are no secrets of importance; there is no lack of communication; there is full understanding. Though most of us fail to love much of anything in this way, the fact that this is a failure suggests it is a necessary condition for an ideal love.

For love of **X** to be love of **X**, it must be based in knowledge of **X**; it must be that the special awareness of the other that is love truly be awareness *of the other*. Call this true love.[8] In perfectly true love, we are not mistaken in any way about the object of our love. Harry loves Juliet because he thinks she is honest and kind and he loves her entertaining and original stories, and that she calls him Harris though his name is Harold. If, in fact, Juliet is not honest and loyal, and all her stories were plagiarized from a book, then his love fails to be true. This is a common enough failing in love, one we all recognize and guard against. We warn our friends or children if we think their loves are based in some form of delusion. We are hurt and confused if we find out that our own love is false. To find our love is not true often makes us fall out of love, even in situations where no

---

5[Nozick, 1989: 7]

6[Hegel, 1948: 306]

7Plato, 1953: *Symposium* 241d]

8Not to be confused with the mythical individuals that await each of us down some glowing sun-dappled path, our true love – the one we are supposed to be with; the one meant for us; the *one*.

deception took place. We generally desire our loves to be true (and we consider this desire to be an important part of what it is to love). The truth of love is a genuine measure: it comes in degrees. Maximally true love knows everything of the loved object; minimally true love knows almost nothing. A love for a person is not true if it is based only on a smile: persons are much more than their smiles. One may truly love the smile, but not the person. Love at first sight is only minimally true. The romanticizing of this type of love is usually accompanied by the assumption that that first sight somehow captured the loved one's essence. "I felt like I'd known them all my lives," they'd say. When this assumption is not made, it is generally agreed that love at first sight must be followed up with a more substantial understanding of the other to be of any great worth.

Furthermore, it is more important to know things essential to the other than things seemingly accidental. I know all of Madonna's songs by heart; it may be fair to say I truly love Madonna's music; but it would be a mistake to claim that I love Madonna the person. Moreover, we can even have knowledge of the essentials of a person, but if we fail to make ourselves aware of those essentials our love is not true. Tristan does know all there is to know about Juliet, but thinks only of her lips. This is not true love. For a love to be true, our knowledge must affect our awareness of the other; it cannot be compartmentalized away. If our lover thinks abortion is permissible, but we are violently opposed, we might have the tendency not to bring that subject up, to try to forget that that is an aspect of our loved one. This love fails to be perfectly true.

Trueness of love applies not just to people, of course, but also to objects. If I claim to love the Mona Lisa, but have never seen it, or make the claim only because I think I should, I don't genuinely love it. If I claim to be a lover of jazz, but have only listened to Bird, this love is not true (though my love of Bird's jazz may be true). We look askance at a person who claims to love things with which she has little experience. We tend to think her desires, if not just a pose, are not really about the object she claims to love. The term dilettante (in the derogatory sense) refers to a person whose love is not true, who merely dabbles in many fields, whose love is based in minimal understandings of intricate subjects.

In conclusion, love for an object fails to be true when it is not really about that object, either because the love is built of false awareness of the object or merely shallow awareness of the object. For love to be love at all, it must be true to some extent. I do not love **X** if I know nothing of **X**. And the more I know the better my love.

3.1.2 Deep Love

"There is only one proof for the presence of love: the depth of the relationship." Erich Fromm[9]

Love that is perfectly true need not be a perfectly ideal love. To see this, consider an example from a recent movie, *Adaptation*. New Yorker journalist, Susan Orleans, being a journalist, spends much of her time involved in the passions of others. It becomes increasingly clear to her and to the audience that Susan has no passions of her own. To fill this lack, she takes a drug made from the stamens of an orchid. This drug is supposed to awaken her passions. The first time she takes the drug, she develops an intense 'relationship' with the dial tone of her phone.[10] She listens and listens to it. She tries to hum along with it. She hangs up and contemplates it. Eventually, she realizes the dial tone is made of two different pitches. She calls a friend to help her hum the dial tone. She has him switch pitches so she can have the chance to hum both the higher and the lower pitch.

Susan is certainly behaving like someone in love. If this is love, it is true; it may, indeed, be perfectly true; there may be nothing else to get from the dial tone. But something, we would all agree, is wrong

---

9[Fromm, 1974]

10Whether this is really supposed to be a passion drug or is just a 'routine' hallucinogenic is irrelevant. Suppose for the moment that the drug's intended effect is to make her love something, *anything* actually.

with this love. One thing that is clearly wrong is that we shouldn't intensely love things of little value, and, clearly, the sound of a dial tone is of little value. But there is another way of describing the failing here: Susan's love for the dial tone is (necessarily) shallow; it is not what I call a deep love.

Harry and Juliet have been married for fifty-three years. Harry's love for his wife has changed over the years. The intensity of the love has lessened in some ways, but his love has deepened. On the whole, he considers this deepening a great gain. Particular expressions on his wife's face are filled with a lifetime of meaning; he knows what she means when she says, "uh–huh" but looks away, and when she says "uh–huh" and purses her lips. When our love has deepened, our knowledge of the loved one has grown.[11] The depth of love is a measure of how much our love encompasses, how much we have when we have the object of our love, how deep our awareness of the other is. As the years go by, Harry learns more and more of Juliet. He comes to have a better and better working understanding of what she is. When he brings her to awareness, it is not just her lips, or her voice, or a particular value of hers that he brings to awareness. It is everything about her, and everything about their relationship, past and present that he brings to mind.

True love of an object is necessary for deep love of that object. Harry's love for Juliet is not deepened by him learning more and more of clocks or black holes or cheese cake, but by learning more of Juliet. Although, a perfectly true love (as of time t) of **X** does not require that one has the maximal possible deep love of **X**. This is a consequence of the fact that certain deep objects can gain in depth over time. Over time people change and the way that they change (not just what they change into) becomes an important part of who they are. Moreover, the ones we love, especially in romantic love, develop connections with us that they did not have when we first loved them. Over time Harry and Juliet develop a shared history that is part of who they are, the time they went skiing on Kilimanjaro, the

---

11In chapter 2, I referred to the depth of knowledge: deep love is not grounded, unfortunately, in merely deep knowledge, but in deep and wide knowledge.

honeymoon, the fight over the broken china, the thousand choices and calculations built around the raising of a child, the sound of the alarm that wakes them both in the morning. "To love someone might be, in part," Nozick says, "to devote alertness to their well-being and *to your connection with them* {italics mine}"[Nozick, 1989]. Love for an object must become partially (especially in romantic love) love for the relationship itself. And, so, no matter how true love is at the outset of a relationship, love can – and, if the relationship is even moderately good, usually will – deepen with time.

True love is not sufficient for deep love; this is because deep love requires a deep object. Katherine's love for the dial tone is true, but fails to be deep. It fails because the object of her love is a shallow objet. A true love for a human being will always be deeper than a true love for a dial tone. To be lost in a dial tone is to be lost in a teacup; to be lost in a person is to be lost in an ocean. There is nothing more for Susan to learn of the dial tone, nothing more to have; she has it all and it is little. True love of smiles is not as deep as true love of faces is not as deep as true love of people. True love of dial tones is not as deep as true love of lullabies is not as deep as true love of symphonies. 'Deep' objects are necessary for deep love. And a deep object, I suggest, is nothing other than a rich object. This is because depth must be something like a measure of knowledge, and the measure of knowledge is, plausibly, richness (see §2.2.2 and §2.2.3).[12] Deep love requires rich knowledge or awareness of the other, and rich knowledge of an object requires a rich object. The dial tone is shallow because I can't learn much about it; I am not aware of much when I am aware of it. A person, on the other hand, is a deep object because I can learn a whole bunch about him.

There are two requirements, then, to be met to have deep love: true love and a rich object of love. True love of a rich object is sufficient for deep love.[13]

12In fact, we will see that it is a measure of the richness of *awareness*. But as rich awareness of an object requires that that object be rich, deep objects must be rich.

13Deep love is more valuable than shallow love. Harry is, all other things being equal, beter off than Susan. A person who spends her life loving shallow things, no matter how truly, might be reasonably called a shallow person. It might reasonably be thought that

3.1.3 Platonists vs. Romantics

Let's explore depth and truth in the context of romantic love. Juliet loves Harry; she wants all of him; she wants to know all of him; she wants her love to be as true as possible. How should she go about achieving this? Martha Nussbaum suggests there are two broad categories of property to which romantic love may attach.[14] Harry cares deeply about ocean preservation and the preservation of beauty in general. He also has the habit of pinching the bridge of his nose when he is frustrated. Which property should Juliet love him for? Which property is more the type of property one needs to know to love Harry? His deep cares and values or the particular traits that make him uniquely himself? Lots of people love beauty, but only Harry pinches his nose in that unique way. We can love our love for (1) his central properties – those properties that drive his character, without which he would truly seem to be a different person – or (2) for particular properties – those properties that make him truly unique, and one-of-a-kind. Nussbaum structures the debate around a critique and defense of Plato's Phaedrus; so, call the first view the Platonic view and the second view the Romantic view.

In the Phaedrus,[15] Socrates claims that the best love is love that attaches to the loved person's deep values and aspirations, and this is because these deep values and desires constitute the genuine person. If we love someone only for her looks, or her money, or her knowledge, or for her taste in chocolates, we fail in an important way to be loving her at all. This is a failing, Socrates says, because we fail to care about the real person, and what really makes up the person's good. A person just is her deep aspirations and values, and so Socrates tells us, a person's good is the satisfaction of those deep values and aspirations.

---

being shallow as a person is a failing because shallow love is a failing.

14[Nussbaum, 1990]

15I am going to follow Nussbaum's interpretation here without defending it. I am concerned more with the philosophical positions than with whether Socrates or Plato held either of them.

To see this, ask yourself, what must we give the other to promote their good? Consider four options. First, we could protect features of the other that we like. This is clearly insufficient. I may like the way you smoke cigarettes, but you deeply desire to quit. Second, we could satisfy the other's desires. Unfortunately, we know that our loved ones can have desires that are not good for them, indeed, that don't even match up with their own deeper desires or values. To satisfy all of the desires of our loved one will not universally promote her good. A third option is to promote what *we* think is good. This option fails to be properly about the other. The other's good, we generally think, must have something to do with who the other is. For our actions to be loving actions, we must in some way be motivated by the other's perspective of the world. What is good for us need not be good for her. This suggests the fourth possibility, we could promote a world that matches up with our loved one's deep values and desires; their good is determined by what they really care about. I think this is right as far as it goes (and lines up wiht our discussion of freedom in Chapter 2) but does it imply Socrates' view of romantic love?

The view is problematic because Socrates' view of love sounds more like love of a value system rather than love of a particular person. Say Harry loves Juliet for her deep value system **V**. But Juliet's sister Jill has a similar if not identical value system **V1**. Is there not a sense in which Harry should love Jill as much as Juliet? Or, rather, isn't there a sense in which Harry *does* love Jill as much as Juliet? Juliet just happens to be the person Harry found that embraces value system **V**. But his love would be the same for anyone else with a sufficiently similar value system. If this is love, it is not properly true. Something important is left out, namely the unique individual.

And this is what the Romantic is concerned with: the unique, perhaps eccentric properties of a person, the particular way he sips his soup, the way his hair moves, the precise thing he said to his boss while quitting, the single joke he repeats a hundred times. When we fall in love, we fall in love with a *particular* person, and the best kind of love is a love that could be only for that person. The things we bring to mind when we bring to mind our loved ones could only be vaguely described as her deep values. We usually bring to mind particular unique behaviors she has; the expressions on her face; the sound of her voice, a particular time that we were with her. Call these properties the *accidentals*. Love cannot be love if it does not attach, in some way, to the accidentals of the other.

But, the Platonist replies, it would be a strange love that *only* knew the other's accidentals. Surely, one can love the other almost fully, even without noticing, for example, that he uses his left hand to open peanut butter and his right to open jelly. But we do not love the other almost fully if, for example, we are unaware that he deeply values taking risks with respect to his financial security. The romantic is probably right to think that all of the properties of the other, even the seemingly inconsequential, should be, ideally, some part of our love for the other, but it is a mistake to think that it is not still more important to pay attention to more fundamental features, the values and deep convictions, of the other.

There is a path between these two views. Juliet has a habit of standing on one leg like a crane when she washes the dishes. Harry loves this about her. Consider three reasons for this love. First, it could be just because he finds the pose attractive. Second, it might be because the whole pose expresses the graceful ease, the unthinking confidence with which Juliet does difficult things; this is a characteristic of Juliet's whole character that he's always liked. Or third, he loves the pose for no other reason than because it is just something that Juliet does.

Suppose it is for the first reason that Harry loves the pose. The pose itself, the particular structure of the pose, is a beautiful thing. But then it is irrelevant that this is a pose of Juliet's. Harry loves Juliet's pose *qua* pose. He would love this pose if anyone were doing it. It is as if Juliet had been given a beautiful watch. To love Juliet only because she has a beautiful watch is clearly a failure of a serious sort. But if the Romantic is pointing to this first option, then she is proposing that we love a person for nothing more than a series of appealing watches she was lucky enough to have been given, watches that have nothing particular to do with who she is.[16]

Consider the third option. Suppose Harry just loves the leg standing because it is Juliet doing the leg standing. This seems better. At least Juliet is in the mix somewhere. Unfortunately this is circular. Harry loves Juliet because he loves (or approves of, or desires, or pays attention to) the unique property **P**, the property of standing on one leg, but Harry loves **P**, the leg standing merely because Juliet is doing the leg standing. But why should Harry care if it's Juliet's? Because he loves her. But he loves her because he loves the property. And so on.[17]

The only plausible option is the second. This is a halfway house between the Romantics and the Platonists. He loves the accidental pose because it suggests a deeper unifying feature of Juliet; yes, because the pose is Juliet's pose, but more importantly, because the pose is an expression of Juliet's character and nature. This is what makes it truly hers. Love is true when you know everything there is to know about the loved one. But we've shown that love is not just about both the deep underlying values and the unique variety of accidentals. This is too simple for two reasons. First, it gives us no explanation for why, as we just mentioned, a deep value is more important than some one eccentric accidental. Second, it does not explain the relation between the accidentals and the deep values. Knowing the connection between the person's deep character and his actions and particular preferences is essential to loving the oth-

---

16Much of our physical appearance is unconnected to our deeper person, and this is why love based on physical appearance can be such a failure. But note that Harry could love the very same watch in either of the other two ways described above. Maybe he likes that *she* likes the watch. Maybe he likes that she takes such good care of the watch. The same can be said of people's physical appearance. To genuinely love someone's looks as that person's looks requires that you love the attitude and behavior that *she* has with respect to her looks; does she exercise, keep herself clean, dress stylishly etc…?

17One could get out of the circle by appealing to some independent process that gets us to fall in love with the person. Once we are in love with the person; we love her unique properties because they are her properties. I think we have a better explanation of things, though. Moreover, there is a limit to what we love just because it is Juliet's. Or rather, there are things that are more Juliet's than others. If Juliet has been hypnotized to cluck on the hour – this action is less hers – than the yoga postures she's spent years trying to perfect; and we should love it less.

er. If we fail to see how the unique little action of our loved one is connected to some aspect of the deeper person we are failing really to love that action as an action of our loved one. To see this, notice how often peculiar habits of one love attract us to other people who have those habits as well. I suggest this is because the peculiar little habit has become connected in our minds with the deep person that we already love. The habit itself has little to no value; but as part of a bigger structure, it has tremendous value.

There is something shallow about a love that only considers the accidentals of a person. But there is something untrue about a love that only considers the deep values of a person.[18] To truly love the depth of a person is not just to love her deep values, nor is it just to love the particular ways that those values are expressed, but to love both for the reason that the one is an expression of the other. To truly love the depth of a person is to love the particulars of a person because those particulars are expressions of that person's deep values. In some ways it mirrors the scientific enterprise: we must go to the particulars for evidence of the deeper person. But once we've come up with our theory of the deeper person,[19] we go back to the particulars to see how the deeper person is expressed. This is a never-ending process and it is how we come to know someone's full richness.

This explains why love can be so difficult if the person we are with is not unified; if we can't see how the person's particular actions are expressions of deeper commitments and aspirations; or, worse, if the person's actions are actually antithetical to his deep values. When

18There is something articifial about the distinction between deep values and accidentals that may becoming clear here. If we consider deep values to be values-of one's-own as discussed earlier, then a deep value *is* unique to the individual because a deep value is *thick*. It is formed from the unique and particular history of that person. Jill and her sister could never have the same value system. Likewise, most accidentals are not separate from one's deep values. If our particualr and unique ways of expressing ourselves are *freely* expressed then they flow from our deepest values and, considered thickly, are part and parcel of our values.

19This sounds too intellectual but is on the right track. Why can you predict your loved one's actions? It is not just because you have complete familiarity with the Keplerian charts; you also have the Newtonian laws. And even if the situation is novel, you generally (hopefully) have a good idea about the way your loved one will act.

people act inexplicably, we feel a distance. We can't understand. But this distance is the precise opposite of love because at the center of love is understanding.

3.2 What is Love?

Deep knowledge of something is not sufficient for deep love. I know a number of things about Hitler's concentrations camps. But I don't love them. There are three important features of love that we have yet to look at: 1) the role of desire – clearly, it is not love if we don't desire something of/from the other, 2) the role of value – clearly the loved one must appear good to us in some way; and 3) the precise type of knowledge that we need to be in love: we have discussed what we need to know of the other, but knowledge of the right things doesn't seem to be sufficient for love. These three features of love are interrelated.

The argument of this section proceeds as follows. Love requires that we see the other as good. The Experience Conjecture entails that seeing state-of-affairs **S** as good is the desire that **S**. If this is true then Harry's experiencing Juliet as good is nothing other than his desire that Juliet be as she is. This, alone, is not sufficient for love. We also want to *have* our loved one. We want to experience her, to fully experience the entirety of her, to get to know her, to be in her presence, to deepen our relationship to her. This is equivalent to seeing *experiencing her* as good. And this is equivalent to desiring to experience her. When we love someone, we see her (her existence) and our experience of her as good. We desire her existence and we desire to experience her. This second desire, I will argue in Chapter 4, is taking pleasure or enjoyment in the other.

3.2.1 Loving Desires

I argue love is made of two desires. A desire for the other and a desire to experience the other. So why these two desires?

First, it is clear we must see the other as good in some way if we love the other. In Chapter 1, I noted the important distinction between believing something is good and seeing it as good. It is not sufficient that we believe the other is good for us to love the other. To love **X** requires I see **X** as good, that I experience **X** as good. If I do not experience **X** as a good thing, clearly I do not love **X**.

But by **(EC)** this means that if I love **X** I desire the existence of **X**. So I will protect **X**'s existence; if **X** does not exist, I will do my best to bring it about.

But this one desire is not enough. There are many things we desire to bring about that we do not love. There are many things we protect though we don't love them. When we love the other, we also want to *have* the other. It is not enough that the other be *somewhere*. We want to have our love with us. This having of love is experiential. My love will not be (fully) satisfied on hearing facts about my loved one second-hand. I want to experience my loved one for myself. So to genuinely love the other we must desire to experience the other. If we have no desire to experience the other (all things being equal), we don't love the other. If I love **X**, I desire the experience of **X**. In Chapter 4, I will argue that this second desire is nothing other than taking pleasure in the other. And this seems right; we do not truly love the other unless experiencing the other is a pleasure. Furthermore, this second desire explains the desire to know the other as deeply as possible. To experience the other, we must have access to the other. To fully experience the other, we must know all there is to know of the other.

A bunch of knowledge about our loved one (or about any object) is not sufficient to genuinely love. Our knowledge must be brought to awareness.[20] It must be experienced and enjoyed. Conscious lov-

---

20"Our experience of another person [in love] includes a large network of individual evaluations continually in progress and *available to consciousness.*" [Singer, 1984: 9]

ing requires, unsurprisingly, that we are conscious of our love. The deeper the love is, the more of the other of which we are conscious.

This also accounts for how we fall out of love. If love were only about knowledge, it would seem that only amnesia could make it disappear. But love is about a particular relation to our knowledge. If our knowledge – or large parts of our knowledge – of the other becomes inert, if we no longer desire to bring it to mind, to experience it, we are no longer wholly in love. Your lover cheats on you. Suddenly, you can see nothing else of her but her dishonesty or images of her with another man or woman. You are incapable of bringing the rest of her to mind, to bring to mind all the things that you have seen as good. When this inability becomes complete, the love is dead though the knowledge is not. Or, alternatively, if you come to a point where you no longer think you have anything to learn of him or of the relationship. You no longer have any desire to bring him to mind; you no longer desire to experience him. When this happens, you no longer seek deeper awareness of him, you no longer seek to spend time with him. You have, in short, stopped loving him.

This also suggests why it is we fall in love. To fall in love is to have suddenly before us an object that we feel like we can fall into, as into a great symphony, as into a great theory, suddenly there is an object before us that we see worthy of intense, engaged, enjoyable study.

Love, then, is a coupled set of desires.[21] The first desire is simply the desire for the other. This desire is a perception that the other is good. The second desire is the desire to experience the other. This desire is a perception that your experience of the other is good. I call this taking pleasure in the other. But perceptions of the other are just that: perceptions, awarenesses of a particular type. To truly perceive the other as good, you must have awareness of the other. When we

---

21 Of course, there are many other desires associated with love and – especially with falling into romantic love – not all of them are strictly loving desires. There is sexual attraction; sometimes, there is a feeling of safety or comfort; sometimes we feel pride that someone likes us etc.... Though, we may not think that any of these desires are bad, we do think that claims of love that are built entirely on these types of desires are lacking in something.

truly love the other we bring to mind as much of the other's richness as we can; we engross[22]ourselves in the richness of the other, and this engrossment is characterized by the sensation that the other is good, and by the sensation that this experience of the other is good.

3.2.2 The Unity View vs. Feature-Based View: Views of Romantic Love

> "What is common to all love is this: your own well-being is tied up with that of someone (or something) you love…. When something bad happens to one you love… something bad also happens to you." Robert Nozick[23]

With this analysis of love in hand, let's apply it to a long-running debate about romantic love. A feature of long-term romantic love is that it can persist even through significant changes in the features of our loved one. But if we love someone for his features, why should we continue loving him when those features disappear? But if we don't love someone for his features, what do we love him for? Why is it that we fall in love with this person rather than another one?

So, consider two views of romantic love. A *feature-based view* of romantic love assumes that romantic love attaches to certain features of the other and that it is in virtue of seeing these features as good that one is in love. This view explains many common aspects of love including why and how one falls in love. The *unity view of love*, on the other hand, claims that romantic love is about more than any particular properties that the loved one has. The unity view says that romantic love is about the loving relationship itself; love is, as Nozick puts it, about the forming of a *we* by the lovers.

The feature-based view of love has the benefit of common sense

---

22The notion of engrossment is central to Nel Noddings' analysis of care. [Noddings, 1984]

23[Nozick, 1989: 8] Also see [Bovens, 2003 #137] for an excellent discussion of this tension.

on its side. I assumed a feature-based view during the earlier discussion of the Platonists and the Romantics. If Juliet loves Susan, must not she see certain properties of Susan as good or desirable?[24] What a strange love it would be if one didn't care at all what the loved one was actually like. And how could one fall in love if not because of features the other has (features, presumably, that appeal to one)? Why else would one desire the other, if not because he has features one finds desirable? When we are hoping to fall in love, we are looking for someone who has certain features; those features play a large part in whether we fall in love or not.

The feature-based view, though, has real difficulty explaining the constancy of romantic love. If love and the desires associated with love are due only to certain features **F**, then why do so many loves remain constant over so many years, even when features **F** have disappeared? Juliet fell in love with Harry back in 1946 in virtue of his stunning good looks and his lightning-fast intellect. Now, it is 2003 and his physical features are changed beyond all recognition and his mind though still alert is far from stellar. Nonetheless, she loves him just as strongly as she ever did. What can a feature-based view say? Love can persist through even the most radical changes.

A second worry for the feature-based view that is not commonly noted is that it is not immediately clear why the lover should care about the welfare of the loved one on this view. If love is about particular features of the other, I should (rationally) care about the protection of those features. And this may entail that I care about the survival of the other as the bearer of those features. But why should I care about the other's broader welfare? Why should I care about the satisfaction of the other's desires, for instance, or the satisfaction of their deep values?[25] If there is nothing more to loving than seeing features **F** as good, there is no room for also seeing the satisfaction of the other's desires as good, much less for seeing the other's good as

---

24Agape is sometimes interpreted as a form of love that is about the other merely as *person*. But romantic love, at the very least, must require more than this. Otherwise, it seems, we would fall in love for anybody and everybody.

25Unless we've fallen in love with someone whose needs just happen to be satisfied by the satisfying of our own. But, though it is possible, this is certainly not necessary for love.

good. But it is essential to love of persons that the other's good becomes our own. But the other's good is more than just the protection of their lovable features.

The feature-based view might claim that the features that we love of the other must be their desires or values. This is a Platonism of a sort, and I've already noted problems with this view: it is unlikely that the only features of the other that we care about are the other's values. But there is a further and more serious problem. Seeing it as good that someone has certain desires is not the same as seeing it as good that those desires are satisfied. Harry might like it about Juliet that she desires to climb Everest because he wants her to aim high, but he might also hope that that desire is never satisfied for fear of her safety. And even if admiring someone's desires did entail admiring the satisfaction of those desires, admiring someone's desires does not entail seeing the other's good as good. Someone's good is more than just the satisfaction of her desires. The feature-based view's failure to capture this aspect of love might be seen as an irremediable flaw.

The unity view doesn't have either of these problems. To be in love is to lose oneself in another. For the unity-view this is what love is: the losing of oneself in the other. It is the coming together of wants and goods; it is the unification of the lovers, and the creation of a third thing that is the relationship, the creation of a *we*.[26] This oneness may be seen as central to romantic love.[27] To be in love, then is not to think or feel about the other in a certain way. It is to have a different and peculiar psychological (or ontological) relation to the other wherein one as a discrete individual no longer exists, wherein one is only one part of something larger which is the love.

The unity view explains the constancy of love. Love is constant

---

26[Nozick, 1989: 68-86]

27Other unity theories come from Plato's *Symposium* (Aristophanes' speech), Montaigne, Hegel, Paul Tillich, Erich Fromm, William Gaylin, J.F.M Hunter, and Mark Fisher. Aristophanes explains love through the myth of the split self; we are all looking to reunify with our other half; all love is this becoming whole again. Mark Fisher claims that there is a total fusion of selves in perfect romantic love where "the lover less and less distinguish[es] his desires... and beliefs from her[s]." This fusion is caused by what he calls "humble benevolence" toward the other. Tillich says, "Love in all its forms is the drive toward the reunion of the separated" 28. Read Sobel for a good survey of the unity view.

because it consists of the creation of a third object which is neither of the original lovers, an object which like an individual person can change and yet remain numerically the same. Juliet loves Harry because Juliet/Harry, the *we*, still exists. Juliet/Harry has changed over time, just as Juliet and Harry have changed. But Juliet's love is not really a thing directed at Harry; nor is Juliet's love really a thing directed at Juliet; nor is either of their loves directed at Juliet/Harry. The love just is Juliet/Harry. This one-ness also explains why the other's welfare is important to us, independently of the other's changing features. The other's good has become our own welfare because we and the other are a unified thing with one set of interests. Of course, he wants to make her happy. Making her happy makes him happy. Of course, she wants him to win the award he's always wanted. His wants are her wants.

There are major and readily apparent problems with the unity-view.[28] First, what relation does this view have to forms of love that are not mutual, requited romantic love? If love is unrequited, how does one form a joint identity? What relation does romantic love bear to non-romantic love? Do we form a *we* with an artwork, with a song, with a forest glade, with a baby? Surely, a painting isn't capable of forming a *we*, is it?

Furthermore (and more disturbingly), it appears to be an accident that we continue to *like* the other. Presumably, when we fall in romantic love, we fall because we do like certain properties of the other. And, intuitively, for it to continue to be love one should, generally, keep on liking the other. But this is not necessary for the formation of a *we*. Suppose that Harry and Tristan are forced to fly a fighter jet together. Harry is the pilot and Tristan is the navigator. They spend months in training learning to work as a team, as a single unit. They succeed; they form a *we* in the sky. They know what's

---

28One problem is that there is no readily apparent connection between what falling in love is and what it is to love. I certainly don't fall in love with someone *because* I am in a *we* with them. That comes after. Nozick solves this problem by appealing to a two-tiered explanation [Bovens, 2003]. When we fall in love, it *is* due to the features of the other. The features of the other are what cause us to form a *we*. Once we have formed the *we*, though, we have fallen, and are now *in* love. In perfect love of this sort, the features of the other no longer really matter.

good for each other and they provide for each other. But Harry thinks Tristan is a jerk; Tristan thinks Harry is a sop. They clearly do not love each other. Moreover, just as a person can hate themselves, they can hate a *we*. If Harry hates the *we* that he forms with Tristan, he does not love Tristan. The unity-view fails to capture the fact that the loved one must be the object of the appropriate psychological attitudes to be genuinely loved.

The unity view cannot respond by adding in a positive evaluation of some sort to the *we* because the unity view is then open to the same objections as the feature-based view. Why does the positive evaluation remain through changes in the person? Why is it there in the first place? The view cannot respond that being part of a *we* automatically makes you like aspects of the other as Tristan and Harry just demonstrated; indeed, being part of an I doesn't even guarantee liking the I.

A further problem along these lines (put forward by Alan Soble) is that love of the *we* doesn't allow for what he calls robust care. To have robust care for person **P** is to care for **P**'s good because it is **P**'s good. The following is not robust care: Juliet buys her lover a piano he has always wanted because she wants a piano in the house; she thinks it looks nice. Clearly, there is no real generosity here because she is acting for the other's good only because it happens to overlap with her good. But if the unity view is correct, then there is just the one *we* in the relationship, and no one else. How can you care for another's good in a non-selfish way if the other's good just is your own good? But robust care and generosity are essential aspects of romantic love. Clearly, we sometimes sacrifice for the sake of our loved one. But on the unity view, one could never sacrifice for the other.

So, both views seem to be in trouble. The feature-based view seems incapable of accounting for the constancy of love. If love is about features **F** of person **P**, and then person **P** changes in such a way that they no longer have such features, why should love remain? But it often does. But to deal with this problem, the unity-view jettisons a central fact about love, namely that it is, at least in part, a particular psychological attitude. Love in all its forms involves some positive evaluation of the other as the other, but the unity view can't explain this.

These are not problems for the view of love put forward in this chapter. I have suggested that love *is* feature-based, but only in the broadest sense. When one loves, one loves the richness of the other person, but to love the full richness of a person is to love all the properties of the other.[29] Love is not about any particular feature of the other that might change. It is about the other itself, complete and entire. To borrow a term from Leibniz, when we love a particular, we are hoping to love its *notion*, the complete set of properties that the actual other has (including all its past and future properties).[30] The notion of the other does not change; it cannot change; it is just what the other is. So, of course, love is constant. Or, to put it yet another way, the fact that a person changes is an important feature of the other, a feature one should love like all her other features as part of her richness.

We generally do fall in love for certain narrow features the other has. But we know what falling in love is now. Falling in love is just the appearance of two coupled desires where no desires were before. Many things can make us have those desires, many different features

---

29This is not to say that we couldn't fall in love, couldn't begin to want the richness of the other, due to much narrower features. And it is also important to note that we don't love the fact that the other is rich, we love the actual richness. To see that **X** is good is not the same as learning that **X** is rich. To see that **X** is good is to see that **X** is rich. And these perceptions are the desires that ground our understanding of love.

30Of course, given the impossibility of knowing the future, we could not even in principle know another's full notion, except, possibly, after their death. Also, I am not endorsing any particular view of time by using Leibniz's words. Leibniz talks as if the future already exists. If it does, the notion at any given time is as I've described it. If the future doesn't exist yet, then the notion isn't fixed yet.

There is, also, an ambiguity that I can mention here as to what constitutes a perfectly true love. A perfectly true love at time t could be one that is based in awareness of all the properties an object has at time t, or a perfectly true love might be a love that is aware of all the properties that the object has ever had or will ever have. I lean towards the last because it explains our desire to continue living and re-experiencing the other even when we know most of what there is to know about them right now. We still want to know what life with them will be like, how they will change, what properties they are going to have. This can also explain, in part, the love of parents for their children. So much of loving a child is waiting to see what they will become, is wanting to know their future properties.

of ourselves or of our context. Nozick is right on this: what makes us fall in love is a small part of what love turns out to be. Love is a special form of study, a type of intense, engaged contemplation. We can be drawn into this devotion by hormones or fear of loneliness or peer pressure. But once the investigation has begun, once we are immersed in the other, in the abstruse complications that make up the actual person, the reason why we came to be so immersed is irrelevant to the study's value or, more importantly, to the fact that it is a study.

If love is an enterprise of engaged investigation, then constancy through change makes perfect sense. Ludwig began his study of WWII because of an interesting story about the British RAF and UFOs. The UFO story led Ludwig to study American volunteers who flew for the British RAF. And that led Ludwig to study the Americans who were captured in the war and their treatment by the Nazis. And that, in turn, led Ludwig to study the concentration camps. If after years of study, Ludwig found out that the UFO story was a fabrication, his reasons for studying WWII, or the value he received from such a study, need not be altered at all (or only very slightly). A study is about gaining better and better knowledge, and the fact that certain initial properties of the subject that brought you to study it originally were not real (or in the case of romantic love, have changed) need not change anything about the value of your continuing study. Because study implicitly assumes that any knowledge will be good (though some knowledge will be more important than other knowledge), change in the object of study is largely irrelevant to whether the study continues. Your continuing to study now is not due to those initial properties, but due to the large store of properties you came to learn later and to your continued belief that further study is warranted and valuable.

Furthermore, the richness of a person is partly the richness of an historical object. The Parthenon changes year by year, losing much of its original beauty, but it will always be connected to the past Parthenon and the history of Athens. This will always be a part of the value of the Parthenon, of what we love when we love it. The history of an object is part of the object's notion, part of its richness, and is an important part of what we love. This is especially true in close human relationships because the history of the loved one is not just the history of the loved one, but is also a history of the lover. You have intimate knowledge of the other's history because it is part of your history, because you lived a big chunk of that history. Falling out of love with something that is not tied up with who you are may be difficult at times, but it amounts, in the end, to just forgetting the other; it amounts to the ability to stop thinking of the other. But when the other's notion is tied up with your notion, falling out of love entails forgetting large parts of yourself. To completely stop loving the other requires us to stop loving part of ourselves. On this view, there comes a certain point in any good relationship where it is not only explicable that love will be constant, but where we would expect it to be constant; where we would be surprised if the love failed entirely.

The present view can also explain why the lover cares about the other's good.

Start with non-living objects. When we love a painting, we come to see its richness as its good, and want to protect its richness; but its richness is its good and so we will do our best to protect its *actual* good. But the same is true of persons: a person's good *is* a person's richness. To promote the other's good is to protect and promote the other's richness, and the richness of his life. But to protect the other's richness is entailed by the fact that you see the other as good, that you see the other's richness as good. So what is it to promote a person's richness?

As noted in the Platonists vs. Romantics section and earlier in the section on free will, to come to know another human being is, in a large part, to come to know what she values; it is to come to know, in other words, her perspective on the world. You can know many things about someone, but if you have no sense of what it might be like to be her, if you cannot understand why certain things seem good to her or bad to her, you fail to really know her. You do not manage to see another's perspective by merely listing a set of value beliefs. Unsurprisingly, to see another's perspective, you need not believe as she believes, but you must see as she sees; most importantly you must see as good what she sees as good. A liberal democrat and a conservative republican are advised in the course of an argument to see things from the other's point of view. They each say, "What, you mean, see the world falsely?" The Democrat and Republican presumably have a pretty good understanding of what the other believes on the topic at issue. It is not ignorance of each other's beliefs that has created the stand-off. The Republican knows the Democrat believes certain things are good; he just thinks those things are not good. The Democrat knows the Republican thinks certain things are good; he just thinks those things are not good. Neither has genuinely taken on the other's perspective because neither sees as good what the other sees as good.

Seeing the world through my lover's eyes, doesn't mean I can't draw significantly different conclusions about the world than he does. I will always be bringing my own understanding to the situation; I will undoubtedly create different theories of the good, I will value different things. For instance, suppose Juliet does go through the work required to understand Harry's perspective on contraception. That is, she really does try to imagine what it would be like to have grown up in his Catholic family, to have had his experiences with sex etc.... She still might draw conclusions that he wouldn't draw because she has her own evidence from her own life to add to the evidence that she is drawing from his life; she has her own experiences of sex and contraception. The rational conclusion to draw based on all of that evidence, Harry's and hers, may be significantly different than the rational conclusion to draw based on merely Harry's evidence. And, so, she will be motivated by the good she sees which might be very different than the good he sees.

This might be seen as a problem: if we have different values, why would we ever act for the other's good? I suggest that this is not a problem, but rather a benefit of the view. The objection turns on a shallow understanding of what constitutes another's good. We don't think a person's good is entirely determined by his own evaluations of his good, even if he's done the best evaluation possible given his evidence. We think that a person's good is tightly connected to what he deeply values or, more likely, to what he should deeply value given his epistemic situation, but we are also aware that given a certain amount of ignorance, a person may be, in principle, incapable of making a full evaluation of his own good. Therefore, the ability of the lover to bring extra evidence to the evidence of the loved one is not a handicap in evaluating the loved one's good, but a benefit.[31] In general, one of the great goods of a healthy romantic relationship is the sudden influx of information about the world. The stories, experiences, behaviors of the other – because we take them seriously, because we don't just note them but attempt to see them as the other sees them – greatly increase our data about the world of the good, about where it resides, and how we can attain it.

Finally, this view of romantic love does allow for robust care; we can desire the other's good for the reason that it is the other's good. By understanding the other's good, I come to see the satisfaction of certain of the other's desires as good. It is true I want to satisfy some of these desires merely because I now see the object of those desires as good for me. I now want to take her on a trip to Greece as she's always wanted, and part of the reason for this may be that coming to know her has made me like Greece. And now going to Greece is something I see as good for me. But, of course, part of my lover's desire and value set is the belief that going to Greece is good for her. And if I've truly come to see as good what she sees as good, I will see it as a good thing that she go to Greece. But this is the essence of generosity: seeing the satisfaction of the other's wants as good in itself. Given her abilities on the piano, and her desires with respect to playing the piano, I can see that, for her, a new piano would be a good. A new piano does me no good because I don't have the skills, but because I understand what it is like to do something she is good

---

31 Indeed, there are certain people we trust to take care of us, that we go to when we need taking care of. Some of these we trust because we know they are good at providing certain things that they and we know we like or value (e.g. lentil soup), but there are others we trust to take care of us because we know that they often can see our good better than we ourselves can. We trust that they can see the world from our point of view well enough that when they add their insight, they will make good decisions for us.

at (from my skills in basketball, say) and I understand what it is like to reproduce beautiful art (from my reading aloud of poetry, maybe), I can understand how, for her, the piano would be a good. In general, then, when we have done the work to see the good as our lover does, we find this changes what we think is good for us, but it also entails that we see the satisfaction of some of the lover's desires as good merely because they are the lover's desires.

The conclusion, then, is that the view I am presenting can explain what both the feature-based view and the unity-view can explain without falling prey to either view's problems. In agreement with the unity-view, when we love we come to see the good of the other as our own good; also, a large part of the reason why there is constancy in good romantic love is that the relationship itself becomes part of the loved object. But the view I am presenting has none of the worries of the unity view. It is perfectly explicable what unrequited love and love for non-human objects are; they are fundamentally the same as requited romantic love. This is because central to love are desires and these desires can, in principle, be directed toward any type of object.

3.2.3 The Strength of Love

> "For fierce as death is love,
> As sure as the tomb its envy.
> Its wounds are wounds of fire,
> of conflagration."
> The Song of Songs, of Solomon (transl. by C. Kelly)[32]

There is a third measure of love that plays a large part in our evaluation of how good a love is, namely, the intensity of the desires associated with love. Call this the strength of love. If one thing is clear about love, it is its power to motivate us. Parents give their lives for a loved child. The lover abandons all other enterprises to win his

---

32[Kelly, C. 2015]

love. The jealous lover kills to keep his love to himself.

While a true love is better than a false love, and a deep love is better than a shallow love, a stronger love will not always be better than a weaker love. The intensity of our desires can be inappropriate. Susan Orleans had an inappropriately intense love for the dial tone. What explains this inappropriateness? If desires are just perceptions of goodness, then one good explanation is that there is a seeming that something is better than it actually is. Susan perceives the dial tone as better than it is; she is having a hallucination of value. Misperceptions are failings.

The inappropriateness, though, is not only due to the simple misalignment of the perception of value and the actual value of the object. If Tristan sees Juliet as having a great good **G** and desires her to that extent, but the perception is not properly connected to Juliet (for instance, if it is based only on her smile), then the desire is still inappropriate *even if Juliet does have value* **G**. So, the appropriateness of a loving desire depends on the proper connection between the object of love and the desires of love.

The proper connection between desire and the object of desire is identical to the proper connection between perception and the object of perception. One requirement for a proper sensory perception is that you have available to you the sensory information necessary to perceive the thing you think you perceive. I cannot see the great pyramids of Egypt as I sit here in Colorado no matter how accurate a pyramid-experience I might have. Tristan can't experience Juliet as good if he doesn't have the proper information necessary for that experience. If I don't know of you, I can't perceive you as good. So, to have appropriately strong love, our desires for the other must be commensurate with the value of the other and must be due to proper awareness of the other.

But to have full awareness of the other is to see the other in his full richness. And if we love him and see him in his full richness, we have a true (and, almost certainly, deep) love for him. And, so, if I love you and perceive you fully, I must have perfectly true and deep love for you. And this perception of your good is the strength of love. And so true and deep love is necessary for the strength of our love to be appropriate. The best love has appropriate strength. And, so, the best love is a true, deep, and appropriately strong love.

3.3 Love and the Good

The view of love put forward solves several of the central problems associated with the analysis of love, and is capable, moreover, of unifying loves across categories. At its center, romantic love is like love of a painting or a cause or a child. And these are all goods in our lives. In this section, I turn to the ultimate goal of the chapter. What can our analysis of love tell us about the good?

To repeat: good things are the things it is appropriate to love. I suggested two ways this fact can give us information about the good. First, does the analysis of love determine the proper objects of love? Yes, the proper objects of love are rich things. Second, the fact that we should love the good is a value fact like other value facts, a fact that needs explaining. If monism is true, the final theory of value must claim that there is some property X that entails that the act of valuing X also has the property X. If it turns out there is only one such X, then, if there is any good at all, X is the good.

The argument of this section is two-fold. First, the better a love is, the deeper the love. Since the object of the best love is the best type of thing, I argue that the better the love is, the better the object of love. But only rich objects can be deeply loved; I conclude that whatever is good, is also rich. The best explanation for this fact, I argue, is that richness is the good. Second, I argue that the best love is the deepest love because deeper love is a richer state of affairs than shallower love.

3.3.1 What Love Loves

"Theories of love are found in the works of scientists, philosophers, and theologians." Mortimer J. Adler

Objects can be worthy of desire for both instrumental and intrinsic reasons. Objects are worthy of love for only intrinsic reasons. Some state-of-affairs **X** can be uncontroversially desire-worthy even if that state-of-affairs is intrinsically disvaluable (or less valuable) because it will lead to something of great value. The Merit Connection does not tell us much about what the good looks like because any type of thing (leaving to the side possible deontological restrictions), given the right circumstances, can be worthy of desire, even things with no real value of their own. We can, and often do, appropriately value intrinsically valueless (or relatively valueless) things for their instrumental effects.

Love, on the other hand, requires that the value of interest is part of the object of love.[33] If you love **X**, it is because you see **X** as good in itself, not because **X** is good for anything else. If you 'love' Juliet for her money, even if you want this money for the purpose of doing a great deal of good, you don't really love Juliet. You may love the 'great deal of good' you are going to do with the money, but you don't love Juliet. Love of the object must be about the object itself.[34] To desire appropriately state-of-affairs-**X**, you need know little to nothing of state-of-affairs **X**. You need only know that **X** leads to some

---

33"Desire wants what it wants for the sake of some private gratification; whereas, love demands in interest in that vague complexity we call another person." [Singer, 1984: 8]

34This is not to say that relations to persons or things cannot be the properties we love about a person or a thing. This is because relations can be inextricably tied up with who or what a thing is. Maybe, I love my snow blower because it so good at blowing snow; that is, I don't just love it because it makes my life easier, but I love it because it is designed so well for its purpose. It's quiet; it's efficient. I've taken apart the engine and put it back together again. I know how every piece of the snow blower makes it better *for blowing snow*. It is clear that the purpose of a thing can be inextricably linked up with what it is and loving something for its purpose does not mean (necessarily) that you don't really love it. Likewise, a person's history and goals are relations, but we can love a person, in part, for her history and goals because her history and goals are an important part of who she is.

good state **Y**. The best love, on the other hand, requires that you bring to awareness the full object of love. It is for this reason that an exploration of love is more likely to tell us something important about what the good actually is. I suggest that it tells us the good must be something like richness.

I begin with the Love Connection:

(LC) The better a love is (all things being equal)[35] the better the object of love and vice versa.

This is clear. Imagine two perfectly true loves; they both have complete access to the other. Clearly the true love that is love of a better object is a more valuable love, is the better love. Harry's true love for Juliet is better than his true love of his hamster.

I've also argued for:

(BL) The better a love is (all other things being equal) the deeper a love and vice versa.

By **(BL)**, and **(LC)**, we get that,

(LC2) The deeper a love is (all other things being equal) the better the object of love is and vice versa.

In addition, we've seen that

(RL) The deeper a love is the richer the object of that love and vice versa.

By **(RL)** and **(LC2)**, we get,

35The *ceteris paribus* clause in each of the claims of this section is for two reasons: 1) to allow for the possibility of misaligned desires, that is, desires that are not in sync with the depth of the love. A deeper love, then, might be less good than a somewhat shallower love if for some reason it were a love whose desires were more out of whack than those of the shallower love. And 2) love can have many instrumental effects. Harry's love of his Hamster may give him important comfort while his love for Juliet could lead him to commit suicide. Instrumentally, Harry's love for the hamster is better than his love of Juliet.

(Conclusion) The better X is (all things being equal) the richer X is.

At love's center is the basic Aristotelian drive, the drive to know. The better a love, the more that drive is satisfied. This means that love, that magical, life affirming, life-changing, sought-after state of awareness is a particular form of engaged knowing. The better it is, the more of this knowing is at its center. The measure of knowing, though, is richness; therefore, the measure of love is richness. In addition, the best love is also true; that is, not only does the best love take the thing it is aware of to be a good thing, it is right to do so. The proper objects of love are good things. And the proper objects of love are rich things. This means that the best things are always rich. There are only two good explanations for this: either richness is the good itself or it is a necessary condition for the good.

The better explanation – especially, given my discussion of the apparent pluralism of value in the preceding chapter – is that richness is not only a necessary, but also a sufficient condition for the good. When we love we seek out richness; we seek out deeper and deeper connections to the rich itself. Every new bit of the other person, every new bit of knowledge (in good love) seems good. Unless love is generally delusional, unless most of our loves and most of the desires associated with love are improper, then the best explanation for that seeming is that those new bits, that increased richness, is good.

3.3.2 Why Loving the Good is Good

Assuming richness is the good, why is it the good? To answer this question, Nozick began with the observation that love connections like **(LC)** are not value neutral.[36] If certain loves are better than other loves, a value theorist needs to explain why in terms of her underlying theory of value. And if this value theorist is a monist, she needs to explain why in terms of one property. So, I need to explain what is rich about **(LC)** and **(LC2)**.

Nozick points us in the following direction. It is better to perceive good things as good, he notes, than it is to perceive bad things as good (or good things as bad). The claim is justified by an appeal to the claim that it is better to have an accurate perception than an inaccurate perception. And this can be explained, as I noted in §2.2.2 and §2.2.3, by an appeal to the claim that richness is the good. Accurate perception is a unification of the world with our awareness.[37] Accurate perception is a richer state of affairs than inaccurate perception because inaccurate perception is not so unified. The pro-attitudes being partly constituted by desires are, therefore, partly constituted by perceptions of value. So, having pro-attitudes for bad things will be less rich than having pro-attitudes toward good things.

All of this is right, but it is an explanation too meager to explain the good of love.[38] Yes, love is partly constituted by perceptions of value; so love is better when those perceptions are unified with the way the world actually is. There is more in need of explanation, though: deeper loves are better than shallower loves and yet both a shallow love and a deep love can be constituted by equally accurate perceptions of the good. I can love a dial tone properly as long as the

---

36[Nozick, 1981: 436].

37Putting to the side, of course, the large number of instrumental reasons that knowledge is better than false belief (or unjustified belief).

38Nozick's explication is slightly more complicated; he allows for a property called disharmony which is an objective bad, so that loving bad things or hating good things is not merely less good then having the proper attitude toward those objects but is bad. I think this is an unnecessary complication, and that everything I need is plausibly contained in the notion of richness outlined in chapter 1. I will discuss the bad in §4.4.1.

love is appropriately weak. If it is appropriately weak, the perception of value at its center is just as accurate as an appropriately strong love for a human. The betterness of deep love cannot be due merely to whether it is truth-tracking about value or not. There is something significantly better about deep love than having a single correct belief or single accurate perception.

But the explanation for this was already given in Chapter 2. Rich knowledge is better than less rich knowledge and better than rich belief. To have a rich, but false, belief system may well be a beautiful thing, and may have genuine value, but when these systems are accurate, the richness is greater. But what can be said about knowledge can also be said about awareness. Rich accurate awareness is better than less rich awareness and better than rich inaccurate awareness. But the best kinds of loves are just instances of rich awareness; they are, as we've seen, awarenesses of richness. To be in deep love is to have a representation of a richness in the world. An accurate representation of a richness is itself rich. Moreover, because the representation is accurate, there is a rich set of connections between the world and your mental state. The very fact that love requires engrossment in valuable things makes love a valuable state, a state that is orders of magnitude more valuable than merely having a single accurate perception of value. And, so, it is clear why the best love is the deepest; it is because the deepest love is the richest love.

3.4 Love, Spinoza and Should

"Blessedness is not the reward of virtue, but virtue itself. We do not enjoy virtue because we keep our lusts in check. On the contrary, it is because we enjoy blessedness that we are able to keep our lusts in check.... Blessedness consists in love towards God." Spinoza, The Ethics

Spinoza argued in **The Ethics** that right action was properly motivated action. Properly motivated action is motivated by the right emotions. He called the right emotions 'active' emotions. According to Spinoza, the active emotions are rational emotions: they promote proper understanding of oneself and the universe, they flow from proper understanding, and they are the emotions that 'define man's power', that is, those emotions that when acted from make the actor free. The prototypical active emotion is love. On the other hand, the wrong emotions to act from he called 'passive' emotions. These emotions are irrational, arise out of 'fragmentary knowledge', and are the source of 'human bondage', man's lack of freedom. The prototypical passive emotion is fear. I want, briefly, to defend this distinction between the emotions. Considerations already put forward both in the preceding discussion of love and the broader value theory being presented here make much of what Spinoza says plausible.

Active emotions broaden our experience of the world and passive emotions narrow our experience of the world. Passive emotions limit the scope of our attention. When lustful, we are not concerned with the other's character or personality or hopes and dreams. Lust directs us to the other's body, often a limited portion of the other's body; it narrows our experience of the person to those features. The more powerful the lust the more powerfully narrowed our experience is. Contrast that with ideal love.

Fear is also a narrowing emotion. When I go to the zoo, I like to admire the lions; I appreciate their fur and their loping movement, the subtle, soil–like variations of color from head to toe, and the way the lion stands out against the rocks and tree branches. In my own way, I love the lions. I like that they are, and I like to experience them as they are. On the other hand, if the lion leaps the barrier and starts running for me, my experience, and, in particular, my desires change rapidly. I no longer appreciate the lion's fur, or its loping run or much else about it. My experience is narrowed to nothing but teeth and claws. Fear, generally, narrows the world down to the danger fear fears. Other emotions that work like lust and fear are anger, hate, jealousy, and all the subtle mixtures and variations of these. My girlfriend didn't wash the dishes; I am angry with her; she is narrowed in my experience to being a 'slob.' I hate members of the Libertarian Party because of my perception that they are cruel to the poor; I think of them as no more than selfish, greedy, pro–business ideologues. Both my girlfriend and Libertarians are much more than my anger and hate allows me, at the moment, to accept.

The passive emotions are not only narrowing, of course; sometimes they are positively hallucinatory. Walking home in the dark, I see lurking figures in the shadows that are not there. Jealous that my girlfriend is cheating on me, I am continually catching her thinking about someone else; I smell colognes in her clothes that do not exist. Angry at my officemate, I see every word as an insult. Feeling lustful, I see every movement as suggestive. It is in these two ways that Spinoza can argue that the passive emotions are 'related to the mind only in so far as it conceives things inadequately.' These emotions narrow and impede our understanding of the world; they actively motivate us to stop looking at the broader world and they fill our minds with false understanding of the broader world. These emotions are old evolutionary tools -- fight, flight, and reproduce -- developed long before understanding was useful to us. When it comes to surviving and reproducing in a wild world, these emotions are useful. But in a world of ideas, self–awareness, reason, language, complicated social relationships, and science, they are blunt instruments at best. The passive emotions tend to actively constrain our understanding.

Active emotions, on the other hand, open us to the objects of our experience; they increase our awareness of the world; they seek understanding. When we feel compassion for a person's suffering, it is because we understand to some extent how they feel; when we feel sympathy, we aim to understand. When we are in awe, our mind tries to grab something just beyond the size of our understanding. When we feel love, we want to experience the other in its entirety, just as it is. The active emotions are expansive states of mind in which, ideally, the full richness of the object is brought into awareness.

One might argue that love can be just as narrowing and hallucinatory as the passive emotions. Take for example, the early stages of romantic love. This is undoubtedly true, in one sense, but is more of a semantic distinction than a real one. As already argued, it is a failure of love when it narrows our view of the object of love. This is not a failure of, say, fear. Indeed, we might think that it is precisely what fear is supposed to do. Likewise with anger and jealousy and lust. The passive emotions are essentially narrowing; the ideal active emotions are broadening. It is the ideal active emotions from which, Spinoza suggests, we act. (Another point: we might think that early stage romantic love is more akin to lust than it is to love as defined in this chapter. There is some evidence that the hormones associated with early romantic love disappear within a couple of years of a committed relationship, but the love, clearly, does not.)

Clearly, love is a richer mental state, all things being equal, than the mental states characterized by the passive emotions. The most obvious reason for this is that love contains more detailed and expansive representations of the world than the narrowing emotions. Experiential evidence of this is overwhelming. If you have ever been consumed by fear, you know how small the mind can become. Indeed, one term for a person suffering from excessive anger and hate is 'small–minded.' When feeling love, on the other hand, the world seems large and miraculous.

Another important reason love is richer is that most of the passive emotions are aversive in nature (not lust, of course). In this sense, the passive emotions are a form of suffering. When you hate somebody, the experience of them is, generally, something unpleasant, something you would choose not to have. Fearing a lion does not make me want to experience the lion or to know more of the lion. Hating a person does not make me want to experience that person or to know more of that person. I would rather not think about what I fear or what I hate; and if I must think of them, I will not think of them in their entirety, but in their hatefulness or scariness. I will discuss the aversive nature of suffering in the next chapter.

Finally, it is essential to love that it seeks understanding of the other, to truly know the other in its fullness. Even lust, which does pull us toward the object of our emotion, both physically and mentally, does not seek understanding of that object. Continuous conscious loving of something moves us on an upward path toward ever richer representations of the loved part of the world. Continuous fearing, hating or lusting after a person leaves us, at best, in stasis. It, generally, doesn't seek new information; hence the mind will move, if it all, in the direction of illusion. For all these reasons, love and active emotions are richer mental states than passive emotions. This accords nicely with the consistent intuition that a life lived in love is better than one lived in fear or hate or lust. The good life will not be symmetrical with respect to passive and active emotions. This lends some plausibility to Spinoza's account of ethics.

3.5 Conclusion

The argument of this chapter has been multiple. First, I worked toward an analysis of love and used this analysis of love to determine the best love. In love, one desires both the existence of the loved one and the deepening of one's awareness of the loved one. These desires must be connected with the world in the correct way. We fail to love in as much as those desires are not constituted by an awareness of the other, in the richness of the other. This entails that the best love is a love fully aware of a rich object.

But we know something else about the best love: it is also attached to a good object. Therefore, good objects are rich objects. The best explanation for this, I suggest, is that the good just is richness. I then explored further evidence for this, by explaining why deep loves were better than shallow loves in terms of a theory that richness is the good. Love for a rich object is itself a rich state; the richer the object of love, the richer the love. Deep love is better than shallow love. And so, in addition to the reasons given in Chapter 2, there are good meta-ethical and moral psychological reasons to think that the good is richness. In addition, I suggested that it is plausible that right action will also be connected to love and richness; namely, right action, however it gets specifically delineated, will be the freest, most loving, and richest action available to any agent at any given time.

4

PLEASURE AND PAIN

Montaigne tells us, "I, who boast of embracing the pleasures of life so assiduously and so particularly, find in them, when I look at them thus minutely, virtually nothing but wind."[1] And, yet, Montaigne agrees with the vast majority of us that a good life is largely determined by its ratio of pleasure to pain. Strange that, that a passing motion of the mind, a stirring of the mental air can carry so much weight in our lives. Indeed, many people's lives are directed by the belief that only pleasure and pain have intrinsic value.

If richness is the good, why should we think that the simple experiences of pleasure and pain have significant value? Pleasure, at least on the face of it, need not have any variety in it at all. Isn't the sensation of pleasure just as unified and simple as an experience of red? Think of the pleasure of a warm bath, the enjoyment of watermelon, the heat of orgasm. There is nothing particularly complex in these experiences, certainly nothing on the order of the other goods we have mentioned. The present view has even more difficulty explaining pain. On the view that richness is the good, nothing is intrinsically bad. There is no property that could count as negative richness.[2] For the richness theorist, the worst things are merely valueless. So, if our generally held assumptions about pleasure and pain are correct, the claim that richness is the only intrinsically valuable

---

1Montaigne [1973]

2Nozick disagrees. He thinks that disharmony is negative unity, not just the lack of unity, and so disharmony can ground our intuitions of badness. [Nozick, 1981: 430-431]

property must be false.[3]

I argue in this chapter that pain and pleasure do not have any significant intrinsic value (though they can have significant instrumental value). There are several *prima facie* good reasons for thinking that pleasure and pain are intrinsically good/bad. I argue that given proper analyses of pleasure and pain (and the proper analyses of taking pleasure in **X** and suffering **X**), these reasons lose their force. The two main reasons for thinking that pleasure and pain have intrinsic values are (1) that pleasure and pain are intrinsically motivational and (2) that pleasure and pain are intuitively valuable/disvaluable.

Pain and pleasure appear intrinsically motivational. This, in itself, gives us two strong reasons to think that pleasure/pain are intrinsically valuable. Why? First, because moral realists are under an obligation to give some explanation of the fact – widely regarded as strange – that the good motivates us. If the good must be intrinsically motivational and pleasure and pain are the only things intrinsically motivational, we have good reason to think they are the good/bad. Findlay puts this same point in another way: what possible explanation could there be for the 'gross empirical accident' that pleasure and pain always motivate us? Why did it turn out that those sensations always move us? One simple explanation would appear to be that those sensations are intrinsically good and bad, and, therefore, motivational.[4]

A second worry for any realist theory of value is that there is widespread disagreement about what is valuable. The universal desirability/undesirability of pleasure/pain is a compelling answer to relativity arguments against objective value. The hedonist can point to pleasure as a counterexample to the claim that there are no universally accepted preferences. Pleasure and pain are states, they can say, that we all like or dislike.

It is often claimed that in addition to our desires for pain and pleasure, we have many direct intuitions that pleasure/pain are good/

3Nozick, surprisingly, seems to accept this. He says, "We should be perfectly happy if the degree of organic unity accounted for 90 percent of the variance of intrinsic value." [Nozick, 1981: 419]

4[Findlay, 1961: 177]

bad.[5] Direct acquaintance with pleasure or pain, or imagined pain or pleasure, is often thought to give us direct evidence of their value. In addition, the contemplation of other people in pleasure (or pain) is intuitively good (or bad). And so, again, if we are realists, and we accept intuitions as evidence, if we accept that there are moral perceptions, we appear to be forced into accepting that pleasure/pain are good/bad.

I begin by looking at pleasure. After outlining in detail the reasons for thinking pleasure valuable, I defend a specific version of a common analysis of pleasure, namely, that the pleasures are just experiences that are desired while we are having them and entirely because of intrinsic features of them. I argue that this analysis both shows that pleasures are not intrinsically motivational (in the appropriate sense) and explains why we would all think (or have the intuition) that pleasure is intrinsically good even if it were not. I then suggest that certain forms of pleasure – namely, pleasure in experiences of the good – are intrinsically valuable, but the value of these pleasures can be captured by the present theory. Except for a few added wrinkles, the arguments against the intrinsic badness of pain are analogous. I conclude that though pain is never intrinsically bad, human suffering generally is, and for reasons explicable by the present theory.

5Of course, given that I have argued that desires serve as our basic observations of fact in the realm of ethics, that they play the role of intuitions, the distinction between intrinsically motivating and intuitively good/bad becomes blurred.

4.1 Mackie: Reasons to Think Pleasure is Intrinsically Valuable

J.L. Mackie's influential book, **Ethics: Inventing Right and Wrong**, lays out the challenge to the moral realist. Mackie thinks these challenges are insurmountable and that they entail moral nihilism.[6] He believes there are no values that "are part of the fabric of the world."[7] His two most serious objections, he calls the 'Argument from Relativity' and 'The Argument from Queerness.' The hedonic realist, unlike realists of every other variety, has ready answers to both of these objections.[8] This is a major advantage hedonism has over other forms of realism. Mackie has laid out conditions for what a realist picture of the world must look like, and hedonism meets those conditions fairly easily. If no other theory can meet those conditions, and if Mackie's conditions are fair (I think, more or less, that they are), then if you are a realist, you must be a hedonist.

4.1.1 The Argument from Relativity

Mackie points to the eternal disagreement over ethical claims, both between cultures and within cultures. This disagreement is best explained, Mackie argues, by the claim that there are no objective values. A good response has to show that either (1) there is not any real disagreement over fundamental ethical claims – that the disagreement is only apparent – or (2) that the disagreement is due to biases, distortions, faulty moral faculties or some other principled

---

6I prefer 'moral nihilist' to the more common 'moral skeptic.' Mackie is not just claiming that there is no way to know about moral facts. He is claiming there are no moral facts. He is not a moral agnostic, but a moral atheist.

7[Mackie, 1977]

8This is not to say that there aren't other answers to these objections. Clearly, I think that there are. But there are no answers as apparently straightforward as the hedonist's answers.

defeater or (3) some combination of both. Mackie argues that (1) is clearly false. A quick scan of the philosophical literature may be the most compelling argument against (1). There seems no significant moral or value claim that has not been hotly debated (including hedonism) by philosophers.

But if the disagreement is as severe as Mackie suggests, then (2) is not going to be as good an explanation of the disagreement as moral nihilism. It only makes sense to claim perceptions are being distorted when there is some set of normal, accurate perceptions from which to measure that distortion. If there is no such set, if there is no way to establish which perceptions are accurate, you should wonder if that type of perception is perception of anything. Imagine a set of clairvoyants called 'past-readers.' Past-readers claim to be able to see into the distant past. We put a dozen of them in a room and ask them to describe what Christ looked like on the cross. They close their eyes; they do the 'past-reader' hum. If they all claim to see Christ on the cross, but none agree on what they see, we have good reason to doubt that they are perceiving anything at all, that they are accessing anything real about the past. But this is analogous to Mackie's understanding of humanity's perception of ethical facts. All humanity feels they have some access to what is right and wrong and yet, in general – the claim is – nobody can agree on what those facts are. If this is true, then unless we have some independent reason for thinking that there are moral facts, the general human conviction that there are such facts gives us little reason to believe that moral facts exist.

Now, the case as presented is overstated. It is not at all obvious that there is not more agreement than Mackie wants to admit, and that there aren't good explanations for the disagreement that does exist.[9] The amount of disagreement that does exist, though, especially in the philosophical literature, still makes one wonder if there are

---

9Rachels presents several explanations for disagreement. The most convincing being that disagreement is due more to differences in non-moral beliefs than to differences in moral claims. Hindus, for the most part, think harming cattle is wrong, and Christians, for the most part, do not. But the Hindu's reasons for thinking it is wrong to harm cattle are based, in part, on their belief that cows are (or might be) their ancestors. The moral

any foundational perceptions in ethics. The challenge Mackie presents to the realist is the challenge to show that there is some moral claim we can all agree on (or, at the very least, that there is something we should – epistemically speaking – all agree on, and that there are good reasons for why in fact we don't). Mackie thinks there is no such a claim.[10]

4.1.2 Argument from Queerness

"An objective good would be sought by anyone acquainted with it, not because of any contingent fact that this person, or every person, is so constituted that he desires this end, but just because the end has to-be-pursuedness built into it."
Mackie[11]

Mackie's second argument is even stronger. The good is, in some important sense, desirable. Mackie pushes this further: the good must be capable of making us desire it. But, Mackie claims, if the good has this property, it is unlike anything in existence. Nothing we know of is intrinsically action-guiding. Rocks and paintings and electrons don't force any motivations on us. If we already desire rocks, we might be motivated by rocks; but rocks *qua* rocks don't motivate us. The whole physical universe is rock-like in this sense. And, so, the moral realist is committed to an ontological pluralism: there are these queer motivating moral facts, and then there is every-

---

principle underlying their belief is, then, the claim that it is wrong to harm one's ancestors. A claim that most Christians would also believe. The disagreement, then, is not a moral disagreement, but a disagreement about good old descriptive facts. Many moral disagreements can be understood in this way. Note for instance the debate over abortion. Suppose that most everyone agrees that killing innocent persons is generally wrong. The disagreement, then, is about the non-moral fact of whether a fetus is, in fact, a person, and not a *moral* disagreement at all. (Ignore, for the purposes of example, Judith Jarvis Thompson, here please.)

10At least, in *Ethics*. In 'Evil and Omnipotence,' he argued that pain grounded a strong argument against the existence of a good God.

11[Mackie, 1977]

thing else, the natural world.

To look at it another way: the widely accepted Humean theory of motivation claims that a belief could never, on its own, motivate us. "It is not contrary to reason," says Hume, "to prefer the destruction of the whole world to the scratching of my finger."[12] For Hume, reason only helps us achieve those ends that we already desire. I noted in Chapter 1 that the having of a belief cannot, on its own, motivate. But if the having of beliefs about moral facts does not entail the having of certain desires, but moral facts do, on their own, somehow motivate us, moral facts are queer, unlike anything in the world. But if you can't find such a fact, then nothing is a moral fact..

So, Mackie has presented a challenge to the moral realist. Show me something that has to-be-pursuedness, he says, or let go of the idea of objective value facts.

4.1.3 The Hedonist Response

The hedonist seems up to the challenge, with strong responses to both of Mackie's worries. In response to the Argument from Relativity, there is almost universal agreement that pleasure is desirable/good. And in response to the Argument from Queerness, pleasure, due to this universal desired-ness, appears to be a natural, normal, everyday property that is intrinsically motivational, that does have to-be-pursuedness built into it.

There are clear differences among people in their preferences. Differences in taste for food, hobbies, sleeping, and sex are found across and within cultures. The taste of spicy pickled pig's foot delights one, but is despised by another. Alcohol makes one person feel on top of the world, and another sleepy and depressed. But these disagreements in taste are not disagreements, the hedonist replies, about pleasure. It is clear that the things we call the pleasures are not universally desired, but pleasure itself, the hedonist claims, *is* univer-

---

12[Hume, 1896: II.iii.3, 416]

sally desired. I don't eat spicy pickled pig's foot because I don't enjoy the taste, because it doesn't give me pleasure; but if I did enjoy the taste, if it did give me pleasure, I would eat spicy pickled pig's foot. There is little to no disagreement that pleasure itself is good, despite the panoply of 'disagreements' about what things are pleasurable.

People will forgo pleasure or endure pain. One might endure the pain of a sprained ankle in the last minutes of a basketball game or deny oneself cake while on a diet. It is sometimes thought that enduring suffering or refusing certain pleasures can strengthen us. But such cases aren't genuine counterexamples to the hedonist. There are, no one would doubt, many instrumental reasons for desiring some suffering or desiring less pleasure. It may be that enduring a bit of pain now will lead to less pain later. It might be that avoiding some pleasure now will lead to more pleasure later. That situations like these undoubtedly occur does not suggest that people don't generally agree that all other things being equal, pleasure is a good, pain a bad, that pleasure is intrinsically likable, and pain intrinsically dislikable. Indeed, the very fact that it requires strength to endure suffering suggests that pain does seem bad and is motivating. And the fact that damaging pleasures are called 'temptations' suggests that pleasure does seem good and is motivating.

Consider Kant's objection to the hedonist.[13] A murderer has been captured and put in prison. Does the situation improve – as the hedonist seems to require – if we give him pleasure? Many think adding pleasure makes the situation worse becasue the man doesn't deserve pleasure. Doesn't this suggest that pleasure is not unconditionally valuable? This is a serious objection to the monistic hedonist, to someone who claims that only pleasure is valuable, but it isn't necessarily a counterexample to the claim that pleasure is an intrinsic value. The intuition does suggest that something other than pleasure is of value as well, something like just-desserts.[14] If you are good and you get pleasure, that is a good thing. It's just. If you are bad and you get pleasure, that's not a good thing. It's unjust. We may

---

13[Kant, 1959: 9-10]
14[Oddie, 2001]

agree that the disvalue of injustice can outweigh (even far outweigh) the good of the prisoner's pleasure, but we needn't say the prisoner's pleasure is valueless. Indeed, the very fact that good people should get pleasure and bad people shouldn't suggests that pleasure is something good because justice is about giving good things to good people and bad things to bad people.

So, the hedonist thinks that what disagreements there are with respect to the claim that pleasure is intrinsically good are theory driven; and they are not widespread. Mackie's appeal to cultural disagreement does not seem to apply in the case of pleasure because value intuitions about pleasure are remarkably uniform. To imagine, all things being equal, a state of pleasure, is to imagine a better state than one without pleasure.[15] If this is true it strongly suggests that pleasure, all by itself, is valuable. Indeed, the disagreement over other values is itself an argument for the hedonist: we disagree about all those other 'values' because they are merely contingently and instrumentally valuable – when valuable at all – in virtue of creating pleasure.

This also suggests a reply to the Argument from Queerness. Mackie missed an everyday element of the world that does have to-be-pursuedness built into it. Pleasure is intrinsically motivational. To feel pleasure will make you want, all other things being equal, to continue feeling it. You aren't really enjoying – taking pleasure in – something unless some part of you wants the experience to continue.

So if you are a moral realist, you might think you have to accept the value of pleasure because it doesn't look like there is anything else out there that has this 'queer' property. Then the moral realist has to be a monistic hedonic realist. If there are any other values in the world, they will be merely instrumental values, instrumental in creating pleasure and avoiding pain. This entails that the theory that richness is the only good is false. Indeed, it suggests that richness is not an intrinsic good at all.

15I have some reservations about this claim that I will mention later. On first glance, though, it is plausible.

4.2 Response to the Hedonist: An Analysis of Pleasure

4.2.1 The Analysis

I've stated the case for hedonism as strongly as possible, but I have already undermined it in other parts of this essay. There is another way that the good might be motivational: namely, through the experience conjecture. There are several reasons to think that the disagreement in other areas is not as severe as suggested. Furthermore, given the analysis of love, there are strong reasons to think that pure hedonism must be too narrow. Could there be any real love in a world where the only good is pleasure (except love for pleasure, and this love, at least with respect to simple pleasures, would always be shallow)? Harry doesn't love Juliet if he likes her because she gives him pleasure. We will take pleasure in experiencing those we love, but that can't be the *reason* we love them. In general, this has always been the worry about hedonism: that it is too narrow, that it can't explain all the things that we think are valuable. If we are hedonists, we can only value those things in as much as they are instrumental to creating pleasure. But we all have intuitions that, at least some of these things are valuable in and of themselves. I suggested in Chapter 2 that a theory of richness can plausibly explain most of our intuitions about what is intrinsically valuable. The hedonist must explain away those intuitions. I suggest that rather than explain all of those intuitions away, we need to explain away our intuitions that pleasure is an intrinsic value. I start by giving an analysis of pleasure.

I begin this analysis by showing that pleasure is not a sensation. The experiences that we take pleasure in are deeply heterogeneous: the taste of cake, the feel of sun on the face, the glow of accomplishment, the scratching of an itch and so on. When we take the time to contemplate these experiences, as Montaigne did, we find it impossible to pinpoint a single aspect of these experiences that is pleasure. We find 'nothing but wind.' "There is virtual unanimity today," claims Brandt, "that pleasure is not an element of experience like a color patch or sound. Just try to examine pleasure itself, in the way you can inspect a red patch itself. It cannot be done. Pleasantness always seems to be pleasantness of something...."[16] Many have agreed.[17]

To feel pleasure is to enjoy something. Call all experiences that are the object of enjoyment the pleasures. When I claim no sensation is the pleasure sensation, I am making two closely related claims. (1) There is no sensation intrinsic to the pleasures themselves that makes them the pleasures; and (2) There is no sensation that comes along on top of – but is separate and distinct from – the pleasures which makes the pleasures pleasurable.

Consider the first claim. I take pleasure in knowing I will die before my son. I also take pleasure in the taste sensations of kung pao tofu. No single sensation is intrinsic to both of these experiences. After all, one experience is characterized by a sensation, the other by a bit of conscious knowledge. The fact that I take pleasure in both, then, cannot be due to the fact that they are both partly constituted by a pleasure patch of sensation because there is no sensation (pleasure or otherwise) of which they are both partly constituted. This is no less obvious when considering more similar experiences such as, for instance, the class of purely physical pleasures. Orgasm and the taste sensations of kung pao tofu share no essential qualia.[18]

Moreover, and more importantly, few, if any, of the sensations that are pleasures are pleasing to everyone. The taste of kung pao

---

16[Brandt, 1959: 305]

17Much of my argument against there being an unique pleasure sensation follows [Feldman, 1997], though many others have argued similarly. Aristotle says, "There is no great value in defining pleasure as a phenomenal event: better to say it is an activity in accordance with the nature of one's condition." [Aristotle, 1985: VII.12 1153a13-15] Ryle says, 'In a word, pleasure is not a sensation at all....' Rem. B Edwards says, "It will be maintained that instead of there being a single quality of pleasantness which all 'pleasures' have in common, there are instead only innumerable qualitatively different feelings which we wish to sustain and repeat.... The distinctive feeling tone of a specific pain or pleasure cannot be fully identified in direct experience...." [Edwards, 1975: 280-281]

18John Hospers has argued that there are two types of pleasure: localized pleasures and non-localized pleasures [Hospers, 1961: 112]. An example of a localized pleasure is the

tofu is, presumably, the same for most people and yet the pleasure each person takes in tofu differs dramatically from person to person. This is true of most of the pleasures. Some people love kung pao tofu and some people loathe it. Some people love beer and some people loathe it. Some people like a hot bath and others loathe it. Is there any reason to think, in any of these cases, that one person is right and the other wrong? Is one of them having a faulty experience? Or is there any reason to think that the objects of their experiences are different? Is the loather missing something in the hot bath? Is the one who likes beer adding something that isn't there? Are they just experiencing completely different things?[19] In general, there is no reason to think that all differences in taste are due to differences in the objects of experience. You and I could feel qualitatively identical taste sensations without both feeling pleasure.

This is made abundantly clear when we consider that pleasure variations over a single type of experience are not only inter-subjective, but also intra-subjective. As I get full, the kung pao tofu doesn't taste any different. My tongue is still receiving the same sensations. It is just that I am no longer taking pleasure in that sensation. If this is true, it shows that there is, generally, nothing intrinsically pleasurable about the experiences intrinsic to the pleasures.[20] The pleasures are nothing other than those things that we generally take pleasure in.

Someone might accept that no sensation is universal to the plea-

---

stimulation of the erogenous zones because it makes sense to ask *where* it feels good. An example of non-localized pleasure is the pleasure we get in listening to a symphony. It doesn't make any sense to ask where we feel that pleasure. Hospers thinks that it is only these non-localized pleasures that are intrinsically good. There may be something to this – although it seems to weaken the hedonist's case against Mackie. But is it a worry for our claim that there is no sensation that is universal to the hedonist's favored pleasures? No. There is no sensation in common to the pleasure I get from knowing I will die before my son and the pleasure I get from listening to a symphony.

19This *may* happen in some cases. For instance, it has been shown that biological differences in people can lead some to think that cilantro tastes like soap. In cases like this, we assume that the likers and loathers *are* having different taste experiences. Cilantro, though, is the exception that proves the rule.

20Some might claim that orgasm or certain drug experiences *are* always accompanied by pleasure. I will consider this at the end of this section.

sures without accepting that there is no sensation universal to pleasure. Surely, they might say, we don't think the sensation of pleasure is universally part of the pleasures, that is, part of the pleasures even when they are not pleasing. But when the pleasures are pleasing, another sensation, namely the pleasure sensation, comes along with the pleasures, comes along on top of the taste of kung pao tofu or the heat of the bath. Sensation **S** is one of the pleasures only when the experience of sensation **S** is accompanied by (and, possibly, the cause of) sensation **P**. What are we to make of this claim?

If one means 'sensation' as sensory experience, the claim is hard to defend. As Feldman points out, a person could take pleasure in all sorts of things even if he were completely anesthetized. Feldman says, "I might take pleasure in the fact that the war in Bosnia has at least temporarily stopped. I might do this even though I am not feeling any sensory pleasure."[21] Or if you allow for such extravagances, imagine a disembodied mind with no sensory apparatus whatsoever, but one that still has introspective experience. It would seem unfair to deny that this creature could take pleasure in a proof of Fermat's last theorem. It would not feel its heart beat faster, it would not feel the flush of excitement in this fact, but why couldn't it enjoy this experience? Pleasure is not a sensation in this sense; we need no sensory experience to be in the state of pleasure.

On the other hand, one can't deny that there is a recognizable experiential state that is pleasure. Surely, it is like something to be enjoying the world. But the what-it's-likeness of enjoyment can't come from sensations, narrowly understood, so it must come from some other element of our conscious experience.

The natural response at this point (and one made many times) is that sensations become pleasures when we have the proper conscious attitude towards them. Let's call that attitude 'enjoyment.' Then:

(PLE) An experience X (sensory or otherwise) is a pleasure at t iff one is enjoying X at t.

---

21 [Feldman, 1997]

So what is enjoyment? The power of hedonism was in its response to the condition that pleasure be intrinsically motivational. This suggests a natural definition of enjoyment:

(ENJ) P enjoys X iff P concurrently desires the experience of X for reasons intrinsic to the experience of X.

The 'for reasons intrinsic to the experience of **X**' clause is necessary. There are many reasons one can desire that an experience continue, and many of those reasons do not entail that we are taking pleasure in the experience. I desire to get well from this flu. I should stay in bed for the day despite the spring-like weather. I desire to stay in bed because I desire to get better. Therefore, I desire to continue experiencing staying in bed, to continue the experience I am having, but I am not, I can assure you, enjoying this experience. It's rather miserable actually. If we want to be in the experience we are having now for reasons purely extrinsic to the experience we are having now, we are not enjoying experience.

The pleasures, on this view, are not anything special in themselves. They are just those things in which we take pleasure and we can take pleasure in almost anything (Though, perhaps not pains. Note why this is, though. Because we assume that pains are intrinsically aversion producing. This lends weight to the definition of pleasures I am about to give. It can't be a pleasure if it doesn't cause us to desire it. So, if a pain entails that we don't desire it, then, of course, it can't be a pleasure. Later, though, I will suggest that pains don't entail aversion.)

To complete our analysis recall once more the experience conjecture. If a desire for **X** is just an experience of **X** as good, then to take pleasure in **X** is just to experience **X** as good for reasons intrinsic to **X**. So,

(ENJ*) P enjoys X iff P concurrently sees (or experiences or perceives) the experience of X as intrinsically good.

Now I feel we've fully captured all the fundamental aspects of pleasure. To experience something as a pleasure is to experience that thing as good, to want it to go on, and you do not desire the experience because of some other desire for things extrinsic to the experience; you desire (and see as good) the experience for no other reason than that it is the experience it is. I claim no great originality to the thesis itself; many others recently and anciently have suggested something similar,[22] but I think once it is properly understood, the reasons for thinking pleasure intrinsically valuable evaporate.

4.2.2 Objections to the Analysis

I want to consider two sets of objections against **(ENJ)**: 1) objections to the claim that the object of the relevant desire is always an experience and 2) objections to the claim that the analysis of enjoyment should be done in terms of desire.

4.2.2.1 First, **(ENJ)** entails the object of enjoyment's relevant desires are our experiences. Doesn't it seem, though, that when enjoying something, say the Parthenon, that the proper objects of the desires that arise are not our experiences but aspects of the Parthenon itself, or of the Parthenon's existence, or of the fact that you are in front of the Parthenon? Feldman, while arguing a different matter, points out that one can be pleased that one is at the Parthenon, or pleased that one has been to the Parthenon.[23] In the second case, the relevant experiences – seeing the Parthenon, feeling the wind in your hair and so on – are no longer; you cannot be desiring *here and now* the experiences of *there and then* concurrent to those ex-

---

22Gilbert, Ryle [1949, 107–108] William Alston [1961, 341–347] Shelly Kagan ["Limits of Well–Being" 1992, 173–174], Richard Brandt[1993, 225], and Tom Carson [1997, 44–45] Also, Sidgwick proposed "to define Pleasure as a feeling which when experienced by intelligent beings, is at least implicitly apprehended as desirable – or – in cases of comparison – preferable." Sidgwick, H. (1962). The methods of ethics. [Chicago], University of Chicago Press, 127.

23Feldman [2004]

periences. It is more plausible, one might think, that when taking pleasure in this past state of affairs the relevant desires are directed not at any present experience, but at the past state of affairs itself, or in this case, your being at the Parthenon.

I begin my response by illuminating a distinction between the attitudes *pleased that p* and *enjoy p*. The first I take it is generally polysemous and is only sometimes synonymous with the second; that is, I can be pleased that p without enjoying p.

It is odd to say 'I am enjoying the fact that I once went to the Parthenon' in a way that it is not odd to say that 'I am pleased that I went to the Parthenon.' Approach this oddness in degrees. Suppose Harry and Juliet are at dinner and Harry says, "I am enjoying the Parthenon." Juliet looks around, puzzled, and noticing no Parthenon within the cafe, asks, "Do you mean you are enjoying a memory of the time we visited the Parthenon? Barring superpowers you have yet to reveal to me, you cannot be presently enjoying the Parthenon itself." "No," Harry replies, "It is not a memory. I am merely enjoying the fact that we went to the Parthenon, but there is no memory involved." "Well, how are you doing that without remembering it?" Juliet replies. To presently enjoy some **X**, Juliet naturally assumes, **X** must be presently experienced in some way. Harry might give any number of answers at this point, but they all require him pointing to some present experience. He might be enjoying picturing himself to be a cultured person because he went to the Parthenon, or imagining what people will think of the fact that he's been, or presently feeling satisfied that he has accomplished some goal of his, or some other such experience. If Harry is meaning to suggest that right now he is literally enjoying a past event, it intimates some spooky direct access to that past event. As this is generally impossible, it is generally impossible to literally enjoy past states of affairs.[24] The same though is true of present states of affairs: the only way we enjoy the world, as **(ENJ)** entails, is via our experiences of it.

On the other hand, I can be pleased that p without feeling any

---

24Though representations of representations make this more complicated. Suppose I am watching a video tape of the Mets winning the 1986 World Series. It is fair

pleasure. I am still pleased that I finished my first marathon in 3:13, just as pleased as I was a year ago and just as pleased as I will be in a year. I have not been feeling pleasure about the fact for that whole time, though (at least not pleasure due to my marathon time). I merely have a certain judgment with respect to my marathon time. 'Pleased that' is not, then, the appropriate attitude to use in defining pleasure because having the attitude does not, in its normal usage, entail having pleasure.

Moving on then. Further evidence that the object of enjoyment's desire is an experience comes from the interchangeability of 'enjoy **X**' and 'enjoy the experience of **X**.' How was the movie? "I enjoyed it," and "I enjoyed the experience," have (generally) identical import.[25] Neither require that you think the movie was good (for instance, I enjoyed the relatively mediocre Troy); both require that you think your experience of the movie was good. And the desire for the experience is more fundamental to enjoyment. If you discovered you had hallucinated the movie, that is, that there was an experience without any real-world object, it would still be true that you had enjoyed your experience (and the imaginary movie), though it might not have been the experience you thought it was. On the other hand, if the movie played, but you never went to it, it would be impossible for you to enjoy it.

Some types of enjoyment, though, seem to require veridical experiences. If this is true, you might think the hallucination response was inadequate. Harry is enjoying watching his daughter Sally

---

usage to say I am enjoying the Mets winning the World Series. It is also fair usage to say I am enjoying a tape of the Mets winning. In addition, it is legitimate to say I am enjoying my experience of the tape of the Mets winning (or my experience of the Mets winning). This is because enjoy x and enjoy an experience of x are generally synonymous.

25Sometimes, we say we enjoyed the *experience* of **X** rather than that we enjoyed **X** to emphasize what we did *not* enjoy, to emphasize that we enjoyed some other aspect of our experience that was not due to **X**. I didn't really enjoy the play, but I enjoyed the experience of going to the play and dressing up, and seeing everyone else dressed up, and sitting in the cool theatre etc… This usage does not undermine my point, though. Clearly, in such cases, I am not really enjoying my experience *of the play*, rather I am enjoying a broader experience of which the play is a part.

graduate from college. If he were to find out that she is not actually graduating, that she has yet to finish a required math class and has been allowed to walk in procession only conditionally, his enjoyment would disappear. This suggests that his enjoyment–relevant desires are (a) either directed at aspects of the world independent of his experiences (the actual graduation) or (b) directed at extrinsic properties of his experience (that they are veridical). Either could constitute a counterexample to (ENJ).

With respect to (a), no one would doubt that the states of affairs we enjoy are often themselves states of affairs we desire. This doesn't mean that the enjoyment itself is constituted by those desires (though, of course, the experience of satisfying desires about the external world are often part of the experience that is the object of the appropriate desire of enjoyment). We can see this because Harry may never find out that his daughter is not graduating. His desire for the world to be a certain way is not satisfied; nonetheless, he enjoys an experience he mistakes for the world turning out the way he wanted. And why does he enjoy this experience? Because his desire for the experience is satisfied. It cannot be necessary for enjoyment that certain external world states of affairs are actual.

One might think this reply does not dismiss objection (b) that Harry desires the experience of his daughter graduating for a property or properties extrinsic to that experience, namely, its being veridical. In reply, note that most (if not all) of our experiences are defined by their intensionality.[26] Harry is having an experience, E, an experience that is essentially of his daughter graduating. When Harry learns that his daughter is not actually graduating, he ceases to have experience E. It is not the case that he continues to have one and the same experience E but now realizes it has different relational properties than he thought and, hence, doesn't enjoy it. Intrinsic to experience E was the intension that it was of his daughter graduating. The experience of his daughter walking in procession without

---

26This is not to say that all experiences are intensional nor that all experiences that are the object of pleasure are intensional. If they are not intensional, though, it no longer makes sense to require of them that they are veridical. Edwards [1979, 87]

graduating is an entirely different — though, of course, importantly similar — experience. Both experiences are largely constituted by sensations of his daughter walking in a graduation procession; indeed, depending on your views of sense data, you might think that the sensory aspects of the experiences are identical. Nonetheless, the experiences are intrinsically different. This intrinsic difference is due to their intensional differences. Intuitively, Harry did not enjoy his daughter's graduation if (1) she graduated but he didn't experience it; (2) she was graduating and he knew she was graduating, but this knowledge was pushed out of consciousness because he had an experience of his daughter failing to graduate (say he is consumed by paranoia that she is fooling him); or (3) he had an experience partly constituted by sensations that would also make up the experience of his daughter graduating, but he knew she was not graduating and hence had the experience of his daughter walking in procession without graduating. The reasons these all fail to be enjoyment is because in each of these cases Harry failed to have an experience of **P** and enjoyment of **P** requires an experience of **P**.

4.2.2.2 Move on to the second worry about **(ENJ)**. Recently Fred Feldman has argued for an attitudinal view of pleasure in which the attitude of enjoyment is left unanalyzed.[27] Feldman is certain that pleasure and desire can come apart. He thinks both that one could concurrently desire **X** for reasons intrinsic to **X** without enjoying it and that one could enjoy **X** without concurrently desiring **X** for reasons intrinsic to **X**. [28] Start with the first. Feldman:

> Suppose many years ago, Bob tasted a certain exotic beer. It had a very unusual taste that he really enjoyed. Then, for many years, he could not find anymore of that beer. He kept looking, though, because he really wanted to experience that taste again. Suppose at last he finds some more of the beer and he goes for it. He is right now drinking the beer and

---

27Feldman's attitude seems to be 'pleased that...' I think this is slightly different than enjoy and not the appropriate attitude to use in evaluating pleasure. [2004]
28Feldman, [2005]

paying careful attention to its taste. Alas, it does nothing for him. Though the beer tastes as he thought it would taste, he simply does not enjoy it… for a moment Bob was intrinsically desiring the taste of the beer, but not enjoying it.[29]

Shortly, thereafter, Bob stops drinking the beer. Feldman's story as a whole is, of course, quite plausible. Things like this happen all the time. But is Feldman's description of what takes place the best? Can I capture the situation with **(ENJ)**? Feldman's first fishy move is at "though the beer tastes as he thought it would taste…" It is a notable feature of our imaginative skills that, though powerful, they are not equal to our perceptual ones. Look out the window then close your eyes. How many leaves are on the trees, what color are they, what color is the hat of the pedestrian going by? Our imaginative memory is a thin sheet to the body underneath that was the original perception. Taste memories are among the most difficult to bring to mind. It is not sufficient for Bob's enjoyment that he be desiring something that refers to the particular taste he is having. That desire might turn out to be for an extrinsic feature of the experience. Suppose Harry desires to have the exact sensory experience he had last Friday at 2 pm, but he can't remember what experience he had last Friday; he is unaware of the intrinsic features of his Friday experience. Suppose he was drinking red rooibos tea at 2 pm last Friday. Suppose Harry is also drinking red rooibos tea now. Harry's desire to be having the experience that he was having last week does not entail that Harry is enjoying the tea now. Why? Because the fact that he had the experience at 2 pm last Friday is an extrinsic feature of that sensory experience; he doesn't even know that the two sensory experiences are one and the same. To enjoy the tea, Harry needs, while drinking the tea, to desire some intrinsic feature of this experience of the tea.

Given our earlier discussion, there are two broad classes of intrinsic features available for Harry to enjoy here. Most commonly, we would say he needs to desire some portion of the distinctive and

---

29Feldman, [2005, 18]

detailed qualitative character of the taste of the tea. If this is the account of the intrinsic feature Harry desires, I take it Harry is enjoying the taste of the tea. The other option is that Harry intrinsically desires an experience of the same intensional character,[30] namely, an experience of himself drinking the tea. If this is the account of the intrinsic features, I take it Harry is enjoying his drinking of the tea. Desires for either of these feature types would mean that Harry was enjoying some aspect of the state of affairs that is Harry drinking red rooibos tea.

So, which intrinsic desire does Feldman intend to give Bob? I think Feldman intends the first, that Bob intrinsically desires the particular taste of the beer. Let's quickly dismiss the second option, then. Suppose Bob just desires the experience of himself drinking this beer at this time in this way, independent of the particular qualities of the taste. Perhaps the experience of being here drinking this beer is a culminating experience, the end of a long search (similar to Harry at his daughter's graduation). In such a case, Bob *would* enjoy the drinking of his beer even though he does not enjoy the taste because he intrinsically desires an experience of himself drinking that beer. If this were Bob's desire, we would expect Bob -- finally having his goal in hand -- to continue drinking his beer. This is not what happens, though, presumably, because he doesn't like the taste. We can conclude, then, that Bob's desires as he begins drinking the beer are not merely about drinking the beer and achieving his goal, but about having certain taste sensations.

So, suppose Bob desires a taste of a detailed and unique qualitative character, call it **T**. Upon drinking the beer, Bob has the experience **T**, but, immediately, decides he does not want to continue having experience **T**. What explanation can one give for Bob's ceasing to desire **T** upon tasting it? Given that Bob learns nothing new upon tasting the beer ("the beer tastes as he thought it would taste"), it is odd, perhaps inexplicable, that his desire for **T** disappears so readily.

30This is not to say that taste sensations do not have intensional character; that is a debate I sidestep. If you think they do, then the distinction I make above is between two different aspects of the intensional character of Harry's experience.

Perhaps, Feldman will tell us that the desire **T** disappears because Bob finds out that he isn't enjoying **T**. If this true, though, then, contra Feldman's description, Bob *didn't* desire **T** for intrinsic reasons of **T** but because **T** might bring enjoyment which is an extrinsic feature of **T** (on most anyone's account of enjoyment).

A natural description of what happens to Bob is that he discovered rather quickly that he didn't desire **T**. Bob's experience was not the one he thought it was going to be. He was not capable of fully imagining **T** beforehand. He inferred from extrinsic properties of his past experience of the beer, namely his once having enjoyed it, that he still wanted that precise sensory experience. Evidently, he was wrong. We do this all the time. We hope something will please as much as we remember it pleasing us. Often, they don't. I will go so far as to say that the desires for particular qualitative experiences that we have before we have the experiences are almost never the same desires we have while undergoing those same experiences. Our concurrent desires have a set of indexical referents unavailable to us until the experience is happening. When I am fully enjoying **E**, I am wanting *that* and *that* and *that*, those particular qualitative aspects of the experience before me now, aspects that it would be almost impossible to enumerate or fully imagine afterward. The best explanation, then, for the common experience of wanting an experience of type **F**, but failing to enjoy token experience **X** of type **F** is that the token experience failed, upon being experienced, to be what one wanted, either because it was different from what remembered or because one 'remembered' it only via extrinsic properties of the experience.

I recap. Bob has made a point of telling himself he will get enjoyment from the beer. On Feldman's description he knows exactly what he will be getting. There must be some explanation for why, after finally getting it, he doesn't want it anymore. Feldman's description, though, gives no explanation. The best explanation is that the experience wasn't what he thought it would be, or that he hadn't really known what the experience would be. The fact is that if Bob is not enjoying his drinking of the beer, he will stop drinking it (all things being equal). **(ENJ)** gives us an explanation for this: when Bob's enjoyment disappears, his intrinsic desires disappear.

A more compelling counterexample to **(ENJ)** would demonstrate Bob's intrinsic desire for **T**; for instance, a case in which Bob continues over a period of time to claim to want the beer for its intrinsic properties all the while asserting that he is not enjoying it would be more problematic for **(ENJ)**. Is this possible? Elsewhere Feldman has considered and dismissed cases that could be turned into such an objection. Consider

> "Suppose a certain chef is trying to make some food taste a certain way. Suppose that chef himself does not find this taste.... pleasant, but he knows that others will enjoy it."[31]

Suppose now that the chef tastes the food. If he has achieved the desired taste, he will be experiencing it while desiring it; yet, he will not enjoy the taste. Suppose it is difficult to maintain the taste throughout the cooking process, and so he must continue to taste the food. He will continue to desire the precise taste he is experiencing, he will continue tasting it, yet never will he enjoy it. After all, he doesn't even like it. Yet he did desire to have this experience, and his desire is intimately associated with features intrinsic to the taste; that is, he wanted to taste precisely the taste he is tasting and it is the fact that it is precisely that taste that makes him desire it. This means, by **(ENJ)**, he is taking pleasure in the taste; and, therefore, the taste is a pleasure. We've already established, though, the taste isn't a pleasure for the chef. Contradiction. Feldman rejects such objections; as do I: despite appearances the chef doesn't intrinsically desire the taste. Rather, the chef desires the taste because of the knowledge it will bring, namely that the taste will make his customers happy. And, so, if the chef is enjoying anything, it is not the taste itself, but a bit of knowledge that the taste gives him. Or, alternatively, he doesn't desire the taste because of the taste's intrinsic features; he desires the pleasure the taste will bring to others. The taste itself is instrumentally valuable because it gives him that knowledge or because it

---

31 [Feldman, 1997: 463]

pleases his guests. But, then, (ENJ) does not entail that the taste is a pleasure for the chef and there is no contradiction.

What about the other direction of (ENJ)? Does enjoying **X** entail intrinsically desiring **X**? Feldman thinks one can experience a genuine pleasure with no desire for that pleasure.

Feldman thinks he can imagine an anti-hedonist who has such strong desires against having pleasurable sensations that when feeling a sensory pleasure he responds,

> "Yes, I can feel it. It does feel pleasant. It is an enjoyable feeling. But I wish it would stop. Not because of consequences or accompaniments, but just for its own sake. I prefer not to have such feelings."

This comment is, on its face, compatible with all I've said until now. "I wish it would stop," does not entail that the anti-hedonist doesn't feel any desire for it. We often want things that we desire to stop. It has been relatively uncontroversial since Plato that one can have a desire for **X** and a desire for not **X** at one and the same time. This means that one can enjoy **X** while having intrinsic desires for not **X**. In such a case, to borrow a phrase from Tal Brewer, one's enjoyment will not be wholehearted, but it will still be enjoyment.[32] I may want the drink for its coolness, but not for its sweetness; hence, I may enjoy the drink even while not intrinsically desiring certain of its qualitative aspects.

Feldman, though, says this person has a complete absence of desires for the sensation and yet it is pleasurable to this person. What can convince us that such a state is possible? What evidence do we have that one can feel the pleasure without any desire whatsoever? None that I can see. A perfectly good explanation of such a character is that he recognizes he is feeling intrinsic desire for a sensation, and, for other reasons, he has decided he doesn't desire to feel such desires. This second desire is stronger than the first. Furthermore, there is good reason to think this person does not have an intrinsic

---

32Who borrowed it from Ryle. Brewer [2003]

desire to be out of his state of pleasure. He seems not to want the pleasure because it is among the pleasures (among 'such feelings'), but being a pleasure is, as I've defined it, an extrinsic aspect of a sensation (though not necessarily of an experience as a whole).

What Feldman needs is a case where a person feels pleasure, and they want the pleasure to stop for no exterior reason; or a case in which a person feels no pull toward the pleasure and would do nothing to continue the experience, not because they have some other philosophy that motivates them to avoid pleasure, but just because the pleasure itself brings about no motivation. The problem with cases like the one Feldman raises is that there is another plausible desire floating around to explain the aversion to pleasure. There is no reason to go the next step and assert that there is no desire for the pleasure. The anti-hedonist, or an extreme self-loather, or an extreme masochist (who wants pain unmixed with any pleasure) are all defined by other desires that can easily be brought to bear in an explanation of the psychological aversion to a particular pleasing experience. What Feldman needs does not seem available.

(Appropriate counterexamples of this sort may be available for similar definitions of pain, though. Aspirin and anti-inflammatories make pain sensations go away. Morphine and other similar drugs, on the other hand, reduce the aversion to pain without reducing the intensity of the pain sensations. This suggests that the motivation and the sensation of pain can come apart. Though such considerations are not conclusive, they genuinely make one wonder about an attitudinal analysis of pain in the way that Feldman's examples do not for pleasure. Why? Because there is no reason to think that morphine motivates one to want pain. There is no obvious set of conflicting desires in the pain case in the way there was for Feldman's pleasure cases.)

I consider one last argument against defining enjoyment in terms of desire. Feldman takes this puzzle from Sidgwick.[33] Consider Feldman's Bob again. He's finally found a beer he likes and is enjoying it. Someone asks him why he wants to experience the taste

---

33Feldman [2005, 18-19]

of the beer. Bob says he wants to experience the taste because it is pleasurable. Surely this is a natural response, similar to responses we've all made. Unfortunately, it is problematic for (ENJ) because the property of being a pleasure is extrinsic to the taste. If Bob's only desire for the beer is its being a pleasure, it wouldn't, by (ENJ), even be a pleasure.

Once again, in reply, there is no reason to think that the only desire Bob has with respect to the beer is the desire for pleasure. Perhaps the only reason Bob wants to taste the beer before he drinks is because he believes it will be a pleasure. Nonetheless, when Bob tastes the beer, it will be, if he is right, a pleasure. If my analysis is correct, he will now intrinsically desire the taste; it will, by (ENJ*), now seem good to him. He may continue to desire the seeming it-self, of course. The fact that Bob desires it for its pleasurableness, though, does not on its own show that Bob does not desire it for any of its intrinsic aspects. Indeed, a natural way to refer to the fact that one is desiring T for intrinsic properties of T is to call it pleasure. If one asks why Bob continues to drink the beer, he can truthfully say, "Because it is a pleasure." If it were not a pleasure, he would not intrinsically desire the taste, and, so, would cease to drink, as he had in the earlier example. Such an explanation of Bob's talk, though, is entirely compatible with my account of pleasure. I would like to add that though there may be times we desire some future experi-ence solely because we think it will be a pleasure, that is far from the norm. There are a thousand things that give Bob pleasure, yet, right now, he wants this particular beer. That suggests he is aiming not only for pleasure but for at least some aspect of the particular expe-riences that will bring him that pleasure, even before he has those experiences.

4.2.2.3 Irwin Goldstein responds to definitions such as I've given with the following:

> There clearly is some limit on the sensation that can be an
> itch or a pain. As pleasure is connected with a desire to seek
> experience, so an itch is connected with a desire to scratch.

But not just any sensation could be an itch with the mere addition of a desire to scratch the area. Nor could just any sensation be a pain. Brush your cheek lightly with your finger and you feel a light sensation which is neither pleasant nor unpleasant. That sensation would never be an intense pain, nor even a mild pain, whatever desire you might introduce.[34]

First note that there is a difference between claiming there are limitations to what can count as a pleasure and claiming that there is a particular sensation that is the pleasure sensation. Nevertheless, if there are limitations on what can count as a pleasure, if the above is true with respect to pleasure, if it is true that not all sensations can be pleasures, then there is a serious objection to defining the pleasures as just those experiences we take pleasure in.[35] But, I claim, that Goldstein is just wrong with respect to the pleasures. All experiences could be under some circumstances pleasurable unless there is something about an experience that makes it impossible to concurrently desire it for reasons intrinsic to it.[36] "I found out I'd won (or lost), what a pleasure!" "He brushed my cheek gently (or roughly), what a pleasure!" "She read me the whole book (or didn't), what a pleasure!" As there is nothing in the vast perversity of human experience that can't be enjoyed, there is no experience that can't be a pleasure.

Goldstein does seem to be right that there is a limitation on what could count as a pain. We can suffer from nausea, for instance, but it is clear to me that nausea – though unpleasant, though a cause of

---

34[Goldstein, 1980: 351]

35There are responses. Say some set of sensations S (perhaps pains) can't be pleasures. This need not be an indictment of our definition if they can't be for the reason that they can't be intrinsically desired. One might think that intrinsically bad experiences couldn't be pleasures or one might argue that there are certain contingent features of our biology that makes it impossible for us to desire S while experiencing S.

36Leave to the side, once more, pain and suffering. It may be we can't take pleasure in pain and so pain can't be a pleasure. Fine, as long as the reason we can't take pleasure in pain is because we can't concurrently desire pain for reasons intrinsic to the pain. If this is true, then pain and suffering do not constitute counterexamples to our definition. On the other hand, if they *can* be concurrently desired for intrinsic reasons than I have no problem accepting them as possible pleasures.

suffering – is not a pain. I return to this when I attempt an analysis of 'displeasurable' sensations. (Also, it's not clear to me that Goldstein's claim that 'mild' sensations can't become intense pains is true. I have in mind examples in the vein of Chinese water torture in which a droplet of water on the forehead becomes a torment. I leave that for later.)

4.2.2.4 One might also object that there is a sensation that is always pleasurable, always motivational, namely orgasm. If this is true, then maybe there is a sensation that is the pleasure sensation, namely, the sensation(s) of orgasm. Assume, then, that the experience of orgasm is an experience that we must take pleasure in. What conclusions should we draw from this? It is not a counterexample to the definition of pleasure given because it is not the case that the other pleasures – even the purely physical ones – have a bit of orgasm in them. As a class, the pleasures cannot be defined by a sensation. One might claim that it is orgasm and not pleasure that is a response to Mackie. But it is rather implausible to assume that the experience of orgasm is the only intrinsic good. It is possible, I presume, to live a life good to some extent – if not to a great extent – without any orgasm at all. Is there another explanation for why all desire orgasm, an error theory as it were? If orgasm is always pleasurable, I suggest this is due to contingent features of human biology/psychology. There are excellent evolutionary reasons to think that we would be built in such a way that we would always desire orgasm. After all one of evolution's main 'purposes' is to get us to reproduce. So why not make it always seem desirable? And so even if orgasm is always pleasurable, it is neither a counterexample to the definition of pleasure given above, nor is it an objection to the theory of the good being presented.

(On the other hand, I personally don't have the intuition that orgasm must be pleasurable. It seems possible to me to imagine the sensations of orgasm without any concurrent desire for them, without anything good about the experience at all. In informal polls I have conducted, I haven't found anyone with strong intuitions in the other direction. Imagine, for instance, an orgasm that doesn't stop. This, some of us feel, would become painful.)

4.2.3 Response to the Hedonist

I am now in a position to respond to the hedonist. Begin with the hedonist claim that pleasure is intrinsically motivational.

If **(PLE)** is right, the sensations that are the pleasures are *not* intrinsically motivational. Pleasures are just whatever we happen to be experiencing when we are enjoying something. The fact that qualitatively identical sensations can be both enjoyed and loathed establishes that the pleasures are not intrinsically motivational. If kung pao tofu is a pleasure at the beginning of the meal, less of a pleasure in the middle of a meal and not a pleasure at all by the end of the meal, then the taste of kung pao tofu is not intrinsically desirable. There is no doubt that when we are taking pleasure in kung pao tofu, the taste of kung pao tofu appears to be the kind of thing that is intrinsically motivational. That's what it is to take pleasure in something, to desire it for its intrinsic properties. But this appearance is clearly mistaken in most cases.

So, suppose the hedonic thesis must be, as Fred Feldman points out, about the good in enjoying the pleasures, about the good of the experience of taking pleasure in **X**, and not the good of **X** itself.[37] So is enjoying **X** an intrinsically motivational state? Yes, in one sense. Enjoyment is intrinsically motivational in precisely the same sense that desires are intrinsically motivational. Enjoyment of **X** is a desire and so to be enjoying **X** is to be motivated.

Unfortunately, this isn't the sense of intrinsically motivational required by Mackie. To be intrinsically motivational is to have intrinsic features that *cause* motivation, not to intrinsically *be* a motivation. To be intrinsically motivational is a property similar to being red. If an object is red and we look at it, we see red (absent defeaters).

37[Feldman, 1997]

If **X** is intrinsically motivational, the mere contemplation or experience of **X** makes one want **X** to some degree (again, absent defeaters). This must be right; otherwise, all desires would be good and we would have an easy answer to antirealists like Mackie. Clearly, though, Mackie isn't doubting that we can be motivated at all.

The experience of enjoying **X** is not intrinsically motivational in the appropriate sense. We desire to take pleasure in good things, but not in bad or worthless things. Imagine taking pleasure in the sound of random dial tones in pay phones around town. Does the thought of this just make you want to do it? Or is there anything intrinsically desirable about taking pleasure in the torture of children? If you were taking pleasure in torture, you would find the experience desirable, but does the thought of taking pleasure in torture now just make you want to do it? In general, the thought of enjoying **X** does not make me want to enjoy **X**. **X** may be bad or worthless. Though I like enjoyment, I want my enjoyment to be of at least somewhat good things. I feel no motivation to take pleasure in torture.

If there is still some part of us that thinks there's something desirable about the dial-tone listening and the torture, I suggest we are still thinking about the pleasure. We might feel that if we really are going to get some pleasure from these things than there is at least some pleasure from these things than there is at least some reason to want to do them. There may be many other reasons not to do those things, of course, but the pleasure gives us some reason. We have this feeling for one of two reasons: either 1) we still think that the pleasures themselves are intrinsically motivational – that is, we think that taking pleasure in listening to dial tones is intrinsically desirable because pleasure is intrinsically desirable and is always present when we are taking pleasure in things; or 2) we think that we should desire that which we believe is good and we assume that the pleasures are good; and so we have a reason to desire taking pleasure in dial tones because that would entail we have something good, namely, pleasure.

I have already shown that (1) is false. The pleasures are not intrinsically desirable. And putting to the side the fact that (2) is begging the question, it is still not the proper understanding of intrinsically desirable. If taking pleasure in **X** is desirable if and only if we believe that **X** is good, then it is not intrinsically desirable. The good, because of Humean considerations, must be motivational all on its own, independently of our beliefs about it. This is what Mackie thinks is so odd about the good, and this is what pleasure had seemed to do for the realist.

Let's move the discussion, now, away from motivations to perceptions of value. The intuitions are strong that pleasure is good. Nothing said so far has changed the fact the pleasures seem good. They do.

I suggest now that the analysis of pleasure gives us good reason to doubt that these seemings are evidentiary. Of course, I say, we have the intuition that pleasure is good; of course, we all experience pleasure as good. That is what pleasure is. We would expect to see pleasure this way – independently of whether the pleasures are good or not. This is because intrinsic to what it is to enjoy **X** is that **X** seems good; and, therefore, intrinsic to what it is for **X** to be a pleasure is that **X** seems good. But the fact that it is analytic to a pleasure that it appear good, does not in itself give us a good reason to think that the pleasures, as a class, are good. The pleasures would seem good whether they were or not.

Perceptions of value are desires and we know that we desire the pleasures only under certain conditions. This means that we have good reason to doubt our perceptions of value with respect to the pleasures. The pleasures seem good if we are taking pleasure in them, but for the large majority of the pleasures, if not all, this perception is contingent on the time and person who is experiencing the pleasure. You taste the kung pao tofu and do not perceive it as good; I taste it and, right now, I do perceive it as good. Later, when I am full, I no longer perceive it as good either. It is clear that our perceptions of value with respect to the pleasures are not reliable.[38]

What about our intuitions with respect to enjoying **X**? Do we see enjoyment as intrinsically valuable? Even if the answer to this

---

38 There is another logical option here, of course. It could be that the pleasures *are* good and that our perceptions of value are *only* accurate when we are enjoying something. But

question were 'yes,' we would have good reason to worry that these perceptions are parasitic on our perceptions that the pleasures are good. And as we have established that those perceptions are unreliable, we would have good reason to think that our perception with respect to the enjoyment would be unreliable. Moreover, we don't see taking pleasure in an arbitrary **X** as good. Taking pleasure in torture, for instance, is not good.[39] In general, we think one should take pleasure in things worthy of pleasure. But if this is true, then enjoyment is not, as a rule, intrinsically good. It will depend on what one is taking pleasure in.

One might respond by claiming that enjoyment in bad things is bad all things considered, but that there is still some good in taking pleasure in **X**, namely, the pleasure (in a response similar to the one we gave to Kant). This response relies again, I think, on our now debunked intuition that there is something good about the sensation of pleasure. We can't use that type of response as there is no pleasure sensation and the sensations that are the pleasures are not intrinsically good. Now there is nothing in the taking-of-pleasure that can retain the value. The pleasures are not necessarily good and desires are not necessarily good (again: there is nothing good about desiring to experience bad things). Nor is there anything good about perceiving good things as bad. But this means that our intuitions give us little to no reason to think that pleasure or taking-pleasure-in **X** are intrinsically good. And once we convince ourselves that we have no real reason to think that enjoying **X** is intrinsically good, we lose all reason to think enjoying **X** as intrinsically desirable.

One might argue that it is not the desiring of pleasure that gives enjoyment its intrinsic value, but desire satisfaction. It is true that when one experiences a pleasure, one is in a state of continuous desire-satisfaction. This is an interesting twist on the more commonly accepted connection between pleasure and desire-satisfac-

---

this is hardly credible. Any experience or sensation can be the object of pleasure, and any pleasure can seem pleasing to any degree. We would be forced to accept, then, that all sensations are good to an arbitrary degree.

39Read [Zimmerman, 1980] for a detailed exploration of the relation between the good of pleasure and the good of the object of pleasure.

tion. It is widely assumed, I think, that a large portion of the value of desire-satisfaction is due to the fact that it is generally pleasing. On this account, though, pleasure is good because it is a case of desire-satisfaction. I am of the view, recall, that desire-satisfaction is of intrinsic value, but the amount of intrinsic value for a particular desire-satisfaction is proportional to the value of the thing desired. I just desired to write the phrase 'the thing desired.' That desire was satisfied, but I think we can all agree that the intrinsic value of that satisfaction was minimal. This is because, I suggest, typing 'the thing desired' is, on its own, minimally valuable. Furthermore, when I desire bad things, the satisfaction of those desires is minimally good (perhaps on some views, even, bad). Though the good of some enjoyment, namely enjoyment of the good, could possibly be explained by the value of desire-satisfaction, any intrinsic value that other enjoyments have must be due to other reasons. I hope I've shown, though, that there are no other reasons.

There are important instrumental reasons to find pleasure valuable. In general, pleasure relaxes us and help us to perform better. In general, the presence of pleasure reduces 'narrowing' emotional states like fear and anger and hate. On the whole, enjoying **X** is an attitude of openness to **X** and allows us to fully engage with the richness of whatever experience we are having. No matter how true these claims are – I think they are generally true – all of these give only instrumental, and contingent, value to pleasure.

The hedonist response to Mackie, then, does not hold up. Pleasure is not intrinsically motivational and the best explanation for the wide agreement that pleasure is a good is not that the pleasure is actually a good, but that pleasures are just analytically the kind of things that seem good, whether they are or not.

4.3 The Good of Pleasure

4.3.1 Enjoying the Good

Because the thesis of these past sections may seem severely revisionary, I want to conclude by briefly noting that a significant number of our common sense beliefs about the value of pleasure are true and their truth is explicable by (ENJ) and the present value theory. The most important of these is the intuition that enjoying good things is good. Nothing I have said to this point has given us any reason to doubt this. Let me suggest that there is some initial plausibility to the claim that pleasure in the good is more than just instrumentally valuable even if pleasure *qua* pleasure is not intrinsically valuable, and even if richness is not the one good. First, enjoyment is a type of appreciation and one of the things the good should motivate in us is an appreciation of it. To appreciate the good is appropriate; appreciation of the good is good in and of itself. Another way of putting this: it should be good to contemplate the good, as Plato would say, and enjoyment of **X** is a type of contemplation of **X**. Second, enjoying the good is to experience the good as good, is for the good to seem good to us, and this is an accurate perception. If there is intrinsic value associated with epistemic norms as most would think, then this enjoyment will be good because it is a good perception. Finally, enjoying a good thing is the satisfaction of a desire for a good thing. If desire-satisfaction is good proportional to the value of the object of the desire, then enjoyment in the good is good proportional to the value of the thing enjoyed. This seems right. If all of this is true, then the way many of us try to bring value into our life is backwards. Rather than making one's life good by adding pleasure to it, one should bring pleasure into one's life as a way of recognizing the good that is already there.[40] Pleasure is a

---

40 Aristotle says we remember that pleasure is merely the crown of the good life. Aristotle

symptom of the good life.

And, of course, all those explanations of the value of pleasure in the good are consistent with the present value theory. I argued in Chapter 1 that if X is a rich object, then an experience E that is full awareness of X is also rich. This is for two reasons: (1) E is isomorphic to X and therefore as richly structured as X and, so, is more or less equivalently valuable to X and (2) the rich causal perceptual connections between X and the experience is the unification of two very different types of thing to form a third rich object: the genuine awareness of X. So, on the theory that richness is the good, there is a set of experiences that are intrinsically good, namely deep experiences of good things. So, if the experience you are taking pleasure in is a deep experience of a rich object, that pleasure is good. (Moreover, unlike the pleasures as a class, these experiences will consistently be experienced as good under normal epistemological conditions. If you do see the richness in the Mona Lisa – the unification of color and setting and character and expression – you will, under normal circumstances, see it as good. If you do see the richness in a person – the unification of his experiences into a set of beliefs and desires, into a perspective on the world, his reasons for being the way that he is – you will, under normal circumstances, see him as good.[41])

It is interesting to note that a hedonist even of a very restricted type can't explain the fact that enjoyment in the good is intrinsically valuable. Assume that taking pleasure in good things is the only intrinsic good. Look at some arbitrary experience of enjoying X. How are we to decide if this is good or not? We must first decide whether X is a good. X is good if and only if it is an experience of taking pleasure in some Y and Y is good. But this is identical to our original question and so leads to a regress. This regress is vicious. Nothing would turn out to be good on this theory of value.

Finally, I would like to tie in the present analysis to my earlier analysis of love. Unsurprisingly, we find that love and pleasure are intimately connected, Recall that conscious loving consists of

---

and T. Irwin (1985). Nicomachean ethics. Indianapolis, Ind., Hackett Pub. Co

41 Barring, as usual, any instrumental 'bads' caused by the Mona Lisa or the person.

two desires: the desire for the other and the desire to experience the other. And an immediate consequence of this is that all conscious loving is partly constituted by enjoying the other. If we are loving the other and are consciously experiencing the other (or experiencing memories of the other), we have a desire to continue that experience; this desire is the taking of pleasure in the experience of the other. And when we have the best love, when we have deep love, we are taking pleasure in our experience of a great good, of a rich object. So, when we are enjoying the right kind of objects with the right kind of awareness, we are loving it, and this is, according to theory and sense, a great good.

4.3.2 Mill's Higher and Lower Pleasures

"The great source of pleasure is variety." Samuel Johnson

Let's return now to a worry I mentioned earlier. If our desires are so unreliable with respect to the pleasures, what reason do we have to trust them as the grounding of our value theory? One quick reply is that they aren't that unreliable outside of the pleasures. In general, we desire rich things. I gave a more detailed answer in Chapter 1. I suggested several reasons why our desires might fail to be accurate, several reasons that applied similarly to normal perception. Those reasons could be put into two classes: failure due to insufficient perceptual information and failure due to spurious information.

First, if our desires do not arise from an accurate or full sensory awareness (or intellectual awareness or memory) of the object, the value judgments we draw with respect to the object are unreliable. Someone shows me the Mona Lisa, but I am seriously distracted thinking about a letter I just received from my lover. It is unlikely if not impossible (given the meaning of 'distracted') that I will have a full awareness of the Mona Lisa, and so when I claim that the Mona Lisa is mediocre, my claim is based in insufficient data. This first reason is an explanation of why we might fail to see good when it is there.

Second, desires can arise not from perception of an object, but for internal reasons that have nothing to do with the object. This is analogous to certain failures of normal perception. If my blood pressure drops and I 'see red,' this is not due to any feature of the external world, but due to the accidents of my own biology/psychology. If pregnant Juliet suddenly desires the taste of pickles, we presume that this is not because of some sudden increase in the value of pickles, or her sudden awareness of their true value, but because of an internal change in her biology which makes her have such a desire.[42] This second reason why desires might be inaccurate explains why we might see good where there isn't any (or bad where there isn't any).

But this second explanation seems to explain why the simple pleasures – those pleasures that appeared to be such powerful counterexamples to our theory of the good – appear good even when they are not. It is when we are hungry that kung pao tofu tastes good. When we are full, it ceases to taste good.[43] It is when we are sexually aroused that orgasm seems desirable. Afterwards, some of us just want sleep. The simple pleasures as a whole serve simple bodily or psychological 'needs.' These needs distort our perception of the value of the object of these needs. The pleasures that are actually good, such as the pleasure we take in a loved one or good art or a mountain, arise due to awareness of a good object. It is the thing itself that makes us want to experience it.

This distinction gives us a fairly good method for defending a version of J. S. Mill's much maligned[44] distinction between the higher and the lower pleasures.

Mill says,

---

42 Though sometimes this may be due to the increased value of her eating pickles for the specific nutrients pickles provide.

43 Sometimes we keep eating something even if we are full because it tastes so good. It is interesting to note that slow eaters have this happen a lot less often. It takes time for the body's signals to get to the brain. We can feel fullness in the stomach without feeling psychological fullness.

44 C.D. Broad says that Mill "was so confused that he probably did not himself know precisely what he meant." [Broad, 1967: 232]

"Of two pleasures, if there be one to which all or almost all who have experience of both give a decided preference, irrespective of any feeling of moral obligation to prefer it, that is the more desirable pleasure. If one of the two is, by those who are competently acquainted with both, placed so far above the other that they prefer it, even though knowing it to be attended with a greater amount of discontent, and would not resign it for any quantity of the other pleasure which their nature is capable of, we are justified in ascribing to the preferred enjoyment a superiority in quality, so far outweighing quantity as to render it, in comparison, of small account."[45]

There are (at least) two qualitatively different kinds of pleasure, Mill suggests. Call these the higher and lower pleasures. The higher pleasures are always better than the lower ones. Among the lower pleasures are all of the physical pleasures we get from such things as eating, drinking, and sex. Among the higher pleasures are all the mental pleasures, "the pleasures of the intellect, of the feelings and imagination, and of the moral sentiments,"[46] as well as aesthetic pleasures and the feelings of achievement.[47]

This is a strange claim for an avowed hedonist to make. How could it be that one pleasure is better than another even if it is "attended by a greater amount of discontent?" If discontent is an amount of displeasure, then if lower pleasure **L** is less in discontent than higher pleasure **H**, it is greater in pleasure than **H**. If pleasure is the only good, then we should conclude that lower pleasure **L** is better. Mill concludes the opposite. He argues that certain pleasures, the higher pleasures, differ in quality from the lower, and this quality makes the higher pleasures superior to the lower ones. This is an odd form of hedonism, a kind of pluralistic hedonism; it's a theory according to which only measures of pleasure are good, but there are two measures (at least) not one. The more intense a pleasure is, the better it is; and the higher in quality a pleasure is, the better it is. Most hedonists find this very odd.

45[Mill, 1971: 19]

46[Mill, 1971: 17]

47[Feagin, 1983]

I am not a hedonist, of course; I deny what Mill wanted most to defend – that pleasure is the sole intrinsic good. On the other hand, Mill was not making his distinction without reason; and, I suggest, it is a worthy insight into the structure of value. One I think the present theory can capture. I suggest that the higher pleasures are just those pleasures that are caused by accurate perceptions of the object of enjoyment. The lower pleasures are those pleasures that are caused by our own internal urgings, that is, by desire hallucinations. The higher pleasures are an accurate perception of goodness, the lower pleasures are a hallucination of goodness. Such a distinction largely maps onto Mill's differences between the physical and mental pleasures. It is eating, drinking, sex and so on that are most likely to be due to our own internal fluctuations and biases. The desire to listen to music, to write a poem, to solve a daunting mathematical puzzle, or the desire for true and deep love, or the desire for a walk through the woods, or the desire to engage in conversation – these desires are less likely to be caused by our biological nature or by deeply internalized psychological needs.

This is not to say that I think Mill was right to make a hard and fast distinction between the physical and the mental.[48] It is not really, in the end, what type of sensation or experience that we are taking pleasure in (physical or mental) that makes the distinction between higher and lower pleasures, but the causes of our taking pleasure in that sensation. Harry and Juliet can both enjoy the same gourmet meal, a fantastic creation of a Brilliant Chef, while doing it in two very different ways. Harry is starving and he enjoys the meal thoroughly as a satisfaction of that hunger, though he would have enjoyed anything with sufficient calories. Juliet, on the other hand, also enjoys the meal thoroughly, but her enjoyment is due to a deep awareness of the delicate taste structure constructed by the Brilliant

---

48Rem B. Edwards has argued that the distinction can be made by using Hospers' division between localized pleasures and non-localized pleasures [Edwards, 1975]. Recall that a localized pleasure is one where we can ask *where* it feels good. This distinction closely maps on to the one we are making – eating, drinking, sex, massage etc… are all localized sensations – but I think it is clearly wrong. Surely the pleasure we get from satisfying a drug addiction is non-localized, and surely it is a lower pleasure, both intuitively and for Mill. Our explanation captures this fact.

Chef. The same meal provides Juliet with a higher pleasure and Harry with a lower pleasure.[49] [50]

But on the whole the highest of the higher pleasures are due to deep awarenesses of rich objects. And it is to these pleasures that Mill suggests "all or almost who have knowledge of both [higher and lower] give decided preference." This claim is important because it suggests that even in the realm of pleasures, the richer pleasures are always preferred. Is this true? Somewhat surprisingly, it is.

There is developing quite a bit of psychological evidence that our favorite experiences are something like the richest ones. Mihaly Csikszentmihalyi has done extensive studies into what people consider to be the best experiences in their lives.[51] People do not rank orgasms as the best times in their life. They do not rank drug experiences as highest. Hot baths are not mentioned. Csikszentmihalyi says, "The best moments usually occur when a person's body or mind is stretched to its limits in a voluntary effort to accomplish something difficult and worthwhile. Optimal experience is thus something we make happen." This could be solving a proof, making art, writing a paper, having an involved conversation with a friend, reading a good book, falling in love. Osborne describes it well,

> "There is, I think, a special sort of pleasure or emotion, associated with heightened vitality and successful concentration, which is apt to accompany the unimpeded and intense acti-

---

49This is not to say, of course, that Juliet can't feel the pleasure of satisfying her hunger as well.

50Now, generally, there *is* good in satisfying hunger, and satisfying thirst. There is good in bringing our body into balance. So why aren't these higher pleasures? If the pleasure is the sensation of hunger satisfaction, then it is a higher pleasure – though its intensity may be distorted. But note that the sensation of hunger-satisfaction is different from pleasure in the taste of kung-pao tofu. To take pleasure in the taste of kung-pao tofu because of our internal hunger is a lower pleasure; the pleasure is not due to awareness of any rich features of the tofu, but due to our own internal 'imbalance.'

51He calls his method the 'Experience Sampling Method.' Subjects are fitted with an electronic pager and required to write down what they are doing and thinking and how they are feeling whenever the pager goes off. It would go off about eight times a day. [Csikszentmihalyi, 1990: 4] I think it is important to note the method because it reduces the likelihood that the respondents are ranking experiences higher that they think they *should* rank higher, and it also reduces the dependence on memory and after the fact evaluations.

vation of any skilled faculty whether it be a bodily function exercised in athletics, a trained gift of craftsmanship, reasoning in logic or mathematics, or the aesthetic faculty (whatever that faculty may be) in aesthetic appreciation. As there are times when we seem to be more alive than others, when we are pervaded by a general sense of pleasant well-being, so at times a particular faculty may be more 'alive,' more intensely engaged, than ordinarily and the concomitant pleasure is more intense and more specific."

The experiences in which we are most thoroughly engaged and which require the most of our attentive resources to experience are the ones that are the best in our life. But these are just what we've called the higher pleasures; this is, actually, just love for whatever we are experiencing. And, so, Mill was right. In general, we prefer the higher pleasures to the lower. We prefer to take pleasure in the actual richness of the world, the richness that requires us to use the full richness of our minds. "I enjoy my life twice as much as others," says Montaigne. "For the enjoyment in life is due to the lesser or greater attention we pay to it."[52]

These pleasures, the pleasures of greater attention, are great goods. Indeed, they may form a great portion of the good life. And, so, the central place that so many have given to pleasure is thoroughly understandable and to a large extent justified. But it is not true that the pleasures as a whole are intrinsically valuable. And the pleasures that are valuable are valuable in virtue of their richness.

52[Montaigne, 1965]

4.4 Suffering and Unpleasantness

Given our discussion of pleasure, it is appropriate to begin our discussion of pain and its relatives by suggesting parallel analyses of unpleasantness (pain is only a special class of unpleasantness) and suffering, and, afterward, look at the complications. I suggest that

(SUF) **P suffers X iff P concurrently desires not to have the experience of X for reasons intrinsic to the experience of X.**

If this is true, then the experience conjecture suggests that every event of suffering is a perception of our present experience as bad. In other word:

(SUF*) **P suffers X iff P concurrently sees (or experiences or perceives) the experience of X as bad for reasons intrinsic to X.**

Something like this is extremely plausible.

Consider the things we suffer. We suffer from embarrassment, from depression, we can suffer an itching, we can suffer insomnia, we can suffer from pain. All of these things, while we are suffering them, are unpleasant – call them, for the sake of symmetry, the displeasures.[53] There is clearly no sensation common to the lot; there is no sensation that is displeasure. The unpleasant sensations and experiences are nothing other than those experiences that are suffered from.

Moreover, the sensations that make up the displeasures are not consistently unpleasant. A certain taste is unpleasant for one and not unpleasant for another, unpleasant for me now, and not unpleas-

---

53Hospers calls all non-localized unpleasantness, 'displeasure,' and localized unpleasantness, 'pain.' But an itch can be a localized unpleasantness, and clearly is not a 'pain,' in a normal sense of the word. Moreover, we do use the word pain to talk about some non-localized unpleasantness. There is mental pain, after all.

ant for me later. My friends' laughter is unpleasant right after they dropped my pants, but not nearly as unpleasant an hour later, and is actually pleasant a decade later. Feeling cold can be invigorating one moment and unpleasant the next. This suggests that the perceptions of value made while suffering are unreliable.

But for the same reasons discussed with respect to pleasure, the perceptions of value that are essential to suffering give us a good explanation for why we would think that suffering and unpleasantness are bad even though they are not. To suffer from **X** is to see **X** as bad – even if **X** is not bad. We should expect, given our analysis, that the displeasures would appear bad. But the fact that it is analytic to the displeasures that we see them as bad need not be a reason on its own to think that they actually are. The fact that we can suffer from almost anything suggests that suffering does not necessarily attach to badness just as enjoyment does not necessarily attach to goodness. Furthermore, suffering is motivational, but only in the sense that all desires are motivational; there is nothing intrinsically undesirable about the displeasures (leaving certain physical displeasures like pain to the side, for the moment). So, if all of this works, we have no immediately obvious reason to think that suffering and unpleasantness are intrinsically bad.

There are complications, though, for the theory of richness that I am sure many readers have already noted. First, why should we have any perceptions of bad at all in a universe of only good things? Are all of our perceptions of bad misguided, all of our aversions and intuitions of wrongness? If yes, my theory seems severely revisionary. At least with the pleasures, I could give several reasons why the pleasures are, or can be, good – and to a great degree. Our pleasure perceptions were not universally faulty. So, is unpleasantness like pleasantness? Are there experiences that we suffer from that are genuinely bad? If there are, it seems they can't be accounted for by the present theory of the good. Second worry: isn't it the case that pain (at least) is a displeasure that is always perceived as bad? Isn't pain always motivational? Doesn't this suggest that pain is bad, whatever we think of the other displeasures?

In the following two sections, I attempt to deal with these worries. First, I argue that our concept of bad rarely, if ever, applies to something that is 'below zero' in value; that is, rarely do we think that bad things are absolutely bad. There are two exceptions to this: wrongness and suffering. I argue that our theory of the good has no difficulty in accounting for the wrongness of actions without resorting to any notion of absolute bad. So, we are left with suffering as the only thing that we actually think of as absolutely bad.

Second, I argue that even if pain is always perceived as bad it does not on its own give us a good reason to think that pain is intrinsically bad. Pain is unpleasant and its unpleasantness is what makes us think it is bad. But unpleasantness is not intrinsically bad, so why should we think pain is intrinsically bad? Moreover, I argue that pain is not always seen as bad. Pain is tightly connected to certain representations of badness, and if those representations can be made to disappear the feeling that pain is bad can be made to disappear.

Finally, I argue that suffering is a consistent and genuine instrumental bad. This is due to the fact that suffering, on the whole, reduces the richness of our experience because suffering is a necessarily distracting experience. Our experience is almost always better, because richer, when we are not suffering.

4.4.1 The Asymmetry of Bad and Good

There is nothing in this world with negative heat. There is, at absolute zero, an absolute absence of heat, but that is as heatless as the world gets. Nonetheless, we have a word for the opposite of heat: 'cold.' We call some temperatures 'cold' even if they are nowhere near absolute zero. Calling a temperature cold, I suggest, is to say that there is a lack of heat. And this usage is relative. If I lived in Minneapolis, I might claim that 32 degrees Fahrenheit isn't cold, but 0 degrees Fahrenheit is. If I lived in Florida, I might find 50 degrees Fahrenheit cold. We use the term 'cold' relatively because there is no absolute sense of cold; there is no sense of cold that means less than zero heat. In Minneapolis, it isn't really cold; there's still a whole bunch of heat around. There is, on the other hand, an absolute sense of heat because we can, legitimately, talk about an objective amount of it.

This asymmetry between 'cold' and 'hot' (or 'cold' and 'heat') is due to our biological nature and the manner in which it interacts with the fundamental nature of reality. Before knowing that heat was mean kinetic energy, it would be perfectly acceptable to theorize about a genuinely cold state of affairs, a state with negative heat. This is because 'cold' and 'hot' originally referred to how things felt. We have two ways (at least) of sensing heat. Something can feel hot or it can feel cold. Given no other knowledge of physics, this might suggest that there are two different properties in the world, being cold and being hot, and that objects in the world could have one property or the other (or, possibly, both). But to conclude this would have been wrong. We have two ways of perceiving one property: heat. We were sure of this only when we discovered what heat was. Of course, many suspected it beforehand. It would be strange, after all, if there were two completely different things in the world such that addition of one always made us feel less of the other, or the removal of one always made us feel more of the other. It was always more plausible to assume one thing causing two different sets of perceptions. Such an assumption nicely explains the relation between cold and heat – they are a measure of the same thing.

Something similar is true with respect to our words 'good' and 'bad.' There is, I claim, only good things and valueless things. There is nothing 'worse than nothing.' Many of us find this counterintuitive. This is understandable because we have aversions, perceptions of badness. Are these perceptions confused? No more than our cold sensations are. When we have a perception of badness, we perceive a lack of good, in the same way that when we have a perception of cold, we perceive a lack of heat. These are, often, veridical perceptions of real states of affairs. Sometimes, when we see things as bad, we are seeing things as less good than usual or than expected, in the same manner as the fellow in Florida who calls it 'cold' because 50 degrees is colder than usual. Sometimes, when we see things as bad it is because we sense they are almost completely lacking in good, in the same manner as when we call Pluto cold because its temperature nears absolute zero. Most of our perceptions of badness are accurate, then – they are measuring genuine value differences. It's just that there isn't anything less good than something of zero value. Just because we have two ways of perceiving value, doesn't mean that there are two value properties, one positive and one negative, the good and the bad. And, on reflection, doesn't this seem plausible? Whenever bad goes away, we see this as good; whenever good goes away, we see this as bad. Why should we assume that there are two different things that perform this fortuitous concert?[54] Doesn't it seem more likely that there is just one thing that we are sensing in two different ways?

So, I claim that there is no absolute bad. This does not mean that there is no objective bad. When the Floridian says that 50 degrees is cold, he means something about the relative temperatures of normal Florida days and 50 degrees. This thing he means may well be objectively true even though 50 degrees actually has quite a bit of heat. When a scientist claims that Pluto is cold, she also means something, and this something, too, may be objectively true even though Pluto actually has quite a bit of heat. When I claim that the meal was bad, I mean it was a worse than I expected or worse than most meals I've had or worse than the average meal or worse than the average meal at this restaurant. Whichever of those things I mean may very well be objectively true even though the meal itself was significantly more valuable than nothing.

There are two sets of prospective counterexamples to this claim about the bad: wrong actions and states of suffering. Here I will consider wrongness. I will look at suffering in the next section. Are wrong actions absolutely bad?

Begin here: the present theory of value can, without any appeal

---

54 This points to a genuine worry about hedonism. Is it really a monistic theory? We are supposed to avoid suffering *and* seek pleasure; sounds dualistic. And from the perspective of one who believes our theory of the good, it seems as silly as trying to stay warm by both avoiding cold *and* seeking heat. You need only do one or the other.

to absolute badness, plausibly account for wrongness. If we accept that the right is grounded in the good, then wrong actions are those actions with a certain relation to value. I don't want to take any position on the precise relation between the Right and the Good. But whatever it turns out to be, the present theory of value will be in good shape. Perhaps, the right action is the one that maximizes value and the wrong actions are those that don't. Or perhaps the right action is any action that creates a certain amount of value or more, and the wrong actions are those that create less value. Perhaps the right action is the action with the most intrinsic value and the wrong actions are those with less value. Perhaps the right action is the one that best appreciates, or contemplates, or loves the good and the wrong actions are those that fail to appreciate or contemplate or love the good. This means a world with only goodness need not be a world with no wrongness. This is made clear by the present theory. Certain actions are, in their nature, things that reduce the richness of the world or prevent richness from coming into being. For example, killing is the destruction of life. Lying is an attempt to prevent knowledge, an attempt to break the unity of mind and world. Destruction is generally the removal of richness and is worse the richer the thing being destroyed. Wrongness – and great wrongness and horrible wrongness – can be easily accounted for by a theory that claims there is nothing intrinsically bad.[55]

Given all of this, it seems that there are no strong counterexamples – outside of cases of suffering – to the claim that our usage of the word 'bad' is generally relative. The sense that there is something really bad is equivalent I suggest to the sense that there is something

---

55What about 'natural evils' like earthquakes? Again, we might think these are absolutely bad because they cause suffering or kill human beings. So, are events of non-human destruction absolutely bad? Well, even on a theory of richness, destruction is close to being *essentially* instrumentally bad (in the relative sense we are using) – that is, there is always some decrease in value associated with random destruction. But just because destruction is inherently connected with loss in value doesn't mean it is worse than nothing. Is it the case that a burning Mona Lisa is worse than nothing? Difficult to say, but I consider it doubtful. Is it the case that a human dying *without suffering* is worse than no human at all? Doubtful. At the very least, I don't think we have strong intuitions either way.

really cold. Further evidence that this is right comes from the fact that the usage of bad is asymmetrical with the usage of the word good. If we think something is good, we think it is better than nothing. If I think a meal is good, or a painting, or an action, or a society, I mean that the addition of that thing adds value to the world. It doesn't really matter how minimally good we think **G** is: if we do think it is good, we clearly mean this in the absolute sense.

We are left with suffering. Some of us have the intuition that if someone is in intense suffering and will continue to be in intense suffering, it would be better that they didn't exist at all. This is an intuition that I want to explain away. But note that given the immediately preceding discussion, it shouldn't be at all surprising to find that suffering is a great and universal bad (relative sense), but not at all a bad (absolute sense). The North Pole is really cold (relative sense), and would appear so to all human observers, but not really cold (absolute sense).

4.4.2 The Asymmetry of Pain and Pleasure

The pleasures turn out to be just those experiences that we desire concurrently for reasons intrinsic to the experience. Something similar cannot be done to define pain, though, without stretching the concept beyond its limits. There are many things we suffer from, many unpleasant things that are not pains. We suffer from embarrassment and fear and depression. Some of these might be plausibly called mental pain, but some are clearly not. Moreover, there are physical sensations that are unpleasant, but not pains. I can suffer an itching without it being a pain. I scratch my poison ivy so fiercely that it bleeds. At first, it just itched (intensely). Now, it hurts as well. Itches and pains are different types of unpleasant sensation. One can suffer horribly from nausea without feeling any pain per se. So, the pains cannot be defined in terms of what we suffer from.

On the other hand, it is at least plausible to think that pains are things that are essentially suffering-inducing. If this is so and suffering is essentially a perception of badness, one might plausibly think that the reason we always see pains as bad is that they are. The reason we don't desire pains is that they are intrinsically undesirable. I respond to this in much the same way I responded to the objection from orgasm given against the definition of pleasure. First, I argue that even if pain is always motivational, this does not give us a good reason to think that pain is intrinsically bad. The better explanation comes from evolutionary biology. Second, there are good reasons to think that the sensations we call pain sensations are not always experienced as bad, are not always motivational.

I propose that the badness of pain is due to the fact that it is unpleasant. If a particular pain were not unpleasant, it would not seem bad. Suppose, then, for the objection, that what we call pain is always motivational. Suppose that whenever we feel pain, we feel some motivation to get out of it. In other words, pain is always unpleasant. I have already noted that many things are unpleasant other than pain. So, it can't be pain sensations alone that make for unpleasantness. Something other than pain sensations must account for unpleasantness. But if it is the unpleasantness that accounts for pain's badness and unpleasantness is not just pain sensations, then we only have reason to think that pain is bad if we have good reason to think that unpleasantness is bad. But for all the reasons that we mentioned in the pleasure section, we don't have good reason to think that unpleasantness is intrinsically bad. We do suffer from unpleasantness; it is in the nature of unpleasantness that we suffer from it, that we think it bad. Still, we have good reason to think that these perceptions are unreliable. And, so, we have good reason to doubt the badness of pain, even if pain is intrinsically unpleasant.

If there is no alternative explanation for pain sensations' consistent undesirability, that undesirability would maintain its evidentiary power. Do we have an alternative explanation for pain's intrinsically motivational nature? Yes, there are strong evolutionary reasons for thinking that sensations associated with pain must appear bad to us, must motivate us. Pain sensations are generally connected to bodily damage and a species would not propagate very well if it did not act strongly to avoid bodily damage. So, if pain sensations are always motivational, it is not because the sensations are bad, but because they are the sensations associated with bad things.

One might respond by claiming that yes, there are evolutionary reasons for making us think that pain is bad, but perhaps evolution just used pain sensations because they were bad, that the badness of pain is, in fact, why we have the particular sensations we have with respect to bodily damage.[56] This seems backwards, though. Imagine a creature that could not feel our pain sensations. Would it be impossible to wire this creature's biology in such a way that it could be motivated to avoid bodily damage? Here's what I would do: whatever sensations the creature felt (they could even be ones we traditionally associate with pleasure), I would wire them directly to its desire centers in such a way that it would always desire to avoid such sensations, that such sensations would always seem bad. The creature would then find these sensations, whatever they were, to be unpleasant. But this unpleasantness wouldn't give us any reason to think that the sensations themselves were bad. Pain sensations would seem bad whether they were or not. But I suggest that something like this is precisely what evolution has done for us. And so, even if pains are necessarily (nomologically) tied up with unpleasantness, it doesn't give us reason to think that pain sensations are intrinsically bad. The perceptions of value we have with respect to pain are undermined because of this strong evolutionary defeater.

Moreover, there is good evidence that things we call pains are *not* intrinsically motivational. Though in the vast majority of cases pain does cause us to suffer, it doesn't always. We are capable of breaking the connection between pain sensations and the seeming badness. Evan Goldstein, a prime defender of the intrinsic disvalue of pain,

---

56"Nature, through evolutionary forces, chose pain over pleasant or tingling sensations to be correlated with harm because pain, being bad and worth avoiding on its own account, is something creatures have reason to avoid on its own merit." [Goldstein, 1980: 361]

admits this:

> "Not disliking those sensations we call 'pains' may seem extraordinary, but this is not reason to say a sensation would not be a pain were it not disliked. The idea of hungering for pain, like that of craving castration, represents an empirical anomaly, a response psychologically queer; it is not self-contradictory, merely linguistically disordered. To welcome or be indifferent to this or any other sensation is imaginable.[57]

Goldstein also cites the case of lobotomy. Lobotomy patients find that the badness of certain pains disappears after the lobotomy even though the pain itself, apparently, remains unchanged. That is, they rank the pains as having the same intensity as before, but no longer feel the same aversion. Hare says with respect to this,

> "If we can understand what it would be for the suffering to be reduced while the sensation remains the same, we can surely understand also what it would be for the suffering or the distress or dislike to be altogether removed without any diminution in the pain sensation."[58]

This is closely related to the way certain pain medicines work. Morphine, for example, does not reduce patient's evaluation of the intensity of pain; it only reduces the badness of the pain; it reduces the patient's aversion to the pain. Again, this suggests that pain sensations can be separated from suffering.

But there are other less perverse or 'empirically anomalous' times when we remove the seeming badness of pain, and so I think it a bit unfair to call non-unpleasant pain 'linguistically disordered.' Indeed, it can be admirable to remove the appearance of badness from pain sensations. Athletic performance provides a good example. When we begin the practice of a certain athletic activity, we may hate the burn in our muscles. After a while, on learning that the pain in our muscles is a good thing – that it is what makes us stronger, that it does us no harm – we find we can actually like the sensation, while still referring to it as pain. Goldstein thinks that this is some-

---

57[Goldstein, 1989: 261-2]
58[Hare, 1972: 87]

how perverse, but if the pain does not signal anything genuinely bad, where is the perversity? Wouldn't it be nice – and even appropriate – if the not-liking went away?

If we accept that pains do not always seem bad, does it undermine the evolutionary explanation for the motivation of our pains? Not at all. All sorts of other biological mechanisms can be undermined through the use of drugs, operations or mental training (heart rate, visual perception, response to cold and so on…). We would expect this. Our biology is not a necessary structure. It is a contingent causal structure. And it is one that is 'designed' to be flexible.

4.4.3 The Bad of Pain and Suffering

What do we do to make pain stop feeling bad? I suggest that we stop seeing the pain as representing or indicating harm to our body. As a marathon runner, I learned to classify pains into two categories: the first category was pains I knew were normal on a difficult run, the burning in the legs, the shortness of breath, and side-aches. These pains – because I knew they were normal and I knew that they didn't lead to any physical damage – failed to seem bad to me. On the other hand, there were pains in my joints, or sharp pains in my muscles that indicated tears, that would make me stop what I was doing, that felt bad.[59] This suggests that at least some of the badness we associate with pain is due to certain representations that come along with the pain. There are two ways this could be: either the pain commonly gives rise to certain representations that there is damage to our body[60] or the sensations of pain are nothing other

59"Untrained athletes may be strongly averse to the strong sensation of 'burning' in a muscle group being exercised but notice little or nothing painful in slight twinges in joints. After, training, athletes tolerate or even enjoy the burning but strongly averse to joint twinges. If there is intrinsic bad in sensations, then the same sensation (burning or twinging) mysteriously acquires or loses the badness after training." [Rudebusch, 1999: 93-4]

60See [Kraut, 1994].

than representations of bodily damage.[61] Since there is still quite a bit of debate about whether qualia are representational, and since I don't need to make a decision with respect to this debate, I am not going to distinguish between these two views. But I find the general picture plausible: physical pain sensations are just those sensations that indicate or represent bodily damage. If this is right, then it gives us a method for distinguishing pain from itches and nausea. Pain is a generally unpleasant sensation that suggests bodily damage, that suggests the breaking of bodily integrity. Nausea is a sensation that suggests some foreign unhealthy substance internally. Itching is the sensation that suggests a foreign, unhealthy substance (or creature) on our skin.[62]

But as bodily damage is a (relative) bad, we are in a position to suggest that some of our intuitions about pain are almost correct. It is not pain that is bad, but what pain represents that is bad. It is fair to say that we don't like bad news. It is reasonable to never want to get bad news. Bad news is intrinsically the type of thing that we would forego if we had the option. But it is not because there is anything intrinsically wrong with bad news itself, with, for instance, the words in bad news. We don't want to get bad news because of what bad news represents. It is the same with pain. If pain represents or indicates bodily damage, then pain is a form of bad news. Nobody wants to feel pain because of what pain represents, not, in the end, because of pain itself. (And so most philosophers have been shooting the messenger.) Bad news fails to be unpleasant when we realize it's false and this explains why I, as a runner, no longer feel the burning in my legs as bad. I realize that the apparent bad news is false.

On the other hand, there is good reason to think that suffering itself is a (relative) bad and not just bad news. Richard Kraut thinks

---

61 This is Rudebusch's view. [Rudebusch, 1999]

62 Further evidence: when we feel pain, initially, do we move to stop the sensation or do we move to stop the perceived damage? If I am sitting next to the fire and feel a sudden burning sensation in my foot, I am immediately afraid that my sock is on fire. I jump up and fling off my sock. I am relieved to find that my foot had not burned, but had only strayed too close to the fire. This relief suggests that a big part of the badness I feared was in what might *actually* happen, and not just in the sensation.

the bad in pain comes from its power as a distraction. "Almost every pain distracts us from devoting full attention to things we care about, and over time pain depresses the level of energy we have."[63] But this is only true of pain when we are suffering from it. If we don't care about the pain, if it is not motivating us in any way, we, presumably, move our attention back to things we do care about. Suffering, on the other hand, does distract us because suffering is essentially motivational. Herein, I suggest, is the real badness of suffering. It makes us incapable of enjoying our life. It makes us incapable of consciously loving the things we love.

Suffering is worse than mere distraction. Mere distraction is not always bad. Suffering is not distracting in the way that a T.V. in a restaurant is distracting. Juliet is trying to pay attention to the conversation she is having with her date, Tristan. He is talking about his dial tone collection. On the television is a show about the threatened extinction of the hammerhead whale. It is quite possible that the show is actually more valuable than Tristan's monologue. She is trying to pay attention to Tristan and so the TV is distracting, but it is not clear that this distraction is a bad thing.

Suffering, on the other hand, is bad because, I suggest, the mental state associated with intense suffering is always less rich than a normal mental state. If you add suffering to a normal, non-suffering mental state, you must reduce its richness. Why should this be? To take pleasure in X is to be fully engaged in experience X. It is to want to know that experience and to be fully open to it. To be suffering from X is the exact opposite; it is to be motivated to leave experience X; it is the want to not know X. The want to not know an experience is not itself narrowing unless that happens to be the experience you are having. When you are suffering there is no way to engage with the full richness of your experience.

Moreover, what we suffer from, prototypically pains, are themselves shallow experiences. I find it impossible to imagine suffering from the full experience of the Mona Lisa. The Mona Lisa might bring up painful memories, it might scare you, it might, if you have a

---

63[Kraut, 1994: 46]

strange reaction to certain pigments, hurt your eyes, but all of these sufferings will be narrow experiences of the Mona Lisa. You can't suffer from a full experience of the Mona Lisa because if you are suffering, it will make you incapable of fully experiencing the Mona Lisa. Suffering turns your eyes away from richness, but to have a full experience of a rich object you need your eyes turned toward the object, hungry for it.

And, indeed, one method for dealing with painful or unpleasant sensations is to open oneself to the sensation. I have often made itches and the badness of minor pains go away by studying the sensation rather than avoiding it. If you are open to the sensation and interested in it, you necessarily have reduced your conscious motivation to be out of the sensation, and, thereby, reduced your suffering. (Also, if you are open to a sensation, you will see that no matter what the sensation, it has a bit of richness, a whiff of beauty. I find it probable that nothing is completely without richness.)

Is this narrowing really what we hate about suffering? Not entirely, of course. In part, we don't like suffering because essential to all suffering is some experience that seems bad. Since this seeming is often mistaken, it means that some part of our perception that suffering is bad is likely to be mistaken. But we also don't like suffering for the very reason that it narrows our life. The first stages of intense suffering are often characterized by fear, but a common description of life during prolonged suffering is boredom. Long-term suffering is a state characterized by monotony, by an inability to engage with the richness of life. If you don't believe this, try to imagine a case of suffering where one is able to engage with the full richness of one's life. Harry has a terminal illness accompanied by intense suffering, but he continues having in-depth conversations with Juliet; he continues composing music and listening intently to his favorite composers; he's learning to cook and so on. He is not just outwardly behaving as if he is fully engaging with the richness of life; he is actually engaging with the full richness of his life. And it isn't that he talks to his wife and then goes into the bathroom and sobs. His consciousness is engaged with his wife, with his music, with his cooking. I personally find it impossible to imagine Harry intensely and continuously suffering during all of this, not while his consciousness is fully or nearly fully engaged in other things. (On the other hand, suppose I am wrong in this. Suppose he really is capable of engaging fully in his conversations and life while all the time intensely suffering. If this is possible, I cease to see the badness in suffering.)

There is further badness that can be associated with suffering. I argued in Chapter 1 that desire satisfaction is a good. Essential to continuous suffering is the thwarting of a desire. The strongest argument, in my mind, for the claim that suffering is an absolute bad is that many of us would prefer unconsciousness to suffering. And we certainly think that it is more humane to use drugs to anesthetize people than to let them suffer. There are even times when many people think it is permissible to allow someone to die – or, even, to kill her – when her suffering is great enough. But if the bad in suffering is due to the narrowing of consciousness, isn't unconsciousness worse? This intuition is partly due, I suggest, to our fear of suffering, a fear that we don't have towards unconsciousness. I suggest it is also partly due to our familiarity with sleep and the in-built human desire to sleep. We don't see sleep as bad for a number of reasons. First, we don't experience sleep (or if we do, it's only during dreaming and dreaming certainly has some richness). Second, we have a built in desire (need) to sleep; falling asleep is one of the simple pleasures. Third, sleep, given our biological natures, is a great instrumental good. But is sleep really so innocuous? Imagine that you didn't have to sleep, that no one had to sleep, but someone had a disease that forced her to spend eight hours of her day in dreamless unconsciousness? Wouldn't this be thought of as a horrible bad? Or, back in the real world, imagine a disease that forced someone to sleep for twenty hours every day as opposed to eight. Or imagine you had the opportunity to need rest for only three hours a day? Wouldn't this be great? Unconsciousness is, I suggest, a great badness that we have become used to because of the necessity. Or rather, we are used to living in Minnesota and, so, 30 degree doesn't seem cold. Nonetheless, that is cold compared to other states.

It is also the case that part of suffering is the wish to have your suffering relieved. And this can be a great wish. Now, as I pointed out in Chapter 2, it can be misguided to think that just because someone has an intense desire that it should be satisfied. On the other hand, it is often the case that a person's intense desires are connected with her deep values. This leads to us thinking that, generally, if someone intensely desires something, we should (absent defeaters) give it to her. Moreover, if we can understand her desire, if it makes sense to us, we are even more likely to feel obligated to give it to them. Intense suffering is accompanied by an intense desire and it is an intense desire that we, more or less, can all understand. To show that people's desires are an important part of our evaluation of the comparative good of unconsciousness and suffering, consider how we feel if someone says they don't want to be given anesthetizing drugs (or don't want to be euthanized). In such a case, it is irrelevant how high she ranks her suffering. Her suffering could be off the figurative charts, but if she tells us she doesn't want to be euthanized or, even, anesthetized, we generally acquiesce to her wishes. We think that she should get to decide, and the world is better if her desires are satisfied, even if that entails intense suffering for her. Freud, on his deathbed, refused pain medication, saying, "I would rather think in torment than not think clearly." Many desires associated with suffering are not that deep. But some of the desires associated with the want to be out of suffering – especially with terminal suffering – are desires about the preservation of dignity, and this can be tightly connected with who we are, with values-of-our-own. When we suffer, we can't be who we are. We aren't free to continue living the way we want. Moreover, we often act in ways counter to the way we want, crying out, contorting our faces, getting angry, being afraid, and so on. It is important that we are able to act in accordance with our values, to be free, to live our lives in accordance with our best image of ourselves. This to me is the value of dignity. Intense suffering often destroys dignity.

And, so, suffering – unlike pain or the unpleasant sensations – is almost always a bad. Suffering almost always reduces the value of our conscious states. It reduces our ability to enjoy the good pleasures. It makes it difficult if not impossible to be in the conscious state of loving, and loving is one of the great goods. To suffer is to have a constantly thwarted desire. It can also make us act in ways that are counter to other of our deep desires, like our desire for dignity. And so, in the end, suffering is a great and consistent bad, but this badness is explicable given the present theory of the good.

4.5 Conclusion: Mackie One More Time

"I can think of nothing less pleasurable than a life devoted to pleasure." John D. Rockefeller

And, so, the reasons stated at the outset of this chapter do not give us reason to be hedonists. They do not give us reason to think that the pleasures and displeasures are of intrinsic value or disvalue. Looking back, maybe one can start to see the oddness in the thought that some simple sensation would be the good or bad. Why should it be that way? Common inverted qualia arguments should have made us suspicious of such a claim. Suppose, per impossible, that there is some quale **P** that is the pleasure sensation. Suppose Tristan and Harry both experience something they call the pleasure sensation whenever they eat Rocky Road ice cream. They both groan in 'pleasure.' They both want to eat more. They both want to continue feeling all the sensations that they are feeling. They both claim to love Rocky Road. But it just so happens that Tristan doesn't experience quale **P** when he eats Rocky Road. He feels some entirely different sensation (it might even be what Harry calls a painful sensation). I have trouble believing that one person is getting a good and the other isn't. Or imagine a pleasure zombie. When he tastes Rocky Road, he gets all the sensations associated with tasting the stuff, and gets all the conscious desires associated with pleasure but he gets no sensation **P**. Does he fail to get the good? Imagine a world of these zombies. Are they missing anything? There are so many qualia out there, perhaps an infinite number, and we don't experience most of them (think of Nagel's bats). What luck, what incredible fortune that we happened to be built to feel the one good!

Now, it is appropriate to ask can the theory of the good presented in this essay answer Mackie's challenge? How is it that the good motivates? And why is it the case that there is so much disagreement about what is good?

The experience conjecture offers an excellent explanation of how the good motivates. If our perception of the good just is a desire, then there is no real puzzle about how the good motivates. The good itself need not have anything extra built into it. To see something good is simply to desire it. Our perceptions of red have certain unique qualitative properties. We call them red sensations. Our perceptions of the good also have certain unique qualitative properties. We call them desires. It is true: desires are not like other perceptions. But color perceptions are not like sound perceptions. And proprioceptive perceptions are not like taste perceptions. To desire is a unique response to a unique stimulus – namely, the good.

The theory that richness is the good makes it likely that there would be quite a bit of Mackie-like disagreement about what the good is. I suggest once again that ethics, like the physical sciences, is primarily an empirical enterprise. It should be no surprise that there is disagreement about what the fundamental theory looks like. It took many years of precise observation and sophisticated theorizing to achieve much agreement in the physical sciences. We should expect no less in the ethical sciences. Moreover, many theories like hedonism or desire-satisfaction utilitarianism seem to assume that we will be able to read the final ethics right off the face of the world, like the reading of a clock. When we see an apple fall from a tree, we are observing, in a sense, gravity. Yes, it is right there for us to see. But all the work of theory comes after this and many other observations. The same is true of ethical theory. Richness is a complex property and a subtle one. It takes quite a bit of theorizing to realize that something like it is the good. And to realize that something like it is the good is only the beginning of the work. Just as realizing that there is some force drawing the apple down is only the beginning of physical science.

I believe we are right now in a position with respect to moral perception similar to the one we were before the scientific revolution – whenever that genuinely began – with respect to normal perception. Drug experiences, hallucinations, differing perceptions at different times were all taken as representing exactly what they seemed to represent. We have come over time to realize how to make our sensory perceptions reliable – something like the scientific method – and as we develop the same skill – and distrust – with respect to our desires, apparent value disagreements should lessen over time.

CONCLUSION

Given recent history in ethics and value theory, there must needs seem something quixotic about the project presented here. It must immediately appear to any trained philosopher, and to most academicians, somewhat audacious to defend a monistic theory of the good that it is not grounded in, or directly dependent upon, some psychological state, a theory, furthermore, that has been missed for thousands of years. But the fact that few have noted it in the past does not mean it is wrong. Many of us – myself included – have been guilty of assuming that the truths of ethics are somehow more accessible than the truths of physics, that the value world is somehow more immediately evident than the physical world. There is no reason to think this. If the final value theory is only half as surprising as quantum mechanics, we should count ourselves lucky.

On a personal note, I have never met a person whose values did not seem such that they could be made intelligible to me. I have always thought that I could be made to see the good that most any person saw. I just require a story, a picture of the world as they see it. With another's pictures in one's mind, the other's motivations become understandable. Perhaps this is unfounded optimism on my part, but it is an optimism repeatedly confirmed. In general, people's actions are intelligible because we can see what makes them think what they are doing is good, why what they're doing seems good to them, even if we are completely convinced they are wrong. This intelligibility suggests, *pace* relativity arguments, that our basic values are, on the whole, more similar than not. I have argued that this is because there is only one underlying property of value, and it is a property that we all, for the most part, have the ability to perceive.

I have touched on a number of the areas needed to establish that richness is the good. Some I have looked at in detail, others clearly require more attention. Important work needs to be done on the analysis of richness. I doubt that it is egregiously wrong as stated, though it may be too vague, as of yet, to be wrong. Further, each of the values addressed in Chapter 2 deserve investigation. Analyses of knowledge and consciousness, of persons and beauty, of freedom and life, are not insignificant challenges; nor is establishing their relation to richness.

We might find, indeed, that keeping the desired value conclusion in mind leads us more surely to the proper analysis. Permit some wild speculation: perhaps the final analysis of knowledge, the final solution to Gettier problems, will entail solutions that involve the organic unity of knowledge. Perhaps the concepts of freedom, persons, consciousness can all be made clearer by recognizing first that they are valuable and, so, connected with richness. I certainly found my understanding of these concepts to improve using such a process. The coupling of philosophical intuition and a proper understanding of value may prove a powerful tool for progress in these areas.

In conclusion, then, there is strong evidence that something like richness must be broadly valuable. Persons, beauty, and consciousness – among other things – are all instances of concentrated richness. And, apparently, this is for what we value them. Given the arguments for monism and given that richness is the appropriate object of love and given the refutation of the hedonistic counterexamples, we are faced with strong reasons to think that richness is not just valuable; it is the only thing valuable.

BIBLIOGRAPHY

Anderson, E. (1993). *Value in Ethics and Economics*. Cambridge, Mass., Harvard University Press.

Anscombe, G. E. M. (1957). *Intention*. Ithaca, N. Y.,, Cornell University Press.

Aristotle and R. Hope (1966). *Metaphysics*. [Ann Arbor], University of Michigan Press.

Aristotle and T. Irwin (1985). *Nicomachean ethics*. Indianapolis, Ind., Hackett Pub. Co.

Aristotle and D. W. Lucas (1968). *Poetics*. Oxford,, Clarendon P.

Bennet, C. (1990). *How to Define Complexity in Physics, and Why. Complexity, Entropy and the Physics of Information*, Santa Fe, Addison-Wesley Publishing Company.

Beardsley, Monroe. (1981) *Aesthetics*. Indianapolis: Hackett

Birkhoff, G. D. (1933). *Aesthetic Measure*. Cambridge, Masbs.,, Harvard University Press.

Boden, M. A. and NetLibrary Inc. (1994). *Dimensions of Creativity*. Cambridge, Mass., MIT Press.

Bovens, L. (2003). "Loves Constancy and Neil Jordan's The Crying Game" (manuscript)

Bradley, A. C. (1909). *Oxford Lectures on Poetry*. London,, Macmillan and Co. limited.

Brandt, R. B. (1959). *Ethical Theory; the Problems of Normative and Critical Ethics*. Englewood Cliffs, N.J.,, Prentice-Hall.

Broad, C. D. (1967). *Five Types of Ethical Theory*. London, Routledge & K. Paul.

Brown, C. (1967). "Leibniz and Aesthetics." Philosophy and Phenomenological Research. S 28: 70-80.

Callicott, J.-B. (1990). "The Case Against Moral Pluralism." Environmental Ethics. Sum 12(2): 99-124.

Callicott, J.-B. (1994). "Moral Monism in Environmental Ethics Defended." Journal of Philosophical Research 19: 51-60.

Coleridge, S. T. (1949). *The Philosophical Lectures of Samuel Tay-*

lor Coleridge, hitherto unpublished. London,, Pilot Press.

Coleridge, S. T. and J. Shawcross (1907). *Biographia Literaria.* London, Oxford University Press.

Cooper, J.-M. (1984). "Plato's Theory of Human Motivation." History of Philosophy Quarterly. JA 1: 3-22.

Csikszentmihalyi, M. (1990). *Flow: The Psychology of Optimal Experience.* New York, Harper & Row.

Dante, A., G. Busnelli, et al. (1964). *Il Convivio.* Firenze F. Le Monnier,.

Dewey, J. (1958). *Art as Experience.* New York, Capricorn Books.

Edwards, R.-B. (1975). "Do Pleasures and Pains Differ Qualitatively?" Journal of Value Inquiry. WINT 9: 270-281.

Feagin, S.-L. (1983). "Mill and Edwards on the Higher Pleasures." Philosophy . AP 58: 244-252.

Feldman, F. (1997). "On the Intrinsic Value of Pleasures." Ethics . Ap 107(3): 448-466.

Findlay, J. N. (1961). *Values and Intentions; a Study in Value-theory and Philosophy of Mind.* London,New York,, Allen & Unwin; Macmillan.

Fine, G. (1989). "Knowledge and Belief in Republic V-VII IN Epistemology (Companions to Ancient Thought: 1).".

Forrest, P. (1991). "Aesthetic Understanding." Philosophy and Phenomenological Research. S 91: 525-540.

Fromm, E. (1974). *The Art of Loving.* New York, Harper & Row.

Goldman, Alan H. (1995) *Aesthetic Value.* Westview Press, Inc. Boulder, Colorado.

Goldstein, I. (1980). "Why People Prefer Pleasure to Pain." Philosophy . JL 55: 349-362.

Goldstein, I. (1989). "Pleasure and Pain: Unconditional, Intrinsic Values." Philosophy and Phenomenological Research. D 50: 255-276.

Gross, M. (1998). *Life on the Edge : Amazing Creatures Thriving in Extreme Environments.* New York, Plenum Trade.

Hare, R. M. (1972). *Essays on the Moral Concepts.* Berkeley,, University of California Press.

Hegel, G. W. F. and T. M. Knox (1948). *On Christianity; Early*

Theological Writings. New York,, Harper.

Hitchcock, D. (1985). "The Good in Plato's "Republic"." Apeiron. FALL 19: 65-92.

Horace, B. Raffel, et al. (1974). *The Art of Poetry*. Albany,, State University of New York Press.

Hospers, J. (1961). *Human Conduct; An Introduction to the Problems of Ethics*. New York,, Harcourt Brace & World.

Hospers, J., Ed. (1967). *The Organic Conception in Aesthetics*. Encyclopedia of Philosophy. New York, Macmillan.

Hume, D., T. H. Green, et al. (1964). *A Treatise of Human Nature ; Being an Attempt to Introduce the Experimental Method of Reasoning into Moral Subjects; and Dialogues Concerning Natural Religion*. Aalen, Scientia Verlag.

Hume, D. and L. A. Selby-Bigge (1896). *A Treatise of Human Nature*. Oxford, Clarendon press.

Hurka, T. (1996). "Monism, Pluralism, and Rational Regret." Ethics . Ap 106(3): 555-575.

James, H. (1951). *The Art of Fiction*. New York.

Kant, I. (1959). *Foundations of the Metaphysics of Morals, and What is Enlightenment?* New York,, Liberal Arts Press.

Kant, I. and J. C. Meredith (1964). *The Critique of Judgement*. Oxford,, Clarendon Press.

Kekes, J. (1993). *The Morality of Pluralism*. Princeton, Princeton University Press.

Kelly, C. (2001). "Organic Unity and the Good in Plato's Republic."

Kelly, C. (2008). "The Impossibility of Incommensurable Values." Philos Stud 137: 369.

Kelly, C. (2014). "Value Monism, Richness, and Environmental Ethics." Les ateliers de l'éthique/The Ethics Forum 9 (2):110-129 (2014)

Kelly, C. (2015). *The Song of Songs, of Solomon*. Los Angeles, Now Experience Books.

Kraut, R.-H. (1994). "Desire and the Human Good." Proceedings and Addresses of the American Philosophical Association. N 68(2):

39-54.

Leibniz, G. W. (1953). *Discourse on Metaphysics*. [Manchester, Eng.], Manchester University Press.

Leibniz, G. W. and R. Latta (1925). *The Monadology and Other Philosophical Writings*. [London, New York, etc.], Oxford university press H. Milford.

Light, A. (1996). "Callicott and Naess on Pluralism." Inquiry . Je 39(2): 273-294.

Lloyd, L. and H. Pagels (1988). "Complexity as Thermondynamic Depth." Annals of Physics 188: 186-213.

Lord, C. (1964). "Organic Unity Reconsidered." Journal of Aesthetics and Art Criticism. SPR 22: 263-268.

Mackie, J. L. (1977). *Ethics: Inventing Right and Wrong*. Harmondsworth ; New York, Penguin.

Marietta-Jr, D.-E. (1993). "Pluralism in Environmental Ethics." Topoi . Mr 12(1): 69-80.

McAleer, Michael. (2001) "Simplicity: Views of Some Nobel Laureates in Economic Science" Simplicity, Inference, and Modelling

Mill, J. S. and S. Gorovitz (1971). *Utilitarianism*. Indianapolis,, Bobbs-Merrill.

Miller, Peter (1982). "Value as Richness: Toward a Value Theory for an Expanded Naturalism in Environmental Ethics" Environmental Ethics 1982 Summer; 4(2): 101-114

Monod, J. (1971). *Change and Necessity: On the Natural Philosophy of Modern Biology*, Knopf.

Montaigne, M. d. and D. M. Frame (1965). *The Complete Essays of Montaigne*. Stanford, Calif., Stanford University Press.

Mikkelson, G.M. (2011). "Weight Species." Volume 33, No 2, 185-196.

Mikkelson, G. M. In press. "Sentience, Life, Richness." In: DesRoches, C. T., F. Jankunis, and B. Williston, editors. New Directions in Canadian Environmental Philosophy. McGill-Queens University. Montréal, QC.

Nietzsche, Frederich (2001). *The Gay Science*. Cambridge University Press.

Noddings, N. (1984). *Caring, a Feminine Approach to Ethics & Moral Education*. Berkeley, University of California Press.

Norton, B.-G. (1995). "Why I am Not a Nonanthropocentrist: Callicott and the Failure of Monistic Inherentism." Environmental Ethics. Wint 17(4): 341-358.

Nozick, R. (1981). *Philosophical Explanations*. Cambridge, Mass., Harvard University Press.

Nozick, R. (1989). *The Examined Life: Philosophical Meditations*. New York, Simon and Schuster.

Nussbaum, M. C. (1990). *Love's Knowledge: Essays on Philosophy and Literature*. New York, Oxford University Press.

Nussbaum, M. C. (2001). *The Fragility of Goodness: Luck and Ethics in Greek Tragedy and Philosophy*. Cambridge ; New York, Cambridge University Press.

Oddie, G. (2001). "Axiological Atomism." Australasian Journal of Philosophy. S 79(3): 313-332.

Oddie, G. (2009). Value, Reality, and Desire. London. Oxford University Press.

Orsini, G. N. G. (1969). "The Organic Conception in Aesthetics." Comparative Literature 21: 1-30.

Orsini, G. N. G., Ed. (1973). *Organicism. Dictionary of the History of Ideas*. New York, Scribners.

Osborne, H. (1952). *Theory of Beauty; an introduction to aesthetics*. London,, Routledge & K. Paul.

Parfit, D. (1984). *Reasons and Persons*. Oxford [Oxfordshire], Clarendon Press.

Parker, D. H. (1968). *The Philosophy of Value*. New York,, Greenwood Press.

Penrose, R. (1991). *The Emperor's New Mind: Concerning Computers, Minds, and the Laws of Physics*. New York, N.Y., U.S.A., Penguin Books.

Penrose, R. (1994). *Shadows of the Mind : a Search for the Missing Science of Consciousness*. Oxford ; New York, Oxford University Press.

Penrose, R. and M. S. Longair (1997). *The Large, the Small and the Human Mind*. Cambridge [England] ; New York, Cambridge University Press.

Plato and W. S. Cobb (1990). *Plato's Sophist*. Savage, Md., Rowan & Littlefield.

Plato and G. M. A. Grube (1974). *The Republic*. Indianapolis,, Hackett Pub. Co.

Plato, B. Jowett, et al. (1953). *Euthyphro, Apology, Crito, Symposium*. Washington, D.C., Regnery Gateway.

Plato, A. Nehamas, et al. (1995). *Phaedrus*. Indianapolis, Hackett.

Plato and C. C. W. Taylor (1976). *Protagoras*. Oxford, Clarendon Press.

Plato, B. A. O. Williams, et al. (1992). *Theaetetus*. Indianapolis, Hackett Pub.

Plotinus, S. Mackenna, et al. (1957). *The Enneads*. New York,, Pantheon Books.

Raz, J. (1986). *The Morality of Freedom*. Oxford [Oxfordshire] New York, Clarendon Press ;Oxford University Press.

Raz, J. (1999). *Engaging Reason: on the Theory of Value and Action*. Oxford ; New York, Oxford University Press.

Rudebusch, G. (1999). *Socrates, Pleasure, and Value*. New York, Oxford University Press.

Santayana, G., W. G. Holzberger, et al. (1988). *The Sense of Beauty: Being the Outlines of Aesthetic Theory*. Cambridge, Mass., MIT Press.

Scanlon, T. (1998). *What We Owe to Each Other*. Cambridge, Mass., Belknap Press of Harvard University Press.

Schaber, P. (1999). "Value Pluralism: Some Problems." The Journal of Value Inquiry 33: 71-78.

Sober, Eliot. (2001). "What is the Problem of Simplicity?" Simplicity, Inference, and Modelling

Sibley, Frank. (1959) "A Contemporary Theory of Aesthetic Concepts," Philosophical Review 68: 421–450.

Sidgwick, H. (1962). *The Methods of Ethics*. [Chicago], University of Chicago Press.

Singer, I. (1984). *The Nature of Love*. Chicago, University of Chicago Press.

Singpurwalla, R. G. K. and Author (2001). "A Compatibilist Theory of Freedom: Values-of-One's-Own".

Smith, M. (1995). *The Moral Problem*. Oxford, UK ; Cambridge, Mass., USA, Blackwell.

Sterling, G. C. (1994). *Ethical Intuitionism and its Critics*. New York, P. Lang.

Stocker, M. (1990). *Plural and Conflicting Values*. Oxford [England] New York, Clarendon Press ;Oxford University Press.

Varner, G.-E. (1991). "No Holism without Pluralism." Environmental Ethics. Sum 91: 175-179.

Wheeler, J. A. (1988). *Information, Physics, Quantum: The Search for Links. Complexity, Entropy and the Physics of Information*, Santa Fe, Addison-Wesley.

Williams, B. A. O. (1973). *Problems of the Self; Philosophical Papers 1956-1972*. Cambridge [Eng.], Cambridge University Press.

Williams, B. A. O. (1985). *Ethics and the Limits of Philosophy*. Cambridge, Mass., Harvard University Press.

Yablo, S., Ed. (1997). *Wide Causation*. Philosophical Perspectives. Boston, Blackwell Publsihers.

Zimmerman, M.-J. (1980). "On the Intrinsic Value of States of Pleasure." Philosophy and Phenomenological Research. S D 41: 26-45.

www.ingramcontent.com/pod-product-compliance
Lightning Source LLC
Chambersburg PA
CBHW031127090426
42738CB00008B/994